A SENSE OF THE HOLY

An Introduction to the Thought of P.T. Forsyth Through His Writing

BY

P.T. FORSYTH, M.A.,D.D.

Foreword by Geoffrey Wainwright

D1566604

WIPF & STOCK PUBLISHERS

Eugene   Pasadena

1996

A Sense of the Holy: An Introduction to the Thought of P. T. Forsyth

ISBN 0-9653517-0-X

Printed by  WIPF & STOCK PUBLISHERS 1996

This book is dedicated to
Bob Cahill–
Joyful Christian,
Lover of God and Good books,
Preacher of the Godspell–
A true Irish bard & Loyal friend,
Thank you so much.

CONTENTS

PREFACE

Is there a revival of interest in the writings of P.T. Forsyth? Throughout the past forty years (since the last Forsyth revival) there has been a small, loyal following, an occasional dissertation offered, a periodic reprint issued. As sellers of used and out-of-print books, we can attest to the high demand for his writings from customers of the Archives Bookshop and Windows Booksellers. T&T Clark's recent publication "Justice the True and Only Mercy: Essays on the Life and Theology of Peter Taylor Forsyth," represents the first major study of Forsyth in twenty years (excepting Clifford Pitt's "hard to find" volume) and may itself point to a Forsyth "renaissance."

Revival or not, it is our own desire to see Forsyth's work available that is driving the publication of this volume. In other words, our motive is not one of financial gain so much as it is to proselytize. We hope that, through this introduction to Forsyth's work, you will join the camp of those who admire Forsyth's genius.

The following collection is an attempt to offer a representative reading that spans Forsyth's most productive years (1895-1918), rather than a collection centered on a single theme. Of course, Forsyth wrote so broadly that this is a rather incomplete representation. Nevertheless, it is our hope that you will find the writings edifying and stimulating. Forsyth tended to be more "striking" than "systematic," we hope that this collection is true to his manner.

Several acknowledgments are due. This project would have never gotten off the ground without the encouragement and support of John Wipf. Thanks are also due to Rich Read and the Church of the Servant

King, true "Forsyth apostles."

"We shall never be real or holy by trying to be either, but only by trusting and loving the Most Holy and Real. The age's soul can only find its forwandered self by trust toward a God forgiving and saving it on the scale of all history in the hell-harrowing, heaven-scaling Cross of Christ."- P.T. Forsyth

FOREWORD

Peter Taylor Forsyth (1848-1921) was a British Congregationalist minister who, until mid life, served five urban parishes and then, in 1901, became Principal of Hackney College in North London. He has been seen as an English forerunner of Karl Barth. Dissatisfied with the liberal forms of Protestantism dominant at the turn of the century, Forsyth realized that the human predicament called for a deeper work of redemption and a more persistent work of continuing grace on God's part–just as the best of the Christian Tradition had in fact always taught. To meet the needs of his time, Forsyth took his cue from the sheer self-gift of God that occurred in the "self-emptying" of Christ narrated by the apostle Paul in Philippians 2. Christ "revealed by redeeming," and the risen Christ now lives for ever to make intercession for us and to bring us, in personal communion, to fulness of life in the Spirit.

Forsyth, unlike Barth, did not write a grand Church Dogmatics; but his work often displays a freshness similar to that of some of the shorter writings of the great Basel theologian. Forsyth's texts make good "spiritual reading," provided that one is open to the theological penetration and profundity that is thereby entailed. In genre, they remain close to what he must have uttered from the pulpit during his pastorates. His chapters on "the soul of prayer" have proved particularly helpful to many.

A first revival of interest in P.T. Forsyth took place in the years after the Second World War, when many of the same issues arose in our churches and culture. The time may well be ripe for Forsyth to speak to us again as we seek to hear and proclaim the distinctively Christian message in a situation of shallowness and fragmentation that cries out for vision and atonement.

In commending this new assembly of Forsyth's writings, I feel nevertheless bound to issue one word of disclaimer. I refer to the occasional outburst of anti-Roman Catholic sentiment from which, whatever its justification in Forsyth's time and place, I at least would wish to dissociate myself in the here and now.

Geoffrey Wainwright

Duke University
Eastertide 1996

THE DIVINE SELF-EMPTYING

1895

> *"Have this mind in you, which was also in Christ Jesus; who, being in the form of God, counted it not a prize to be on an equality with God, but emptied himself, taking the form of a servant, being made in the likeness of men- and being found in fashion as a man he humbled himself, becoming obedient even unto death."*
>
> — *PHIL. 2:5-8.*

This is one of the hardest sayings in the New Testament, because one of the greatest. All great things are hard. It takes us into a region where human thought seems to fail, human analogies break down, and human speech sounds meaningless. It has been asked, for instance, if there is any real or possible process answering to the words, "emptied Himself". Can any being divest himself of his own nature, or will himself out of his own mode of being? Moreover, can we be sure that we know exactly the allusions in Paul's mind which give point to his words and phrases? The *form* of God and the *fashion* of a man, the *fashion* of a man and the *likeness*—in what do they differ? The equality with God—was it something He had and laid down, or something He might have had, but forbore to claim? The discussion on the passage has been immense.

But do not go away from this or any other difficulty with the notion that because all is not clear, all is quite dark. Because some meanings are disputed do not suppose that all sense is hopeless and all value lost. Because we do not clearly grasp do not suppose that we cannot be mightily seized and held. Exact interpretation may be difficult, but great principles and powers may be so radiant that exactness is lost in a flood of glory, and we are apprehended of more than we apprehend.

For instance, there is the great question of limitation within the Godhead which is here raised. It is said sometimes that any kind of a limit put on Godhead is a denial of Godhead. If God accept limitation He empties Himself to the point of vacuity. And some, therefore, stumble at the idea of personality in God, because it seems to limit and narrow Him to human dimensions. While others, going further, not only fail to grasp the philosophy of a Divine personality, but fail to respond to the reality of it, which is much more serious. Others, again, seeing the great limitations in the Christ of the gospels, cannot admit His Godhead. They see Him limited in power, and in knowledge, and in His span of life. Some things He could not do, some things He did not know, and an early limit was put by death upon a life which promised to be so great, good, and blessed. Besides, His cause moves slowly to-day in the world. It spreads at huge cost and difficulty. It looks as if it took His utmost effort to win the results we see, which seem so unsatisfactory for two thousand years of Divine action. "And is the thing we see salvation?" The limits upon His power and success seem so great, whether in His life or in His influence since, that some cannot believe in His Godhead, even when they honour His character and ideals. They think His worth far greater than His power. They think He meant more than He could do, and reached at more than He could grasp. And that, again, leads them seriously to question if worth and power will ever combine; if might will ever be on the side of right in all the order of things. They are not sure if Christ will ever be King. For to believe in Christ means to believe that His right is the final might, and to lose faith in Christ is to doubt whether right ever can or will rule in humanity at all. Belief in a righteous, glorious future for our race stands or falls, practically, with belief in Jesus Christ. If it do not for you it will for your descendants. So the question is a grave one. Are His limitations the result of weakness or of power?

I.—LIMITATION A POWER AND NOT A DEFECT

Well, notice here that Christ's emptying of Himself is not regarded as the loss of His true Godhead, but the condition of it. Godhead is what we worship. Christ's emptying of Himself has placed Him in the centre of human worship. Therefore He is of Godhead. We worship Him as the Crucified—through the cross, not in spite of the cross. It has won Him, both by the heart's instinct and by God's will, the name *Lord,* which is above every name; and it is above in a sense which lifts Him out of the mere human category, and puts other men in the position, not of admirers, but worshippers. Christ's emptying of Himself is therefore treated as one of the powers of His Godhead, not a denial of it. He could not have emptied Himself but for His Godhead. It was His superhuman power, glory, and bliss that made Him able thus to limit His power. The cross is the overflow of exultant Godhead, its purple blossom. Its sorrow is the outlet for Divinest joy, the relief to exuberant Deity.

I think this is the authentic sign and seal
Of Godship, that it ever waxes glad,
And more glad, until gladness blossoms, bursts
Into a rage to suffer for mankind,
And recommence at sorrow.

If we can neither do this nor comprehend it, it is because we are man and not God. We could only understand it by being able to do it. The Father alone knoweth the Son in such a matter, and understands how it was done. The act is a part and sign of Christ's Divine greatness. It is no negation of that greatness. It is a most Divine thing that the eternal Christ should consent to be weak, ignorant, short-lived. It should not come between us and the faith of His divinity at all, when we read true greatness, true Godhead, right. So we have the principle that limitation is a *power* of Godhead, not a curtailment of it. Among the infinite powers of the Omnipotent must be the power to limit Himself, and among His glories the grace to bend and die. Incarnation is not impossible to the Infinite; it is necessary. If He could not become incarnate His infinitude would be partial and limited. It would not be complete. It would be limited to all that is outside human nature. It would be limited by human nature in the sense of not being able to enter it, of being stopped at its gates. God would be curtailed to the extent of His creation. And that would be a more fatal limitation to His power than any He could suffer from being in it. He may be in without being locked in. But if He must be out it is because He is locked out, and effectually limited by a rival power. The power to limit Himself into man is an essential part of His infinite power. Without it He could not create. And creation is the beginning of Incarnation. It is God's self-concentration. Limitation or concentration is one of the surest signs of power. Vague power, aimless and wild, is not divine. "'Tis within limits that the master shows," says Goethe, in speaking of the great geniuses who have perfected their art in a form so small as the sonnet.

II.—THE DIVINE PERSONALITY

(1) Let me risk some repetition on this matter. And first as to God's *personality.* It is said that He cannot be personal, because personality

means limitation, and the Infinite and Almighty cannot be limited. If He could He would cease to be either, and so to be God. Well, so much as this may be granted. If there be any other power than God that can limit God, then there are two Gods, neither of them the Almighty; and so there is no God, as the word has been, and craves to be, understood. I pass over the very disputable point whether personality is in its nature finite because the individual personalities we meet are so. That would lead me too far. I would only ask, supposing we do find limitation in God, must it follow that it is due to some power outside God? Is the Infinite Will the one will that has no self-determination?

On the contrary, the limitation in God is due to God Himself. Self-limitation is one of the infinite powers of Godhead. If God were not personal, if He did not contain the mighty concentrative lines of personality, He would be less than God. He would be a waste, ineffectual force, without form and void. He could, indeed, hardly be force even, which must work in lines. He would be a dim essence, and empty substance, a gaseous abstraction without contents, without feature, interest, or life. He would be without order, for order is limitation. But surely order is the Divine presence in the world, not its absence. Law is His law, not another's law laid on Him. And personality is law and order in their highest terms. Limitation is no more undivine or incompatible with infinity in the one case than in the other. Divine law, indeed, when we express it in moral terms, what is it other than God's self-control?

Personality is thus essential to any ordered Godhead. It is an aspect of the self-limitation which must be among the powers of the Eternal, and of the self-command which must always be the condition of power in any moral being, finite or infinite. If God ceased to be personal, He would be parting with power, He would lose hold on Himself, He would lose character, He would become foreign to all we mean by moral power, hope, or progress, and He would be so far weak, and not strong. What hope for the moral future if the cross, which is the extremity of Divine self-command, and so the condition of Divine conquest, were really found to be utterly alien to the nature of Godhead?

But, on the other hand, God is not imprisoned in His personality. That were a crude Deism, and only another form of weakness. His is a *free* personality. It is free in the sense that it has not the narrow range we associate with finite personalities. And it is free in the ethical sense. It is not stamped upon Him by a god beyond God—

In truth the prison unto which we doom
Ourselves no prison is.

The limits we freely lay upon ourselves, or accept freely, are part of our dignity. They are responsibility, and there is no dignity without that. The limited freedom of the married is a higher form than the unlimited freedom of celibates, who want to do as they like. The ordered freedom of a loving family is more free and worthy than the freedom of the lonely lodger with a latchkey. The limited freedom of a simple life is nobler than the unchartered liberty of luxury, free to indulge each whim. And so the infinite freedom and power of God is not a thing of immunities and abstractions, withdrawn from the world of nature and man. It is the power to live and move, with harmonious ease and completed being, in and through all the rich contents of nature, soul, and will, and finally to subdue them all to His own nature and purpose. Power, in the shape of genius or art, can never be released from ordinary moral conditions. Indeed, we rightly demand in such cases a deeper respect for the fundamental moralities of life. Still more must Omnipotence show itself at home within and not outside the limits of the world and life. It is not Omnipotence if it cannot empty itself of immunities and descend and be found in fashion as nature or man. If it resented this, and were incapable of it, it would be moral impotence, moral anarchy in particular, and consequently a spiritual pretender.

(2) When we speak of the *Incarnation* it is only another aspect of the same thing. The same infinite power as makes Godhead personal or creative, makes it incarnate. Godhead in emptying itself must have power to divest itself of certain attributes like omniscience, and to be found in fashion as a man, with human weakness, ignorance, and risk. There are many things which we know better than Christ did, and yet we rightly worship Him as the Incarnate Son of God. If the incarnation is not possible, then Theism is not.

III.—THE INCARNATION AND ITS MORAL REALITY

I task you a little with this. Many are exercised about such things, which lame their faith. They are hampered by metaphysical difficulties which they have not enough metaphysics to keep in their proper place, and they make them a standard of faith. They come to Christ and propose to subject Him to certain rational tests and demands. Whereas Christ never concerned Himself about the rationality of His demands or tests; but He wanted religion, faith, surrender to Himself, obedience to God. Perhaps He would have gone respectfully by those who wanted to accept or reject Him by a standard of absolute ethics or absolute reason; and He would have discoursed to the poor in spirit and the really religious about the great matters of conscience, truth, and moral reality. They thought and spoke in His language, He in theirs. Ethical and metaphysical science are good and indispensable, but I doubt if Christ would have understood their speech, as they certainly often misunderstand His. He never spoke of Himself as the universal Reason. In the very gospel which is prefaced with the Eternity and Deity of the Logos, He never alludes to Himself in that way at all. But He did speak of Himself as the universal Judge and Lord. He claimed to be an authority for the *conscience,* not for the intellect. He does rule mind in the long run. But it is indirectly, from His seat in the conscience. It is because the conscience rules the intellect, and by the conscience reason stands or falls.

So I beg you particularly to observe that this bold phrase of Paul's, thrust into the interior of the Godhead, is not a metaphysical one. It is not rational. It is moral. He speaks of Christ "emptying Himself", but he is not tracing a philosophic process. He has nothing to say about the passage of the Infinite into the finite, and the resumption of the finite by the Infinite again. There is not a suggestion of the vast unconscious becoming self-conscious in the finite, and so on. He was not brought up in the schools of Alexandria, nor was He the precursor of modern speculation. He was not in this passage running away from religious and practical ends, or indulging in an excursion into the metaphysics of deity. He was urging, with the mightiest motive He could think of the temper, so essentially Christian, of humility. I know our current, and especially our educated Christianity has forgotten the centrality of that virtue. Does it shine out in the great intellectual centres of this Christian country? Has it leavened and subdued the pagan selfhood and pride of the natural man, say, in the professional classes? Is the absence of it as fatal as it should be to Christian repute? It is not a Christian accomplishment or luxury, but a necessary element in Christian character. If it were not at the very centre of Christian character and ideal would Paul have gone to the very centre of the Godhead to find the great and final motive for it?

These Philippian Christians were but lately pagan. They had the moral uncouthness of the pagan amid their outward civilisation. You can get plenty of moral barbarism, mere militant self-assertion, yea, unspeakable grossness, amid much aesthetic and mental culture. Paul is urging on them the refinement so essential to Christian character, refinement which was not mere delicacy of sentiment, but the moral quality of true humility. He knows it is a hard thing, but he knows it is central. So he brings to bear the sublimest as well as the most moving of motives. He places before the Philippian Christians the tender, mighty, and solemn renunciations which were in the very bosom of Godhead itself. He colours with the crimson of sacrifice the pale centres of Deity; and, led by the Holy Ghost, he declares God to be "human at the red-ripe of His heart."[1] Mark the point. He does not philosophize about the divine *essence*. He deals with a living Godhead. He shows us the *motive* of the divine *action*. He does not carry us into the substance of Deity by metaphysics, but into the heart and conscience, the act and motive, of God by faith. He says Christ in the Godhead emptied Himself. And though we cannot go far in the interpretation of such a vast suggestion, we can take care that it is the right kind of interpretation we put on it. And we find the key to the right kind of interpretation in the other word, "humbled Himself, and became obedient."

There are two phrases, "He emptied Himself," and "He humbled Himself." They do not mean the same. The first refers to something that took place in the bosom of Godhead before Jesus was born, before the foundation of the world; the second refers to the earthly human life of Jesus, its spirit, principle, and visible aspect. And it is by the second that Paul mounts up to the first. It is the heavenly that *accounts* for the earthly, that is true; but it is the earthly that *brings home* to us the heavenly no less. The humility of Christ's life and death was a palpable thing, intelligible to people who had any due moral perception. It fascinated them. It grew upon them. It opened out and deepened inward. It was a great and eloquent moral fact, a great and significant spiritual word. And it carried Paul beyond the world, beyond humanity, to what was at the root of it, what went on in the unseen Godhead before the foundation of the world. And it made him feel that whatever else was done there, in the self-limiting of Godhead, it was in its nature a great *moral* act; a great moral renunciation, an act of the same *kind* as that life-long humiliation in which the will of Christ achieved depth after depth of free devotion up to a death of shame. The great eternal act of Christ in heaven and Godhead, before and beyond history, was of a like *nature* to the long act of will by which He went down to death in His human history. It was an act of heart and will, of free resolve, of self-limitation, self-contraction as it were, self-divesting, self-humiliation, self-subordination. We are prone to think

---

1.   Browning: *The Ring and the Book*, Bk. I (altered).

of humility as a feature of those who have very little will of their own, and who always take the path of least resistance. No wonder, then, that we make so little of humility. But Paul thinks of it as the supreme act and expression of the supreme will under human conditions, the greatest thing the greatest will could do. He thinks of it, not as a sentiment, not as a sense of weakness, not as an occasional mood, but as the great ethical act, which forms the real connection, common term, and the *reconciliation* between God and man.

IV.—THE INCARNATION AS THE MIRACLE OF GRACE IS NOT IN THE BIRTH, BUT IN THE DEATH OF CHRIST.

The reconciliation between God and man lay in that great spiritual *act* of Christ's humiliation, an act which drew upon His whole person and gave effect to it. Looking forward, the moral effect of that act on us is our central Christian virtue of humility.

> For that which men think weakness within strength,
> But angels know for strength and stronger yet—
> What were it else but the first things made new,
> But repetition of the miracle,
> The Divine instance of self-sacrifice
> That never ends and aye begins for man?

And, looking backwards, it is the key to that self-emptying in eternity which is the principle of the Incarnation. This puts a great and neglected truth which I am at some pains to urge. Paul does not take the Incarnation as a special mode of two co-existing natures, human and divine, and make it the means of explaining the humiliation, the cross. That is the way of the philosophic theologian, who illuminates the Word by starting, not from Christ, but from rational truths and principles. But Paul starts with Christ, with His actual historic humiliation. From that footing he is caught into reaches beyond time and the world. He discovers that the key to the nature of the incarnation is to be found in the humiliation. The two acts are really one and the same act as seen from time and from eternity. Their nature is one. If the humiliation was a great act of will and obedience, then the Incarnation is the same, rather than an adjustment of two natures in one person. If the humiliation was moral in its central feature, then the central feature of the Incarnation was not metaphysical, but moral also. It also was an act of will, of obedience, of self subordination in the sublimest terms. Now, granting all Christ's miracles, yet there was nothing in that sense miraculous about the long act of *humiliation* in which Christ's whole life went down to death. However miracle may have been associated with it, miracle was not of its essence. It was moral, and not miraculous, in its grandeur. It was moving rather than striking. He refused the miraculous aid of legions of angels in the crisis of His work. Redemption was a *spiritual* conflict and victory in a great *moral* war. The humiliation was as little miraculous as metaphysical. It was one of us that was labouring, fighting, trusting, dying, conquering; but it was Godhead as one of us. And we must apply the same principle, if we follow Paul, to the *Incarnation*. It is in redemption that we find the nature of the Incarnation. It was not any feature of miracle that made its essence, its value, its power. It was the moral element of self-emptying. It was the sublime act of Christ's will and God's will combined, of Son and Father ever one. The central impulse, quality, and virtue of the Incarnation was not in any process undergone by Divine substance, or any intricate relation set up between two natures, or any circumstance attending the mode by which Jesus was born into the world. You may hold a variety of views on those heads and yet miss the power of His Incarnation in them all. The centre of the Incarnation is where Christ placed the focus of His work—not at the beginning of His life, but at its end; not in the manger, but in the cross. The key to the Incarnation is not in the cradle, but in the cross. The light on Bethlehem falls from Calvary. The virtue lies in some act done by Christ; and He Himself did no act in His birth, but in His death He did *the* act of the universe. The soul of the Incarnation does not lie in His being born of a pure virgin; but it lies in the death of His pure soul and the perfect obedience of His will as a propitiation for the sins of the world. God was in Christ as reconciler, not as prodigy. The key to the Incarnation lies, not in the miracle performed on His mother, but in the act of redemption performed by Himself. Christ's great work on our behalf was not in assuming our nature at birth, but in what He did with the nature we call assumed. Men were not redeemed by Christ being *born* as He was, but by His *dying* as He did. It is that which establishes His power over us sinners. It is that which makes His real value to our souls, because it is there that He atones, expiates, reconciles. It is that which gives chief value to His entrance in the world—not that He was miraculously born, but that He was born to die and redeem. The saving humiliation was not that of the manger but of the cross. It was a humiliation not inflicted or imposed, but achieved. And the self-emptying behind all was one to be explained, not by anything happening to Him in His humble birth, but by what happened *through* Him in His humiliating death. If He had not been born in that way, and yet had died as He did, He would still have been our reconciliation with God, our Redeemer from the curse, and our Saviour from the sin of the soul and of the race.

The power of His Incarnation has become so weak among men, for one reason, because its explanation has been sought at the wrong end of His life. The wonder has been transferred from Good Friday to Christmas, from the festival of the second birth *to* the festival of the first, from redemption to nativity, from the fellowship of His death *to* the sentiment of His babyhood. And so we hear sometimes that Christianity is a religion for women and children, and for men in the moods when they are less men and more mild.

V.—THE SON'S SUBORDINATION AND ITS PRACTICAL BEARINGS

I want to press the lesson home in this way, this moral way, this practical way. We are not all thinkers, but we are all moralists in some way. We have sins to be forgiven, and we have duties to be done. And duties are determined for us by those moral relations from which not one is exempt. How can we know our duty except we know our moral relations? How can we know our duty to God without our relation to Him?

Christ emptied Himself, we are told. In doing so He did on a higher and previous plane what He did also in the humiliation of His historic life. And there is a paraphrase of the words given for our help. The phrases run in balanced pairs in this difficult passage. And the counter phrase to "emptied Himself" is "He counted not equality with God a *thing to be mapped at.*" He was of God-head, "in the form of God," within the pale of Godhead, but in Paul's thought He did not possess equality with God, with God the Father. What He emptied Himself of was, not the equality, but the form, the glory, the immunity of Godhead. He put that off, and put on the contrasted form and apparent dignity of a servant. Of course the Son must be subordinate to the Father, though both are in the same Divine form or family. And the true son is one who realises that subordination. He did not regard equality as a prize, something to be snatched at. Lucifer, according to the story, the first of all the angels, did so regard it. He exalted himself above all that was called God, and fell from heaven's household and glory.

Adam, in the other story, also regarded this equality as an object of burning ambition. "Eat, and ye shall be as gods," he was told, and he ate, and his eyes were opened, but his God was hid. Christ as Son had no such passion. He did not aspire to equality of power or knowledge, but to obedience. And so He kept and enhanced that glory which He had with the Father before the world was.

Notice, then, I have the practical point still in view. He was of Godhead, but He sought no equality with God. The glory of Godhead He had, but it was the Godlike glory of subordination. There is place and order in the Godhead, and he kept it. Subordination *is* godlike. He was in the category of God, but He did not claim the immunities of God. The Son would not oust the Father. In a word, *He was not inferior to God, but He was subordinate. Subordination is not inferiority.*

Oh, if you could but learn that in this your day, how many griefs, heart-burnings, rebuffs, failures, and soul bitterness it would save you and your posterity!

Subordination is *not* inferiority, and it is godlike. The principle is imbedded in the very cohesion of the Eternal Trinity, and it is inseparable from the unity, fraternity, and true equality of men. It is not a mark of inferiority to be subordinate, to have an authority, to obey. It is Divine. To suffer no lord or master— that is Satanic; to discard all control but superior force is the demonic form of sin, which soon passes into the brutal. To have no loyalty is to have no dignity, and in the end no manhood.

You hear wild talk among youths that they are free rational beings, and are not going to be a whit more subordinate than they can help, to father, tutor, master, or faith of any kind. The end of which is a hard, coarse individualism, a selfishness gradually growing arrogant (if it be not that *to* begin with), the rupture of family life, filial faith, homely duty, and kindly rule, and the dissolution of all the fine loyalties of the soul for which great men worthily die.

And you hear wild talk in the like vein among women, who start the regeneration of their sex by declaring subordination to be unwomanly, a relic of slavery, a badge of inferiority; as if insubordination were any more lovely in woman than in man, and as if women specially could afford to discard loveliness. I am not going here into special applications, or even into necessary qualifications. I am only laying down the Christian principle, rooted in the very nature of God, and essential to the manhood and womanhood He has made. Without the spirit of subordination there is no true godlikeness, no nobleness of manhood, no charm of womanhood. And the true inferiority is insubordination, and the spirit which will have no authority and resents all control.

A very able yet timid writer (I mean A. J. Balfour) said in a philosophic work, "If we would find the quality in which we most notably excel the brute creation, we should look for it, not so much in our faculty of convincing and being convinced by the exercise of reasoning, as in our capacity for influencing and being influenced through the action of Authority." With which I heartily agree, so long as by authority is meant what Paul means here, the moral authority of character, of a living personality, of the living law and the living Lord, whose name of Lord, because of His dying, is above all lordship, and whose humiliation is the Eternal Authority, as His cross is the final judge of all things and all men.

VI. THE GOD OF THE FUTURE THE GIVING GOD

I will close on the keynote, "He emptied Himself". The one thing which it is the business of Revelation to let us know about the depths of eternal Godhead is this, that its Divinest power is the power to resign, to sacrifice, to descend, to obey, to save. The key to the prehistoric Godhead is the historic Jesus, and His historic obedience, even to the historic cross. And I could almost think that the deepest error which has blinded and lamed Christianity in the world, the root of every other perversion and failure, is indicated here. It is in having conceived of God as a Being whose first and Divinest work was to *receive* sacrifice instead of offering it—one who demanded sacrifices He had never made. Deep into the fabric of Christian thought and habit has struck this pagan strain, that it is God's one royal work to accept sacrifice, and man's one saving duty to offer it. The Christian note is quite other. In the face of all the paganisms, ancient and modern, civil or ecclesiastical, it is bold and original in the extreme. It not only carries into Godhead the power of sacrifice, but it declares this priestliness to be the very saving power of God, the root of all that is glorious in everlasting glory, or kingly in the King of kings. "God so loved that He *gave*." The Divine King is King because He is Priest. That is the marrow of the Christian revelation, the originality of the Christian vision, the sublimity and finality of the Christian faith. And the Church will not gain the power of which the Spirit has made her dream till she has become permeated with this truth in its fulness. It is not enough that it be held by an enlightened student, saint, or community here and there. It is only when the soul of that truth has fused and recast the whole Church of every land that its revolutionary power upon the creed and practice of Christendom will appear. And society will then be dominated, not by spirits whose best life has been spent in the acquisition of things for the lack of which men and brethren round them are dying, but by that unrequited elect, that great unpaid, whose life is a long surrender and whose fate is to be long misunderstood; who do not clamour for their deserts, because the wages of their sin would be death, and also because their faith is that it is a godlier thing to give than to receive; but they empty themselves to make room in themselves and the world for the fulness and glory of God in the cross of Christ the Lord. ❦

THE HOLY FATHER

1897

ST. JOHN 17:2

When the 103rd Psalm says "Like as a father pitieth his children, so the Lord pitieth them that fear Him," it comes home to a time like our own. It is one of those gleams of vision in which the soul of Israel outran the spirit of its age. It transcended its own genius. It rose from the covenant God to the father God. It uttered an *intuition* whose source was *inspiration,* and which in the fulness of time rose into the *revelation* of God's first and last relation to the world. The music, heart, and passion of it lives for ever in Christ—endless pity, endless promise, endless power—lingering, searching pity, loving and lifting promise, weariless power and peace.

But it points beyond itself. There is a height and a depth in the Father beyond His utmost pity and His kindest love. He is *Holy* Father and Redeemer, and it is His holiness of fatherhood that is the source of our redemption and sonship. It is not their obstacle. "Thou, O Lord, art our Holy One, *therefore* we shall not die." He is father of pity to human weakness, still more father of grace to human sin, but chiefly father of holy joy to our Lord Jesus Christ. The New Testament name and idea of God is not simply "Our Father", but "the God and Father of our Lord and Saviour Jesus Christ." And Christ's own prayer was "Holy Father." That was Christ's central thought of God, and He knew God as He is. The new revelation in the cross was more than "God is love". It was this "Holy Father." That is, God at His divinest, as He was to Christ, as He was in Christ.

In the Old Testament God is father often enough as well as in other faiths. And in the 103rd Psalm it appears in a more original and tender way than I can stop to point out. But it is with many limitations. The name, for instance, is as yet imported into God rather than revealed from Him. He is *like* a father more than He is a father. And He is Israel's father only. "Them that fear Him" means Israel. But the chief limitation is this. The name is not yet evangelized. Fatherhood is not yet brought into direct connection with holiness, sin, sacrifice, redemption—only with weakness. The pity of the Father is connected with the allusion to our frail frame in those few verses, not with our transgression and the forgiveness which is the burden of the psalm. God is Father, and He is holy, but it is not as Holy Father that He redeems. Fatherhood in the Old Testament neither demands sacrifice nor makes it, but in the New Testament the Holy Father does both. The holiness is the root of love, fatherhood, sacrifice, and redemption.

The ethical standard is becoming supreme with us today, not only in conduct, but also in theology. We may welcome the change. It carries us farther—to a standard truly spiritual. It plants us on God's holiness as His perfect nature, His eternal spirit, His ruling self and moving centre. We have been over engrossed with a mere distributive equity, which has made God the Lord Chief Justice of the world. Or we have recoiled from that to a love slack and over-sweet. But this lifts us up to a more spiritual and personal standard, to the Fatherly holiness whose satisfaction in a Holy Son is the great work and true soul of Godhead. The divine Father is the holy. And the Holy Father's first care is holiness. The first charge on a Redeemer is satisfaction to that holiness. The Holy Father is one who does and must atone. Atonement wears a new glory when read in Christ's own light. We see it flowing in grief *from that very holiness* of the Father to which it returns in praise. As Holy Father He is the eternal Father and maker of sacrifice no less than of man. He offers a sacrifice rent from His own heart. It is made to Him by no third party ("for who hath first given unto Him"), but by Himself in His Son; and it is made to no foreign power, but to His own holy nature and law. Fatherhood is not bought from holiness by any cross; it is holiness itself that pays. It is love that expiates. "Do not say, 'God is love. Why atone?' The New Testament says, 'God has atoned. What love!'" The ruling passion of the Saviors holy God is this passion to atone and to redeem.

All this and more is in that "Holy Father" which is the last word in the naming of God. The Church of to-day has gained greatly in its sense of the love of God. There are still great things waiting when she has moved on as far again, to the *holiness* whose outward movement is love, which love is but the passion to impart. You can go behind love to holiness, but behind holiness you cannot go. It is the true consuming fire. Any real belief in the Incarnation is a belief in the ultimacy, centrality, and supremacy of holiness for God and man. We may come to holiness by way of love, but we only come to love by reason of holiness. We may be all aglow for the coming of the kingdom, but there is a prior petition. It is the kingdom's one condition, "Hallowed be Thy Name." That hallowing was done in Christ's death which founded the kingdom. We are in some danger of inverting the order of these prayers to-day. "Thy kingdom come is not the first petition. The kingdom comes from the satisfaction of holiness. It does not make it. "God is Love" is not the whole gospel. Love is not evangelical till it has dealt with holy law. In the midst of the rainbow is a throne. There is a kind of consecration which would live close to the Father, but it does not always take seriously enough the holiness which *makes* the fatherhood of the cross—awful, inexhaustible, and eternal, as full of judgment as of salvation.

We cannot put too much into that word Father. It is the sum and marrow of all Christian divinity. It is more than natural paternity spiritualized. It is a supernatural word altogether when the cross becomes its key. But we may easily put into it too little. That is what we all do in some way. Only once has enough been put into it. And that was in the faith and work of Christ,"Father, forgive them." "Father"—that was His faith. "Forgive them"— that was His work. The soul of divine fatherhood is forgiveness by holiness. It is evangelical. It is a matter of grace meeting sin by sacrifice to holiness, more even than of love meeting need by service to man. To *correct* and revive that truth, to restore it to its place in the proportion of faith, would be to restore passion to our preaching, solemnity to our tenderness, real power to our energy, and moral virility to our piety. Our piety is too weak in the face of the virile passions it should rule. The chief lack of religion to-day is authority; and it must find that in the cross or nowhere, in the real nature of the cross, in its relation to the holy demand of God.

We put too little into that word Father, either when we think below the level of natural fatherhood, or when we rise no higher than that level.

I

By thinking below that level; when we do not rise to regard God as Father at all.

Few of us now make that mistake in theory. But most do in practice. Their *practical* thought of God is not always as Father even if they speak much of the Fatherhood. By practical I mean what really and experimentally affects their religion, colours their habit of soul, moulds their silent tone of mind, helps and sustains their secret heart. They treat God as power, judge, king, providence of a sort. He is for them at most a rectorial Deity. But it is the few perhaps who in their living centre and chronic movement of the soul experience sonship as the very tune of their heart, the fashion and livery of their will. Most Christians are not worldlings, but they are hardly sons. They are only in the position of the disciples who stood between Judaism and Pentecost, who received Christ but had not as yet the Holy Ghost. They are not sons but have only received power to become sons. The fatherhood has not broken out upon them through the cross and caught them away into its universal heaven. The great mass of religion, real and practical as it may be, is not yet sonship. It is more or less earnest, active, compassionate. It is Catholic or it is Protestant; it is ecclesiastical, political or pietist; it is eager for the kingdom and set on some form of God's will. Its philanthropy ranges from the deepest and most devoted sacrifice to a kind of charity which is mainly institutional, fashionable, heartless, and on the way to become as hollow as Dickens in his one-eyed way saw it might be. But what it does not enough realise in experience (the preacher himself accuses his own) is the centre and summary of God's will and kingdom, the fellowship with the Father and with His Son Jesus Christ. But prior to the true doing of the will is the trusting of it. "This is the will of God that ye should believe in His Son Jesus Christ." This is His commandment that we should love— really love, and not simply do the works which are inspired and suggested by those who have loved.

But to dwell on that is happily no longer the chief need of the hour.

II

We put too little into the name Father, when we think no higher than natural fatherhood at its heavenly best. It was not by a father or all earth's fatherhood that God revealed Himself. That would have been but manifestation, not revelation. It was by a son and a cross—whose message is the true supernatural of the world. What I mean is that we make too little of the Father when we do not rise beyond *love* to *grace*— which is holy love, suffering hate and redeeming it. The true supernatural is not the miraculous, but the miracle for whose sake miracles exist. It is not prodigy in nature but the grace of God in history. It has no direct relation to natural law. Miracle is not a scientific idea but a religious. An event is a miracle not by its relation to law but to grace. The Incarnation would be equally a miracle, however Jesus entered the world. It is not nature that is the true region of the supernatural, but history, and history not as a chain of events, but as the spiritual career of the soul or of the race. That is the true region of the supernatural. It lies in the action of God's will upon men's wills, not upon natural law. It is the work of God's grace upon men's sin. The miracle of the world is not that God should love His children or even His prodigals. Do not even the publicans likewise? But it is that He should love, forgive, and redeem His enemies; that His heart should atone for them to His own holy nature; that He should consecrate, a suffering greater even than they devised all the suffering they might have to endure; and by their central sin and its judgment destroy sin at its centre. That would be miracle if nature's laws were no more. That is Fatherhood when we speak of God. That is the fatherhood whose life, motive, and security is holiness. That fatherhood is the one mystery and miracle. To nature it is absolutely foreign, impossible, and incredible. Of all things it is least a matter of course. It is a matter of conflict, of conquest, of revelation, credible only by the aid of the spirit that inspired it. It is the fatherhood of the cross, with the grace which that fatherhood shows and the atonement it finds.

Between us and the Holy Father there comes what does not come between us and any earthly father—sin. Sin, hell, curse, and wrath! The wrath and curse of God not on sin only, but on the soul. O you may correct the theology of it as you will, but you cannot wipe—not all the perfumes of progress can hide—the reality of these things from the history of the soul, or from its future. They abide with us because the Holy Father will not leave us, because grace is the "hound of heavens." They are a function of that holiness which is love's own ground of hope. We do not and cannot SIN against natural fatherhood, however ill we may treat it. Sin is unknown to nature, to natural relations, natural love. Nature includes no holiness; and it is holiness that makes sin sin. It was not against his father that the prodigal *sinned;* and his treatment is not the whole sum of sin's cure. He truly says "I have sinned *against* heaven and *before* thee"—*against* heaven, but only *before* his father. It is not the whole fulness of the Gospel that we have in that priceless parable. Christianity is the religion of redemption, and it is not redemption we have there, only forgiveness. If it were the whole, then Christ could be dispensed with in the Gospel, for He is not there. And the father is not put

before us as a *holy* father, but as good, patient, wise, and infinitely kind—
a magnified and most natural man. He does not stand for the whole of
God, nor even for the whole grace of God. He stands not at all for the *cost
to* a Holy God of His grace, but only for the utter freeness of it. Nor is He
presented as Trustee of the world's moral order, of History's destiny, of
Humanity's moral soul and future, or of Eternity's holy law. He feels but
personal grief and wounded affection. It is an individual matter; and
redemption is not. It is a matter between two individuals, and redemption
is not. A soul can neither be saved nor sanctified without a world. To
redeem, the sin must be destroyed, a universe reorganized. Yet the
treatment of a world of sin, a sinful race, does not here arise. Nor are any
steps taken by the father to cause repentance. And it is a question
altogether whether the leading motive in the parable historically did not
lie in the elder brother and his treatment; whether its centre of gravity is
not at the close; whether that is not the foreground which called the
picture into existence, and for whose sake the wonderful background is
there.

We put too little into fatherhood then if we treat it simply as
boundless, patient, waiting, willing love. It is more than the love which
accepts either beneficence (like Faust's) as repentance, or repentance as
atonement, and eagerly cuts confession short thus— "Let us say no more
about it. Pray do not mention it. Let bygones be bygones." Forgiveness,
fatherhood, for *the race,* does not mean, with all its simplicity, just a clean
page and a fresh start and a sympathetic allowance for things. God does
not forgive "everything considered". To understand all is not to forgive
all. That is mere literary ethics, not the moralist's, certainly not the
Christian theologian's. There was more fatherhood in the cross (where
holiness met guilt) than in the prodigal's father (where love met shame).
There was more fatherhood for our souls in the desertion of the cross than
in that which melts our hearts in the prodigal's embrace. It is not a father's
sensitive love only that we have wounded, but His holy law. Man is not a
mere runaway, but a rebel; not a pitiful coward, but a bold and bitter
mutineer. Does not Kant confess as a moralist the radical evil in man, and
Carlyle speak of his infinite damnability? There is many a living
Mephistopheles in Europe. And the horror of the cursed, cursed, cursed
Sultan[1] belongs to the human race—to the solidarity of the race.
"Miserable sinners," which the slight individualist boggles at in his

---

1. Abdul Hamid, for the Armenius atrocities, 1895-6.

prayers, is a poor confession when we remember that we are voicing in our public worship the sin of the race. Forgiving is not just forgetting. It is not canceling the past. It is not mere amnesty and restoration. There is something broken in which a soul's sin shatters a world. Such is a soul's grandeur, and so great is the fall thereof; so seamless is the robe of righteousness, so ubiquitous and indefectible the moral order which makes man man. Account must be had, somewhere and by somebody, of that holiness of God which is the dignity of fatherhood and soul of manhood.

There are debts that cannot simply be written off and left unrecovered. There is a spiritual order whose judgments are the one guarantee for mankind and its future. That law of holiness can by no means whatever be either warned off or bought off in its claim. God cannot simply waive it as to the past, nor is it enough if He simply *declare* it for all time. In His own eternal nature it has an undying claim to which He must *give effect* in due judgment somewhere, if He is to redeem a world. The enforcement of God's holiness by judgment is as essential to a *universal and eternal* Fatherhood as is the outflow of His love. It was not cursed suffering only that fell on the Saviour, it was holy judgment. The Holy Father dealt there with the world's sin on (not in) a worldsoul. God in Christ judged sin as a Holy Father seeking penalty only for holiness' sake. He gathered it in one there, and brought it to issue, focused thus, with His unity of holy law. The misery and death which the sinner bears blindly, sullenly, resentfully, was there understood with the understanding of Holy God; the guilt was seen as God sees it; the judgment was accepted as God's judgment, borne, owned and glorified before the world as holy, fatherly, just, and good. That final witness of holiness to holiness amid sin's last wreck, penalty, and agony—that is expiation as the Father made it in the Son, not changing His *feeling,* but by crisis, by judgment, eternally changing His *relations* with the world.

III

It is at once easier and harder for God to forgive than man. Harder, because He is holy and feels the wound; easier, because He is holy and feels the moral power. In any case it is beyond us. It involves a sacrifice which costs more than sin-struck souls could pay. Sin steadily maims the sense of holiness and the power of sacrifice to it. And even if man by any sacrifice, or even penitence, could mend the moral order he has broken, it would be royal for him no more. It would be supreme and commanding for him no more. If we could heal our own conscience, it would no more be our king. If we could satisfy the moral order we disturbed, our insufferable self-satisfaction would derange it straightway.We should be (as Luther said) "the proudest jackasses under heaven." We may sorrow and amen, but we cannot atone and reconcile. Why, we cannot atone to each other, to our own injured or neglected dead, for instance, our silent inaccessible dead. I think of Carlyle's stricken widowerhood. Neither by hand nor heart can we come at them, nor bring them a whole lone life's amends. Our jealous God monopolises the right of atoning to them for us. We cannot even beseech their forgiveness. We cannot offer them ours. We cannot pray to them, we can but pray for them. We can but pray God to atone to them for us. We may live, like Carlyle, to eighty in a long, penitent widowerhood, and *then* we cannot atone to our wronged or lonely dead, nor smooth a feather of the angels who tarried with us, and we never knew them for angels till they had flown. And there may be broken hearts that live on sweetly to forgive their seducer, but which he can never mend, he can never atone. Nay, we cannot atone to our own souls for the wrong we have done them. We sin—and for us inexpiably— against our own souls. How much less, then, can we atone to our injured, neglected, sin-stung God. If our theology would let us, our conscience would not. The past cannot be erased, cannot be altered, cannot be repaired. There it stands. It can only be atoned; and never by us. If our repentance atoned, it would lose the humility which makes it worth most. It is atonement that makes repentance, not repentance that makes atonement. No man can save his brother's soul—no, nor his own. When Christ knew and said that He could, He knew Himself to be more than man. Man's debt no man can pay. Even God could not just cancel it. None could pay it but the prodigal's Father for him. For the debt was obedience, holiness, not suffering. Penalty only expiates crime, not sin. There was owed that debt to holiness, that atonement to holiness which is so misconstrued when we make it due to justice, or demanded by justice alone. Justice wants penalty, holiness wants holiness in the midst of penalty. It wants a soul's own perfect holiness in the midst of penalty due to other souls; it wants loving obedience amid the penalty of loveless defiance. God alone could fulfill for us the holy law He never broke, and pay the cost He never incurred.

And He has paid it, so freely and completely that His grace in forgiving is as full and free to us as if it had cost Him nothing, as if it had been just kindness. The cost is so perfectly and freely borne that it never appears in a way to mar the graciousness of grace, or deflower the Father's love. The quality of mercy is not strained.

That artist who works with such consummate ease, swiftness, and grace, how did he come by it? By hours and years of cost, in practice, in drudgery, slavery, self mastery, self-sacrifice, by a life he would often describe as one of labour and sorrow more than joy. But the master's art keeps all that out of sight. The grace He offers you is not to be spoiled by the obtrusion of such cost.

The friend you receive, and think nothing in the house too good for him—do you let him know of that trouble with the cook, of those hours of wakeful contrivance by which you earn the means of spending your hospitality on him, of that weakness of body which you master every time you laugh with him, that heartache which you keep down while you make everything so pleasant for him?

So God does not mar His grace by always thrusting on us what it cost. Some part of the failure and decay of evangelicanism (not to say Christianity) is due to the glib parade and unreal obtrusion of solemnities in redemption, about which Christ and His apostles held fine reserve. Even of sin, which is a commonplace of religious talk, Christ never spoke except in connection with its forgiveness. But reserve is not denial. The parable of the Prodigal is there, like every other parable, not to embody a complete system, but to light up one point in particular, which is the *freeness* of God's grace, the grace of it, the bloom upon the Fatherhood. The parable does not teach us that this grace cost nothing, that no superhuman satisfaction was required, that atonement is a rabbinic fiction. Rabbinic! Must it be fiction because rabbinic? It comes ill from liberal thought, this railing at Rabbinism. If God was not moving in the Rabbinic thought of Christ's day, what reason have we to say He moved in Buddhism, or moves in the thought of to-day? But as to the parable, it only tells us that grace is as free as love, that it could not flow more free if it had cost nothing, that the Almighty mastery of redemption is awful but entire, and altogether lovely. We have other reasons to know that if it had cost nothing, it could not have been so free. There is no precious freedom that costs nothing. Without blood, without cost, no remission, no release, no finding of the self, no possessing of the soul, no self-possession, no ease, grace, royalty, or liberty in the soul's matter or style. Without cross no crown for the soul. It is equally true of God and man. Grace does mean cost—but cost completely triumphantly met. Take God's grace in its fulness, richness, kindness. You cannot put too much freedom into the grace of the Father. The ease of its manner rests on the mighty gravity of its matter. Art conceals art. The art in forgiving, the utter grace of it, conceals the art of redeeming, the dread labour, sorrow, and secret of it.

IV

Revelation has its great reserves as conditions of its power. They are not forbidden ground, but they are not flashed in our eyes. Both Christ and the New Testament are disappointingly reticent about the cost of grace, the "plan of salvation," the "theory of Atonement," the precise way and sense in which Christ bore our curse before God, and took away the guilt of the world. Yet such truth (if there be a Holy Ghost and Church) we must have and we can. The saved conscience craves it for its moral world. It is quite necessary for *the Church's* faith, and at last for the individuals. If you never realize at all the cost of grace, you run some risk of making grace of none effect. After all, we are "scarcely saved." To go back to the parable which immortalizes the freeness of grace. What should you think of the forgiven son, who, as the pardoned years went on, never took his mercy seriously enough to give a thought to what he had brought on his father or God? If he never cared to go behind that free forgiveness which met him and feasted him without an upbraiding word; if he never sought to look deep into those eyes which had followed him, watched him, and spied him so far; if he was never moved by the amazing welcome to put himself in the depths of his Father's place; if he took it all with a light heart, and told the world that in forgiveness he felt nothing but gladness; if he said that that was all we know and all we need to know; if the swift forgiveness of God made it easy for him to forgive himself and just forget his past; if the generous, patient father never became for him the Holy Father; if he felt it was needless and fruitless to enter into the dread depths of sin with the altar candle of the Lord, or explore the miracle of the Father's grace— what should you think of him then?

Give him, of course, a year or two, if need be, to revel in this glad and sweet surprise. Give to his soul (if need be) a holy honeymoon. But if the years go on and he show no thirst to search those things which the angels desire to look into, but cannot (being unhuman and unredeemed); if he never seek to measure the latent meaning of it all for the Redeemer, and give no sign of being deepened in conscience as the fruit of being redeemed there; if there be no trace of his coming to himself in a sense still deeper than when he turned among the swine; if he go on with a mere readiness of religious emotion, and a levity of religious intelligence which cares not to measure his sin by the finer standards of the Father's spirit, or gauge the holy severity of the love he spurned; if he learn nothing of the Lord's controversy and His mortal moral strife; if he weigh nothing of the sin of the world in the scales of eternal redemption—if his career in grace were such as that, what should we think of him then? Should we not have reason to doubt whether he was not disappointing the Father again, if he was not falling from grace in another way, and this time in a religious way? He might take the genial cultured way of a natural goodness with philanthropy for repentance, an easy optimism, a beautiful Fatherhood, tasteful piety, social refinement, varied interest, ethical sympathies, æsthetic charm, and a conscience more enlightened than saved. Or he might take the pietist's way. And then is the risk fanciful of his sinking, perhaps, in the ill-educated cases, through a fluent religionist into a flimsy saint, lapped in soft airs, taking a clique for the kingdom, and sold to the religious nothings of the hour with all their stupefying power; with no deepness of earth, no pilgrim's progress, no passion of sacred blood, no grasp on real life, no grim wrestling, no power with God, no mastery of the soul, no insight, no measure of it, no real power to retain for himself, or for others to compel a belief in the soul, its reality or its Redeemer? And even if an individual is saved from these perils of religious impressionism, a church which acted so would not escape.

V

The parable of the Prodigal puts before us the rich freeness of God's grace in a story. But Christ Himself sets it before us in a living soul, as the living grace eternal in our midst. Did Christ utter His whole self in that parable, His whole mind and experience of His work, His whole sense of the depths and heights of sin, grace and glory? If He was the great gospel, could He put His whole self into any parable? No, nor into all the parables and all the precepts taken together. There came, when words had proved fruitless *for* teaching, and parables failures, the last great enacted parable of the Supper, the last great prayers of the garden, and the last great miracles of the cross and the tomb. When Christ came to these things, do you think there was no more in His mind about the cost of Fatherhood than He put into the story of His prodigal? There was a world more. Peter years after spoke, as the Lord the Spirit taught him, of the costly blood of Christ. And it is a strain repeated in the thought of every apostle. Indeed, they saw the life and words of Christ, not only irradiated by His death, but in the radiance even lost or obscured. *The* word of the gospel was not so much the words of Jesus as the one compendiary word of the cross showing forth the righteousness of God, and doing a work for us which is the source and ground of any work in us. The mere space given to the Passion in the gospels shows that to the company of Jesus He was more of a Mediator than even a Teacher, and that the Holy Ghost came from His cross more than from His doctrine.

Still, it remains true that from Christ Himself we have almost nothing in proportion about the holy cost of Fatherhood, the Godward action of His suffering and death. What most engrossed Him, even at the close, He said least of. It was not man's need of Him, nor His action on man. It was God's need of Him; God's real need of His sorrow, God's holy will for His obedience, the action of His cross on the holiness of God. For Christ the first effect of His cross was not on man, else He would have had more to say about it. It was on the Father. And at the end that grew His closest concern. Yet He has little or nothing to say of it for our theological satisfaction. We have but a word or two to show that the nature of the cross and atonement was prayer, that the act into which He put His whole life and soul was in its essence prayer—a dealing with God. We have but a few words wrung from the agony of this clear, sure, resolute, silent man, though in keeping with the attitude of His whole life. But a few words— and these only as it were overheard, not said for transmission, and, like ourselves, "scarcely saved." It is a reticence which is only intelligible if the Son was dealing with the Father in an objective way, apart from the effect of His act and agony upon us. It is in some contrast with the tone of the epistles, reticent as they are. And it has moved the humanism of the day to dispute the entire legitimacy of the succession between epistle and gospel, to rescue the Christ of the gospels from the Christ of the epistles, to save Christ from Paul, and Christ's religion from New Testament Rabbinism.

Well, I will leave on one side the suggestion that the disciples did not understand enough of Christ's words about His death to remember them all as they might. I will not say there is nothing in the suggestion. The gospels were not meant for a finished portrait of Christ, or a complete manual of His truth. They were but supplementary in their origin. It is unhistoric to treat them as sole and complete. They were written for people who had already received the gospel, or had the epistles, in order to fill out their knowledge of Christ. They were less to convey saving knowledge than to enrich it, because the apostles were passing away and leaving no successors behind. Besides, we must remember when we think of the disproportion in the contents of these small memoirs that though we need Christ's work of grace *more,* we need His tenderness and His teaching *oftener* in the Christian life. The weight of the gospels is in their compressed close. But whatever may be in such suggestions is not all. I venture to offer one or two considerations of a different kind in explanation.

VI

It would not be like the grace of God, it would be ungracious, if He came forgiving man and yet laying more stress on what it cost Him to do it than His joy, fulness, and freedom in doing it. You find poor human creatures who never can overlook your mistake without conveying to you that it is as much as they can do. They think no little of themselves for doing it. They take care that you shall never forget their magnanimity in doing it. They keep the cost of your forgiveness ever before you. And the result is that it is not forgiveness at all. How miserable a thing it is instead! How this spirit takes the charm from the reconciliation! How it destroys the grace of it! How penurious the heart it betrays! How it shrivels the magnanimity it parades! How grudging, how ungodlike it is! How unfatherly! What an un-gracious way of dealing with the graceless!

That is not God's way of forgiveness. His Fatherhood has the grand manner. It has not only distinction, but delicacy. He leaves us to *find out* in great measure what it cost—slowly, with the quickened heart of the forgiven, to find that out. Christ never told His disciples He was Messiah till it was borne in on them by contact with Him. He never told them till, by the working of the actual Messiahship upon them, they found it out. Revelation came home to them as discovery. It burst from experience. So gracious is God with His revelation that He actually lets it come home to us as if we had discovered it. That is His fine manner— so to give as if we had found. His shining may even be forgotten in our seeing. And so in a way with our forgiveness it dawns on us. Its freedom gives us the power to see its cost. The crown of the new life is the power not only to enjoy it but to prize it. It is borne in on the forgiven. It is a truth of experience. It is reconciliation taking account of itself. The first condition of forgiveness is not an adequate comprehension of the Atonement, and a due sense of the cost. That is not saving faith. Any adequate idea on that head comes only to the saved. The cross becomes a theology only by beginning as a religion. The condition of forgiveness is answering the grace and freedom of it with a like free, humble, and joyful heart. It is taking the freedom of it home, and not the cost. It is committing ourselves to God's self-committal to us. It is taking God at His word—at His living word, Christ—His urgent, reticent, gracious, masterful word, Christ.

It was left to the redeemed, to His apostles especially, sanctified by a new life, vision, and measure of all things, it was left to all the faithful as their true successors, to dwell on the costly side of the Christ's work, to draw out the hidden wealth of the Father's grace, and the demands of the Father's nature in Christ's cross, and to magnify what the Fatherhood cost both Father and Son. It was indeed even then the teaching of Christ. The earthly Christ was not the all of Christ. The whole Christ was there, but not all that is in Christ. *Totus Christus sed non totum quod in eo est,* says Calvin. He taught Paul in the spirit as truly as He taught the disciples in the flesh. And in Paul He had perhaps a more teachable disciple than they were—a more sensitive pupil, a more adequate soul, and possibly even on points a more trusty reporter of His truths than they. There is an insight into the meaning of His work opened up by the humbled and grateful experience of those first saints whom that work re-made. And they certainly confess that it was the work of the cross more than the words of His mouth that made them what they were. The cross produced in them its own commentary, theology, and exposition And it was left to them to provide that theology as the exposition not of a theme, but of the life and spirit which took possession of them from the cross.

And is that not just as it should be? It is for the redeemed to magnify the cost, the preciousness, of redeeming grace. It is not for the Redeemer. It would be ungracious in Him to do so. He brought the grace to us, and brought it as grace, not as cost; He offered it as a finished thing, rich and ripe, in its fulness and freeness of beauty, love, sorrow, and searching power. For Him to dwell on the cost, who paid it, and to do so while paying it would have been to rob grace of its graciousness, to impair its wonder, amplitude, and spell. But would it not have been just as ungracious, as much of a reflection on grace, if it had made no apostle or saint leap forward, to go behind the constraining liberating, re-creating *charm* of grace, and to draw out for our worship the cost of it—what holy Fatherhood paid in forgiving and what He was too generous to obtrude, till it pricked the conscience and woke the wonder of the forgiven? To dwell on that would have been inconsistent with the humility of Christ, or the reserve which is half the power of His revelation. But not to dwell on it or pierce into it in hushed joy would have been just as inconsistent with the true humility and gratitude of the forgiven.

VII

And this leads me to the second consideration. The doer of a great deed is one who has least to say about it, however he may instruct those who are called to tell of it. Christ came not to *say* something, but to *do* something. His revelation was action more than instruction. He revealed by redeeming. The thing He did was not simply to make us aware of God's disposition in an impressive way. It was not to *declare* forgiveness. It was certainly not to *explain* forgiveness. And it was not even to *bestow* forgiveness. It was to *effect* forgiveness, to set up the relation of forgiveness both in God and man. You cannot set up a relation between souls without affecting and changing both sides, even if on one side the disposition existed before, and led to the act that reconciled. The great mass of Christ's work was like a stable iceberg. It was hidden. It was His dealing with God, not man. The great thing was done with God. It was independent of our knowledge of it. The greatest thing ever done in the world was done out of sight. The most ever done for us was done behind our backs. Only it was we who had turned our backs. Doing this for us was the first condition of doing anything with us.

Now the doers of these great deeds have little to say of them. They are not speechless, not meaningless, but silent men, Heroes are not their own heralds. The Redeemer was not His own apostle. He spoke most of His Father, much of Himself as His Father's Son, little of His achievements, and of the pain and cost of them next to nothing at all.

The more the Gospel says to us, the more we are impressed with its silence. There is a form of the thirst for souls, of religious eagerness, of evangelical haste and pious impatience which is far too voluble and active to be impressive. It is more youthful than faithful, more ardent than sagacious, more energetic than inspired. It would express everything and at once in word or deed. They forgot that the ardent lucid noon hides the solemn stars, and heaven's true majesty of night, no less than does the thickest cloud. Of this there is no sign in Christ. His institutions were not devised in the interest of the world's speedy evangelization. He could wait for the souls He redeemed as well as for the God He revealed. The waiting energy of the Church is just as faithful as its forward movements, and at certain times more needful. Faith has ever a holy indifference and a masterly negligence which rest on the infinitude of divine care and the completeness of Christ's work.

Christ exhibited God, He did not expound Him. He was His witness, not His apologist. He acted on God and for God; He was a power more than a prophet, and a prophet more than a polemist. He did more to reveal than to interpret. And His revelation was in work more than in word, in a soul more than a scheme. He gave a living Spirit more than a living truth, the Holy Spirit more than a vital principle. In Him God gave Himself, He did not explain Himself. He *was* the revelation, He did not elaborate it. To see Him was to see the Father, not to see how He could be the Father. We have the benefit of the achievement. We love and trust its doer. We might trust Him less if He had more to say about it. Our faith is trust in Christ who died, rather than trust in the faith of a Christ. It is trust in a Christ who effected forgiveness by His work, not who explained forgiveness in His word, or kept His act incessantly in our ears. It was not for the Redeemer to be eloquent, or even explicit, about His own work. He did it, and it acts for ever. It set up no new affection in God, but a new and creative relation on both sides of the spiritual world. It gave man a new relation to God, and God, a new relation, though not a new feeling to man. It did not make God our Father, but it made it possible for the Father to treat sinners as sons.

But the great crisis itself transpired in the secret place of the Most High; and the silence of the gospels reflects the Saviour's own reserve. It is the stillness of a quiet, earnest, strong, retiring man. Yea, it is the silence of the unworldly and unseen, the shadow of the holiest, the gaze of the Cherubim, the hush of the great white throne of holy wars in high places, of far off spiritual things—slow, subtle, solemn, spiritual things. The silence of the first creation no man heard or saw. That silence is repeated in the second. It is the silence of the moving heavens, of the rising sun, of the Resurrection in the cool, dim dawn of the Church's faith and love, of all the mightiest action of the Holy Ghost—yea, of His witness borne in your hearts in this hour when I speak these holy names and presume to call these awful powers. if ye call upon the Father, pass the time of your sojourning here in fear— in reverent and godly fear. For this holy Fatherhood is at its heart the consuming fire.

VIII

I add, with some misgiving, one consideration more. The reserve of Christ in the gospels is part of the silence and isolation which filled the cup of His suffering. He had nobody to speak to about it. Nobody could understand. He had no Paul among His disciples. Peter and John were not yet born into this. Yea, at the last the Father Himself grew silent to Him, and communion ceased, though faith and prayer did not. Sigh or brief soliloquy alone remained. He had to consume the smoke of His own torment and ours. His lonely silence was a needful part of His precious agony, of His suffering work. It was a condition of His work's success. Its dumb submission was essential to His complete practical recognition of the holiness of the judgment He bore. It was part of that perfect obedient praise of the Father's righteousness which rose in human extremity from His faith and love. There was more praise in the tenacity of this dumb solitude than when He rejoiced in spirit and said: "I thank Thee, O Father, Lord of Heaven and Earth." It was holiness owning holiness under the *unspeakable* load of human guilt. It was an essential part of the holy judgment He bore, that it should be borne alone with the Father veiled, the future veiled and (may I say) with some *explicit* sense veiled to Himself of that value which the occultation of His glory and knowledge was having for God and for man. Yes, it was, perhaps, part of His work's perfect glory not to know, to be silent in the agony of knowing only the Father's will and not the Father's way. His self-emptying meant self-limitation in knowledge as in other things. I have already applied to Christ's consciousness the words which Calvin applies to His ubiquity: "The whole Christ was there, but not all that is in Christ was there." And this repudiation of entire knowledge may well have been a vital element in the agony of the great act. It was an act that drew not upon His theology, but on the spiritual resources of His moral personality in its superhuman obedience and trust. His silence may have been due to voluntary ignorance, to nescience by holy and omnipotent consent. It was, perhaps, the abyss of His self-emptying, the triumph of His superhuman humiliation, His utter exercise of those self-imposed limitations which made His incarnation, the negative exertion of His will's omnipotence in all that was needful to redeem. It was perhaps His power through positive trust to curb the passion to know, His acquiescence by faith in some theological ignorance, His consent not *explicitly* to see *how* His mortal obedience expiated and redeemed, His certainty only that it did, that the Holy Father had need of it for His holiness, for His kingdom, for His sons. Had He seen all, He could have suffered but little. To have known in detail at that hour the whole meaning, power, and effect of His sorrow would have been to quench it in the glory that could really only come with salvation, when He had sounded its darkness and risen on the other side. The tree of knowledge is not the tree of life.

And so this silence was the draining of sorrow's cup. To see all would be to suffer none. And to utter suffering is to escape some. To confide it is to ease it. To die alone is the death in death. Silence is sorrow's crown of sorrow, and can be more pathetic than death. And the silence of the gospels reflects the Saviour's true dying, His utter suffering, His nescience, His loneliness, His certainty in darkness, His trust, His perfect obedience. As the brevity of His life was part of His greatness, so the lack in the gospels is the condition of their greater perfection; it is a part of their completeness as a reflection of the Redeemer. And the silence of both reflects the awful silence, the hiding of the Father and the future which was the crowning condition of redemption, and the last worst test of holy obedience and dying trust. It was not the Father's anger but His holy love, unspeakable by word or look, to be uttered only by deed, by Resurrection. As Christ's love could only speak silently at last in the *act* and mystery of dying, so God could only answer silently in the mysterious *act* of raising Him from the dead. And this was more than comforting Him in death, for it was raising Him from death's utmost desolation, from death comfortless, the deadliest death, death's sharpest sting and utmost power. Deep called unto deep, and the Will that died addressed and evoked the Will that raised Him up again in silent antiphon which is now the standing balance and order of the spiritual world for ever.

So it did not become the Captain of our salvation to say much about the cost of His grace or the agony of Fatherhood. And it did become the saved to say very much about it indeed. And it becomes the Church always not only to enjoy the Father's grace, but to learn to prize it. We must gain some reasonable sense of the mystery we cannot fathom. We must weigh the gravity of sin in the face of holiness, for the sake of worshipping the Saviour's grace, and love's earnestness about its holy law. It is not in this effort that the Church has departed from the Holy Ghost or gone back from the teaching of the gospels. The Church may wander far; but, as even Goethe said, she must ever return to adjust her compass at the cross. She cannot rest satisfied with the impressionism of the cross. The cross is not there just for religious effect. The Church takes her moral bearings there. She discovers God's moral world and authority there. She reconstructs man's conscience from there, from the word, revelation and nature of the cross, not its sound and music and effect alone. In an instinct so central, so persistent as this, has the Church been misled? Then either she has not had the Holy Ghost, or the Holy Ghost in her has been false to the work of Christ and its true nature and power.

IX

We put too little, therefore, into the Fatherhood of God if we say He is the Father of us sinners without more ado, that nothing beyond our repentance was due to His holiness, that His love could be trusted if He let His holiness go, that He could show His heart's affections by simply choosing not to press His nature's demands.

We put too little into Fatherhood none the less if we think that the satisfaction of Christ was the source and cause of the Father's grace instead of its fruit.

And we likewise put too little into it if we dwell on the cost of forgiveness to God till we lose all sense of the grace in grace, its fulness, freedom, and spell, its tenderness, patience, and utter magnanimity with us.

But too much no son of man can put into that hallowed Fatherhood which is the whole of God and the fulness of Christ. It is the very nature and totality of Godhead, and the source of man's redemption. Its solemn love is the burden of the Saviour's bloody passion, and it is the consecration of man's red-ripe passion for man. No name so fits our whole soul's whole God. Humanism has nothing so human, Christ has nothing so superhuman as this *"Holy Father"*. It wraps the world like the warm waters of the cleansing sea. They touch the horrors of the nether earth below, and above reflect the heaven's endless smile. It is ever like

The moving waters at their priest-like task
Of pure ablution round earth's human shores.[1]

We cannot simplify it on that name, we cannot exhaust it. It is the deepest name and the dearest. It speaks to child, maid, and man. It is the tenderest, sternest, broadest, most sublime. It stamps our humanest part as our godliest. The life of home, country, humanity, of church and kingdom, of action, passion, conscience, our human ties and duties, tender or heroic—that is what now bears God's monogram in us—the moral soul with all its love, care, grace, devotion, grandeur, woe and joy. The old dear names in their new creation are the divinest still, and the nearest at our need. They are the holiest and most human too. Father, mother, wife, child, lover and maid—that is the old story of which the world never grows weary. Of the tale of romance and of renunciation we do not weary. Two lovers whispering by an orchard wall, these weeping their first-born dead or lost, these chilled and estranged for ever, or these at last grown grey and sleeping together at the foot of the hill—such things outlast in their interest for us all the centuries of human care and crime. They outlive our folly, noise and sin, earth's triumph, glories, failures, fevers and frosts. But not only so. They are immortal also in God. They are hid with Christ in God. Eternity does not draw a sponge over the heart. Our great passions are laid up beneath the altar of the Father's passion to redeem. They are smoothed out there where all crooked things are made straight. For us with our faith in Christ's Holy Father, love is not what the pessimists make it—Nature duping the individual in the interests of the species. It belongs to the eternal. Our brief life translates passion into affection, and our affections into moral worth. It spiritualizes, consecrates them. If life do that, how much more eternity! If life can thus reveal, wherefore not death? If life hallow, how much more does God the Holy! It is His own life that flows in these undying loves and ties. They will not give us the Father, but the Holy Father gives us them a thousandfold. Their perpetual song is but the echo of the Spirit, the murmur in the winding heart of the solemn, ceaseless river, which gladdens the city of God, and its fulness is the music of the world. Our first love and our last, its young dream and its old sorrow, are eternalised in our Alpha and Omega, the Eternal Father, the Holy Redeemer. *There* also is the fountain of the sainthood that weds mankind, has the world for its parish, and lays

---

1. Keats, Sonnet, *Bright Star.*

down its life for those who are neither kith nor kin but thankless and evil. Holy Father! It means a household God in a house not made with hands, the king of a righteous kingdom of loving hearts, a social God with a social gospel, a triune God who is an eternal home and society in Himself. Love, loss, fatherhood, motherhood, wifehood, widowhood, home, country, and the heroisms that renounce these, are all eternal in the heavens. They are embalmed for ever in the heart of the infinite Father, once bereaved of His Son, and the Eternal Son, once orphaned of His Father. That is the holy love, sure of itself, which we need to correct the malady of our oversensitive age.

Never did human pity and affection mean so much as to-day; but neither to-day nor to-morrow will it be dear or solemn enough for that primeval, endless love of God. The grace of the Holy Eternal Father has but one image among men, and it is the holy face of Jesus and Him as crucified. The cause of the cross was not only that man was lost, nor that God is love, but also that the Father is holy. Holiness is love's end, and it is only because He is holy that His Fatherhood is inexhaustible and our loves endure. Holiness is that in the love of God which fixes it and assures it for ever. If holiness fail not, then love cannot. If it cannot be put by, then love cannot fade. The holiness which demanded that Christ should die is, by its satisfaction, our one guarantee of the love that cannot die. If God had taken His holiness lightly, how could we be sure He would never be light of love? But He that spared not His own Son, how shall He not with Him also give us all things, and be to us all things which love should crave? There never was a more tender time than the present. But when we read behind the cross, and not only feel it, the heart of fatherhood is that *moral* tenderness which is so much more than pity, which not only weeps, soothes, and helps— but forgives, and forgives as one who in forgiving has to atone and redeem. To-day we are learning new depths of that *moral* tenderness which is the soul of grace, and that *holy* kindness which is the source of Atonement. The cross has more than the moral majesty that broods on earth's solemnities, renunciations, pities, sorrows, and tragic purifications. It brought into history eternal redemption. We never understood as we do to-day the father of the child; perhaps we never were so ready to believe in the father of the prodigal. But also we never had such promise of understanding the Father of the Saviour.

The Father of our childhood and weakness we beautifully understand. Could it be put more movingly than in Coventry Patmore's poem. He had punished his little son and put him to bed, "his mother, who was patient, being dead". Sore himself, he went to see the child, and found him asleep, with all the queer and trivial contents of a little boy's pocket set out beside him to comfort him.

> "So when that night I prayed
> To God, I wept, and said:
> Ah! when at last we lie with tranced breath,
> Not vexing Thee in death,
> And Thou rememberest of what toys
> We made our joys,
> How weakly understood
> Thy great commanded good—
> Then, Fatherly not less
> Than I whom Thou hast moulded from the clay,
> Thou'lt leave Thy wrath and say,
> 'I will be sorry for their childishness.' "

That is most sweet and poignant pathos. And it is neither too keen nor too kind for the pity of God to His *weak* children. It melts us. It is very sacred.

But there is a deeper, tenderer note. It is the grace of God to His prodigals and rebels. "I, even I, am He that blotteth out thy transgressions, and thy sins and thine iniquities will I remember no more." That bows us. It takes us into the Holy Place.

But One takes us behind that into the holiest of all. Deepest of all, tenderest, most solemn, glorious, silent, and eternal is the Father's joy in the Holy Son obedient on the sinful cross.

That joy is the Father's love of His own holiness. It is His blessed and only form of self-love.

It is all beyond thought, beyond poetry, beyond Scripture, beyond speech. God Himself in that mighty joy refrains from words. He could utter it only in act, in raising Christ from the dead by the spirit of holiness. He met the Son's great act by a greater. Deep answered deep. We can feel it and worship it at the last only in the power and silence of the same Holy Ghost. May He never fail us, but keep us burning unconsumed, sure, wise, kind, and strong, in His endless peace and power. ❦

THE LIVING CHRIST

1897

"Fear not: I am the first and the last, and the living one. I was dead; and see, I am alive for evermore; and have the keys of the unseen and of death."—REV. 1: 17-18.

This is a bundle of paradoxes—contradictions which do not exclude but include each other; nay, which *need* each other.

It is thus that God includes and needs man; the infinite strength needs and includes infinite weakness. To meet our weakness God did not stoop *from* Himself, but *in* Himself.

So also God is the least apparent and yet the most real of powers in the world and life. No God—atheism—is the most plausible and the most incredible of creeds.

Thus also Christ is the most provoking and elusive of beings, but the most haunting, the least to be got rid of. To mere inquiry how fugitive, to faith how near, how steady, how mighty, for time and for eternity! And the cross of Christ, the great absurdity of history, is the centre and solution of history.

Christian faith is a mass of contradictions and a glorious tissue of harmony. It is easy to make it seem ridiculous to common sense. But it is fatal for religion to appeal to common sense.

Our faith is faith in a Christ who is and who is not, in a dead man who is our living God, in the living God who died, in one who was humiliated into eternal exaltation, who in extremest weakness realized and revealed the supreme power of heaven and earth.

What is this faith in this Christ?

It is faith:—

I. IN A HISTORIC CHRIST.

II. IN A LIVING CHRIST.

III. IN A CHRIST PERSONAL TO EACH OF US.

I.—THE HISTORIC CHRIST

There *was* such a man. The story of Him is not an invention. Even if it were conceded that everything told of Him is not literally true, *He* was a reality. His figure is real and palpable in history. There is a distinct and powerful character among the great figures of the past— called Jesus, living in a certain land, at a certain time, with certain aims, doctrines, actions, ways of life, and manner of death.

Moreover, this man is prolonged into posterity. He has had a vast influence in history. You could not deny *that,* even if you were among those that reject the influence for themselves.

But no serious mind or conscience either denies or deplores that influence in the past as a whole. To deplore Christ is to renounce the right to moral consideration. Even if He is not the Redeemer, He has been a vast blessing. He deserves more attention and gratitude than Plato, Aristotle, Dante, Shakespeare, Newton, or any of the heroes of culture and civilization. He has done more for the race, for humanity as humanity. Even if you question His power in eternity, you cannot deny the blessing He has been for time, through those who believed in Him as above and beyond time.

None of the most precious boons of civilization would have been here to-day without Christianity, without Christ. He came in and raised a new civilization out of the wreck of the old. He saved the soul of the old, moreover. Christian Europe has lost nothing essential from Greece or Rome. And it enshrines and embalms their soul. That would remain true, even if His new civilization was presently going to be superseded. It is Christianity that is the continuity of the old world and the new. And it is Christianity that has made the modern nations and all their achievements possible.

Especially is this so with the achievements of love and their growth. There is much to disappoint, especially in the spectacle of modern Europe—the Europe of the newspapers. But even there, ask what would have been had Christianity not come in when it did, had it not worked in these centuries as the principle it is. It has failed to put down war. It has even caused some wars and bitter persecutions. So far, yes. But it has done so chiefly by the infection and corruption of political ideas and methods. Politics have well nigh destroyed Christianity. But the tide has really turned, though not much more. Politics have begun to undergo conversion. The recent Machiavelism of some Christian states has shocked the Christian conscience, and roused more than a few to feel that if Christianity do not master the State, the State will destroy Christianity. This has long been apparent in Church politics; it is now coming slowly home in the politics of the State. And as to war, there is nothing else that even promises to put down war. Democracy and self-interest do not do so, and do not tend to do so. Democracies are even more liable to fits of blind passion than monarchs. And it should be remembered that it was the Christian pulpit and the Christian principle in the press and elsewhere that recently prevented a war between the two great democracies of the world.[1]

There is a Europe, there is a Christendom which does not appear in the newspapers, even in the religious press. Journalism is not so much blind to it as shy of it. It is of vast, silent, spreading influence. It is the Europe, the Christendom of Faith—the civilization of the Spirit, the true Church of the heart and soul. That is the Europe, the America, that makes the real difference from the past, the real promise for the future. It is the Europe that most directly owns the influence of Christ in its heart, its conduct, its faith, and its hope, in life private and public.

Nobody has ever exerted such an influence, whether you like it or whether you do not. And it is an effect produced by One who went in the face of human nature. He gave effect, it is true, to certain vast, deep human *tendencies;* but so far as human *prejudices and tastes* go, He went in their teeth. Here is what Professor Freeman said: "You say, Am I still a believer? Certainly. That is, I believe the Christian religion to be from God, in a sense beyond that in which all things are from God. One cannot study history without seeing this. The fact that there was a Holy Roman Empire—that is, the fact that the Roman Empire could ever become holy in a Christian sense—is enough...I compare it with Islam, which is in the

---

1. In 1895 a grave dispute between Britain and the United States of America concerning the boundaries of Venezuela, was eventually settled by arbitration largely through the influence of the American journalist Godkin, editor of the *New York Evening Post.*

like sort the Arabian religion, the religion of all countries that have come under Arabian influences, and of none other. But mark the difference. Islam succeeds by the most obvious causes; by appealing to all that was good and bad in the Arab of the seventh century. Christianity, on the other hand, went right in the teeth of all that was good and bad in the Roman of the fourth century. Yet it succeeded; and I cannot account for its success by any ordinary cause. As I said in one of my published lectures, "For Caesar Augustus to be led to worship a crucified Jew was a greater miracle than the cleaving of rocks or the raising of the dead."

What a personality that was! If you only study it as a historian might Napoleon, it is an incomparable personality. Think of all that has come from Christ in the way of blessing, in the way of counterworking the curse and corruption, and error which His very followers have infused into His name. Think out with just and careful appreciation the blessing flowing directly from His memory and influence to-day. What a personality! And you cannot get more out than was in. If so much has been got out, how much must there have been in that miraculous soul! And how much remains!

All this may be recognised by a dead faith, what you might call the plebeian faith of the ordinary able man, a poor but honest faith, a faith merely historic and intelligent, as a mere matter of observation. Christ as a historic force is now on a height from which He can never again be displaced. So much the new study of history has done.

But this is hardly faith. It is not living faith. It is not the kind of response Christ died to evoke. It is not the kind of faith that has made even its own meagre kind possible. It is not the kind that has perpetuated His influence, and made His power survive deep in the general heart of man.

On some who study Christ as a mere figure in history there dawns another kind of influence from Him. They begin as historians, as critics, they end as sympathizers, advocates, enthusiasts. They came to embalm Him with their spices, and they stay to worship, and return to confess. They are touched, seized, suborned as His witnesses. They can no more be as impartial as if it were Napoleon, Socrates. The ordinary able man may merely discuss Him. The prizeman, in the pulpit or elsewhere, may make of Him a declamation. But no human-hearted man, no man of soul can really be impartial in dealing with Christ. Our sympathies are engaged, captured, preoccupied. We cannot hold this Man at arm's length. The historic Christ stirs in humane minds a faith, a response, which makes mere criticism difficult or impossible. The critic yields to the discovery that this awful and ultimate critic of his soul never judged men impartially, but always with a bias in their favour, and with a view to their escape. "The Lord is our Judge...He will save us." We cannot view Him in dry light, or discuss Him in cold blood. There comes forth the prelude of a living faith. This Man acts on the heart. He wakes admiration, fear, love, and, above all, faith, trust. He is found to haunt life as no other does. He becomes an unseen spectator and standard of all we do and devise. His beauty terror, dignity, and invincibility pervade us. His love, mercy faithfulness, master us. His indomitable grace survives death and rises again in us. He becomes an imaginative ideal, and then a moral imperative. His principle of Divine Sonship becomes the base of a new religion.

But this is a principle which is inseparable from His Person. He introduced it into history, and He goes down the stream of history with it in His soul. He carries it; it does not carry Him. He does not set it afloat and leave it. Where it is He is. Where He is, it is. Through Him it circulates among leal hearts as current coin. But many separate the two. They are at a stage at which they answer to His principle more than to His Person. They think more of His present legacy than of His present life. Christianity is not for them identical with Christ. He is beautiful, sublime, wise, wonderful, mighty; He affects them strangely, and more than they quite realise and own. He is Preacher, He is Example; nay, He is the incarnation of His principle. But He is not yet the incarnation of God. They do not yet say, "My Lord and my God."

Now these have no dead faith. Yet they have not a living faith: they are "Wandering between two worlds, one dead, The other powerless to be born."[1]

They are much more than critics and historians. But they are not yet the property of Christ, slaves like Paul, devotees like John. They believe in the Christ that lived and was dead. But they do not believe in the absolute Victor, Redeemer, and King, in the Christ that liveth for evermore, with the keys of hell and death. A living faith is not mere sympathy with a historic Christ. It is not admiration, reverence, love of that great ideal. It is not the acceptance of His principle, or the assent to His truth. Nay, response to a merely historic Christ is not adequate even to that Christ. It does not meet His claims. It is not the whole response His teaching wakes, or His work evokes, or His character compels, or His soul sought. Faith in

---

1. Matthew Arnold: *Stanzas from the Grande Chartreuse.*

the Christian principle is not the living faith in Christ. We may hold truth as it is in Jesus, and miss it as Jesus, miss Jesus as Himself the Truth alive for evermore.

II.—THE LIVING CHRIST

When we speak of the difference between a dead faith and a living, what we really mean is a difference in the *object* of our faith more than in its kind. The object determines the kind. The great fundamental difference is between a dead Christ and a living. Living faith is faith in a living Christ. It is only a living Christ that calls out a living faith, a faith with stay and power— especially power.

Do not fret yourself examining your faith, trying its limbs, feeling its pulse, watching its colour, measuring its work. See rather that it is set on a living Christ. Care for that Christ and He will care for your faith. Realise a living Christ, and He will produce in you a living faith. Visit His holy sepulchre in Scripture, and as you pore and wait He will surprise you from behind with His immortal life. A living faith, a living Christianity, a living Christendom, means a living Christ. Christianity is more than Christendom, but Christ is more than Christianity. The truth of Christ is more than its appreciation by any age of the Christian Church. But Christ Himself is more than Christianity. He is more than any truth that can be told about Him, any principle He embodies, or any deeds done in His name. Faith in Christ is faith neither in Christendom (or a Church) nor in Christianity (or a system of creed or conduct). But it is faith in the practical reality of His unseen Person, now living, reigning, guiding from His unseen throne the history and the hearts of men to the Kingdom of God.

He acts in many ways. He acts by His historic character. He acts by His historic Church. But still more He acts by His Eternal Person and Holy Ghost. This living Lord is invisible, invincible, and immortal; He is royal, and at the last irresistible; He is infinitely patient because of infinite power and grace; He acts not only on the large course of human events, but directly on living souls and wills, whether humble or refractory; and He rejoices alike in the love of His Father and the love of His Redeemed, and in the communion of both.

To realize this is more than faith in a historic Christ. But it is what faith in a historic Christ arrives at when it grows up and comes to its own, when it finds its true self and soul, its meaning and fulness, its wisdom and stature in an eternal light.

Why may I say so? Is it all a piece of pulpit dogmatism?

The Christian preacher is bound to say it because it is certain that Christ believed and said it.

He believed and said He was more than a historic servant of God raised for a temporary purpose and then done with. He knew and said that He was before the world ("Before Abraham was, I am"), and that He would outlive the world and be King of the adoring love of the souls He made His own. All things were delivered to Him of His Father. And all things include sin, death, the devil, and mankind. "All power is given Me in heaven and on earth." He would be with His own as the Father was with Him. He went to prepare a place for them, and would come again to take them to it. From heaven He would be still on earth in His kingdom, to watch, guide, and bless. Without Him they could do nothing. And such doctrine does not depend on the fourth gospel alone.

What did all that kind of teaching mean? Either that He was what I have said, or that He was the victim of some egoistic delusion. But if He was a megalomaniac of this kind, what is the worth of His teaching on all else? If He was deceived about Himself, how can you put any value on what He said about the Father, about man, about the world? "Is He to be believed when He spoke of everything but Himself?" Nay, if He was deluded about Himself when He made Himself so central to His truth, He is trustworthy about nothing, and only suggestive in greater or less degree.

You cannot stop with faith in a merely historic Christ if you are in earnest about the matter. Your heart will not let you, and your reason will not. Your historic Christ was one who called Himself much more than historic. And if He was wrong, then He ceases to be an object of entire admiration, and becomes an object of some *pity*. He exercises our patience, and not our trust. Faith in a *merely* historic Christ destroys itself because it makes Christ a mistaken enthusiast. And no mistaken enthusiast can be an object of faith. Unless, indeed, you think so meanly of human nature that you can believe that for centuries it has made a God of such a soul, and taken His craze for its creed, till we have found Him out to-day.

To treat Christ as a mere historic person is not Christianity. It is another gospel from the whole Church's, from the New Testament's, from Christ's own.

Humanity will never part with Christ now. But it can only keep Him by taking His word on a point like this. If it do not trust Him there, it dissolves Him, and cannot hold Him even as a hero or a saint, to say nothing of a Saviour. He becomes less than the ideal man of yesterday if He be not the Redeemer and King to-day and for ever.

If you dismiss Him because He is in collision with the laws of your universe, these laws must not be denied. But are they the laws of the soul as well? Must your soul not be told that He too is a universe, and not simply a fact, or a factor, in ours? If He enter life, it is that life may enter Him. He is a world within the world, the destiny awaiting the world, the truth which the world is working out. He is the order within the order of things, prescribing their order at the last.

That one Face, far from vanish rather grows,
Or decomposes but to recompose,
Become my universe that feels and knows."[1]

Such is living faith in a living Christ. If such a soul live, it must be as Eternal King of the spiritual world. Redeemed Humanity would for ever elect Him King if they could forget that it was He who elected them. He is King, Law, and Principle of the spiritual world. Or else He is lost. His reign is either absolute or doomed.

If He is not living, faith must dwindle and die. Do you think you can feed living faith on a dead Christ? You say, perhaps, living faith in God may now go on, even if we lost some faith in Christ. What! could living faith go on in a God who could let such an one as Christ die, who could disappoint the confident faith of Christ Himself that God would raise Him up to glorious life? How can you have living faith in such a God? Is He the Father if His most glorious, only begotten Son be dead? A poor and undivine Fatherhood! Not so very much mightier than our own if it has to see its best beloved perish and cannot help. If God did not raise Christ, but failed Him after such a faith, how can He be more than a perhaps to any faith of ours? No; living faith, even in God, is faith in a living Christ. It is only such faith that can escape extinction. If He be a living Christ, He is not simply an immortal soul. He is not one among many immortals, not even the first among His peers. It is for those nearest Him that He is most peerless. He is King of the whole realm of the soul, and it is He that keeps our faith alive.

If it be not so, if He is only kept alive by our faith, that faith itself

---

1. Browning: *Apparent Failure*, Epilogue, Third Speaker.

must sink under such a task—the task of keeping Christ immortal. If He is not the living, reigning Christ, He is a Christ growing weaker as the ages move on and He recedes into the past. He becomes less and less a power for faith. As He grows more distant, faith in Him grows more dim. If He be not a living Christ, then every generation makes His influence more indirect. It is transmitted to us through more and more people, and as humanity increases He decreases. More souls are interposed between our souls and Him, and absorb His limited light. He becomes lost and smothered in His Church and its corruptions, like any Buddha. The world moves on and leaves Him behind, moves on and outgrows Him. He becomes chiefly a scholar's Christ. It may even become a hope and an effort with us that we should outgrow Him. Great as He was for His own age, if He be not the living and reigning Christ we may, and even must, hope to reach a point of spiritual perfection beyond His, a communion more intimate with the Father, because knowing more of His will. We may even hope one day to be in a position to do more for His principle than His opportunities allowed Him to do. And each age will flatter itself that it has done so, that it has left Him behind, outdone His work, and can search the soul as He did not. There are no few to be found to-day who would say, for instance, that dramatists like Shakespeare or Ibsen have a knowledge of the heart Christ never had or has.

Well, this is a frame of mind fatal at least to Christ's place as Redeemer. It may esteem Him as Benefactor, but it displaces Him as Redeemer. It clears the ground for a totally new religion. It clears the ground, but it empties the soul, disappoints it, crushes its hope. If Christ were no Redeemer, it would need more than another such Christ: only to utter the sob of disappointment and despair that must rise in passion from the human soul as it awakes to its centuries of illusion, feels its spiritual chagrin, and resigns its eternal hopes. What soul could utter on the true scale of his soul the universal woe, "We trusted it had been He who should have redeemed mankind"? For it is just a Redeemer that we most need from God, and a living Redeemer. It is not a teacher, a living example we need, not a benefactor, not an ideal.

Nay, I will go farther. It is not simply a redemption we need. If Christ had come to perform a certain work of redemption, and then had ceased to be; if He had come to satisfy a divine justice with a holy victim, and had then passed into nothingness after satisfying the conditions and leaving the way free for God's love to go forth; if He had come to perform certain preliminaries of our salvation, and not for ever to be our Salvation—then we should have had in Him neither the Redemption nor Salvation that we need. We need a living Redeemer to take each one of us to God, to be for every one to-day all that He could have been upon earth to any one in that great yesterday, and to be for ever what He is to-day. We need a living Redeemer to plead for us in God, not against God, but against our accusing conscience, to be our Advocate with the Father against our self-condemnation. We need Him as the human conscience of God to come to our rescue against our conscience—and the more so as our conscience is quickened, socialised, exalted, and aggravated by solidarity with all the damnation of the world. Conscience makes us men and heroes. Yes, but it is conscience, too, that mocks our manhood with the memory of our sin, our neighbour's, and our kind's. If we were left alone with our conscience it would do more, on the whole, to overwhelm us than to redeem us or support us. We need some surety more sure and merciful and universal than our conscience. We need something more worthy than our natural moral manhood. We need to be made "more sure that we are Christ's than that we are men", more the servants of Christ's conscience than the heroes of our own, more penitents than stalwarts, more saints than ironsides. That is our need of a Redeemer, of a living human Redeemer, a moral owner and King, a living Christ, a Lord and Master more immortal than ourselves, and the root of all that makes our immortality other than a burden. We need a living Redeemer. We need Him for a living faith. And we need Him, as I have already said, *for a living God*—for the reality of a living God.

Yes, to lose the living Christ is to lose the living God, and so on to lose our human soul and future. Whatever enfeebles the hold of Christ on the world now relaxes its sense of God. To escape from Christ is only to be lost in the vague; it is not to ascend to God. It is faith in Christ that has kept belief in a God from dying out in the world. It is never the arguments of the thinkers or the intuitions of the saints that have done that. If Christ grow distant and dim, the sense of a living personal God, of Christ's God and Father, fades from the soul, and the power of God decays from life. And what happens then? We lose faith in man—in each other, and in ourselves. To lose the sense of God is, in course of time, to lose faith even in our own selves, our confident, defiant selves. The soul that in its own strength defies God, dismisses Him from life, has taken the greatest step to losing faith in itself. How is that? It is thus. What I have said is, lose the living personal God, as in losing Christ you would lose Him, and you lose your own soul, your very self-confidence. And it is thus. Make your God not a living God, but a force, a blind, heartless power, or even an irresponsive idea, and you make Him something your heart and will can have no intercourse with. Will can only commune with will, heart with heart. Make your ideal of Humanity an abstraction, not a living soul like Christ's, and you reduce Humanity, as you would reduce God, to a mere ideal or a mere power. You make God and man at their highest something the heart cannot converse with. You rob them of personality. Yet they remain all the time powers greater than the simple soul. So that the great practical feature and experience of the soul, its personality, is something of inferior worth to the world and its powers. In its nature as living soul, personality falls below the Almighty power of the universe. But once let the human soul be sure of that and it is all over with it. It will soon lose power to stand up against such a universe, against the spectacle of nature, against the shocks of life. The universe will roll over it. It loses confidence in itself, because it lost faith in a living God. The soul is lost because it lost God, the living God; and it lost Him because it lost His revealed Humanity—the living Christ as its Mediator and Redeemer with Him for ever.

Mediator and Redeemer! must we not go farther even than that with an ever-living Christ? Yes, one step farther. Intercessor! Steward and Key-bearer of the spiritual world! "He ever liveth to make intercession for us." It is an ever-lasting Redemption, and therefore it is a ceaseless Intercession.

The Intercession of Christ

The intercession of Christ is simply the prolonged energy of His redeeming work. The soul of Atonement is prayer. The standing relation of Christ to God is prayer. The perpetual energy of His Spirit is prayer. It is prayer (and *His* prayer) that releases for us the opportunities and the powers of the spiritual world. It is the intercession of Christ that is the moving force within all the spiritual evolution of history. It is the risen Redeemer that has the keys of the world unseen—the keys which admit it to history as well as open it to man. The key of the unseen is prayer. That is the energy of the will which opens both the soul to the kingdom and the kingdom to the soul. But never our prayer. It is a prayer for us, not by us.

It is Christ the Intercessor that has the key of the unseen—to deliver *from* death, to deliver *into* fulness of spiritual life. The Redeemer would be less than eternal if He were not Intercessor. The living Christ could not live and not redeem, not intercede. Redemption would be a mere act in time if it were not prolonged as the native and congenial energy of the Redeemer's soul in the Intercession of Eternity. Do not picture Christ the Intercessor as a kneeling figure beseeching God for us. It is God within God; God in self-communion; God's soliloquy on our behalf; His word to Himself, which is His deed for us. Rise to think of His intercession as the standing and inexhaustible energy of the divine soul as Redeemer, its native quality, divinity, and occupation through all the variety of the spiritual world for ever. The priestly atonement of Christ was final, but it was final in the sense of working incessantly, insuperably on, not in its echoes and results with us, but in the self-sustained energies of His own Almighty and immortal Spirit. This is the priesthood which is the end of priesthood, and its consummation the satisfaction of the priestly idea. The chief reason why we resent an ecclesiastical priesthood is not because it impairs our independence, but because it challenges the true, final, and sufficient priesthood and intercession of the Redeemer. It deadens the vitality for us of the living Christ. It darkens the glory of His Reconciliation, beclouds the spirit-world, seals up the soul by sealing the powers of death and the unseen, and taking out of the Saviour's hand the key that opens the spirit-world. The intercession of saints is only an attempt to pick the lock, and the sacrifice of the Mass only a forcing of the bolt which freely yields to the intercession of the Redeemer alone.

III.—THE CHRIST PERSONAL TO US

Faith in Christ (as a last word) is faith in a Christ personal to us.

We must have the historic Christ and more. We must have the living Christ. But a living Christ who only ruled His kingdom in the unseen by *general laws* would be no sufficient Saviour. He must be personal to us. He must be our Saviour, in *our* situation, *our* needs, loves, shames, sins. He must not only live but mingle with *our* lives. He must charge Himself with *our* souls. We believe in the Holy Ghost. We have in Christ as the Spirit the Sanctifier of our single lives, the Reader of our hearts, the Helper of our most private straits, the Inspirer of our most deep and sacred confessions. We must have one to wring from us "My Lord and my God." We need not only the risen Christ, but the returned Christ; not only the historic Christ, nor the heavenly, but the spiritual, the intimate, the Husband of the soul in its daily vigour, its daily conflict, its daily fear, its daily joy, its daily sorrow, its daily faith, hope, love. We need, O how we need, a Lord and Master, a Lover and King of our single, inmost, shameful, precious souls, the Giver and Goal of our most personal salvation, a Conscience within our conscience, and a Heart amidst our heart and its ruins and its resurrection.

That is the Christ we need, and, thank God for His unspeakable gift, that is the Christ we have.

CHRISTIAN PERFECTION

1899

"Whosoever abideth in Him sinneth not... Whosoever is born of God cannot sin."

1 JOHN 3: 6, 9.

THE SIN OF THE REGENERATE

This is one of the hard sayings which are so fascinating in the Bible. It raises one of the problems that are so engaging to our moral thoughts, and one of the anomalies that are so irritating and depressing to our moral experience.

Statements like these texts seem to be met with every kind of contradiction:—

1. In the first place, there is the contradiction offered by John himself.'If we say that we have no sin, we deceive ourselves, and the truth is not in us. If we confess our sins, He is faithful and just to forgive us our sins. If we say that we have not sinned, we make Him a liar.' We are to keep confessing, even as sons of God, which means that we keep sinning; for we cannot be urged to confess over and over sins we did before conversion, and which we had forgiven us as we entered on peace with God by faith. The children of God in John's own view keep sinning; yet here you have it, 'Whoso is born of God cannot sin.'

2. In the next place, there is the contradiction offered by our own experience. We know that we sin as surely as we know our life in Christ. As often as we confess Christ we have to confess Him as Saviour and as Eternal Saviour. We have to come as penitents. Our blessedness is always a salvation, not a mere donation. And we have new sins to confess since we last confessed His salvation and took His forgiveness. We cannot deny that we abide in Him, that would be to deny our faith altogether. But just as little can we deny our daily sin, that it is our fault if we are not more

after His mind. If a Christian's sin mean his severance from Christ, then the more Christian we feel the more severed we must be; because the more Christian we are in conscience the more sensitive we are to our sin, and therefore the less we must feel that we abide in Him and are born of Him, if this text have its face value.

And our own experience is only enlarged by what we know of the experience of greater saints than ourselves. The history of holiness is a record of self-abasements on daily cause. It is a story of triumph and joy, but it is a daily humiliation all the same, and a real, concrete humiliation; not a vague and sentimental self-accusation, but a definite self-indictment as the fruit of a serious self-examination.

3. Moreover, texts like these seem in contradiction with the very nature of faith itself. We are told sometimes that it is faithless on our part not to expect sinlessness in this life from the power of God's grace, deliverance entire not only from sin's guilt but from sin's power, not only from its power but even its presence. But it is just the other way. To say 'I have now no sin' is to give up that relation to God which is the essence of faith, and to stand upon a new and subtle kind of legalism. The man who says that tries to enter on a relation to God which is higher than faith, and therefore he falls out of faith. There is no higher relation possible. Love is but faith in its supreme and perfect form. It is the impassioned expression on the face of faith. There is but one attitude of conformity to the will of God, and that is faith: a faith that, being itself an act of will and obedience, always works outward into love. To go beyond that is to step outside the right relation to God. Faith is not the mere sense of dependence on God, but something much more definite, positive, and real. It is the sinner's trust in God the Redeemer. Once a sinner always a sinner—in this sense at least, that he who has but once sinned can never be as if he had never sinned. His very blessedness to all eternity is a different thing from the blessedness of the sinless. The man whose iniquity is not imputed is a very different being from the man whose iniquity was never committed. One sin is, in a sense, a sin in all. The whole nature is affected by it, and always. Pardon is not the cure of a passing illness, but a new birth in which the whole constitution is changed. It is not the dispersion of a cloud by the same sunny action as lights the ground. It was I who, at my will's centre, did that thing. It was my will and self that was put into it. My act was not the freak of some point on my circumference. It came from my centre. It was my unitary, indivisible self that was involved and is infected. Faith is the attitude of

that same self and will of me to God. And as it has become a sinful self through me or my race of me's, therefore for ever faith is not the faith of the sinless but of the redeemed, not of the holy but of the sanctified, the faith and the love of those who have been forgiven much, forgiven often and long, forgiven always. The very nature of faith is trust of a Saviour, who is not the saviour of my past but of my soul; and it is trust for forgiveness, for forgiveness not only of the old life but of the new. That life is only what it is by reason of grace; and grace is not simple benediction, but blessing as the fruit of incessant forgiveness. It is the same forgiving grace that sanctifies us sinners in heaven and has mercy upon us on earth.

It is a fatal mistake to think of holiness as a possession which we have distinct from our faith, and conferred upon it. That is a Catholic idea still saturating Protestant pietism, and making a ready soil for the virus of Rome and the plague of unethical sacraments. Faith is the very highest form of our dependence on God. We never outgrow it. We refine it, but we never transcend it. Whatever other fruits of the Spirit we show, they grow upon faith, and faith which is in its nature repentance. Penitence, faith, sanctification, always co-exist; they do not destroy and succeed each other; they are phases of the one process of God in the one soul. It is untrue to think of holiness or sinlessness as a possession, a quality, an experience of the soul, and so distinct from a previous and qualifying faith. There is no such separate experience. Every Christian experience is an experience of faith; that is, it is an experience of what we have not. Faith is always in opposition to seeing, possessing, experiencing. A faith wholly experimental has its perils. It varies too much with our subjectivity. It is not our experience of holiness that makes us believe in the Holy Ghost. It is a matter of faith that we are God's children; there is plenty of experience in us against it. That we are justified and reborn is matter of faith. The spirit we have is no possession of ours. It is God's Spirit, and it is ours by an act of faith. To claim sinlessness as the perfect state superseding faith is to fall from faith, not to rise from it. It is because we have sin that we believe—as belief must go in a religion whose nature is for ever revealed as Redemption. Our perfection is not to rival the Perfect, but to trust Him. Our holiness is not a matter of imitation but of worship. Any sinlessness of ours is the adoration of His. The holiest have ever been so because they dared not feel they were. Their sanctity grew unconsciously from their worship of His. All saw it but themselves. The eye is the beauty of the face because it sees everything but itself; and if it betray self-consciousness the charm is dimmed. The height of sinlessness means the deepest sense of sin. If we ever came to any such stage as conscious sinlessness we should be placing ourselves alongside Christ, not at His feet. We should have 'life in ourselves', with Him but not through Him, or through Him only historically. We should pass out of faith into experience, or actual, personal possession like our common integrity. We should be self-sufficient. We should cease to live on a constant look to God in Christ, and repentance would cease. We should be near the fall that so often comes to the sinless. We should be in the moral peril of those who, feeling they have attained this sinlessness, are ready to call each impulse good and lawful, as born from the Spirit with which they are now possessed. Moral perceptions are confused. Evil is called good because it is deduced from the Spirit. 'Out of a state of holiness can come no sin. I may do what I am moved to do and it is not sin.'

All this is contrary to the true nature of faith in a Saviour and His righteousness as the standing essence of the Christian life.

4. Perfection is not sinlessness. The 'perfect' in the New Testament are certainly not the sinless. And God, though He wills that we be perfect, has not appointed sinlessness as His object with us in this world. His object is communion with us through faith. And sin must abide, even while it is being conquered, as an occasion for faith. Every defect of ours is a motive for faith. To cease to feel defect is to cease to trust. To cease to feel the root of sin would be to have one motive the less to cast us on God for keeping. Every need is there in order to rouse the need for God. And we need God chiefly, not as a means to an end, not to satisfy earthly need, to keep the world going, to comfort us, or to help us to the higher moral levels. We do not need God chiefly as a means even to our own holiness. But we need God for Himself. He Himself is the end. We need chiefly communion with Him; which is not confined to the perfectly holy but is open to all in faith, and possible along with cleaving sin. To treat a living person as an end, to seek him for himself, has but one meaning. It is to love him, to have our desire and energy rest in him, to have our personal finality in him. So it is that we need and seek God, not His help nor His gifts—even of sanctity, but Himself. His great object with us is not our sinlessness but our communion. "Give me thy heart." He does not offer us communion to make us holy; He makes us holy for the sake of communion.

It has pleased God to leave us in our sin (though not to our sin) that we may be driven to seek more than His help, namely Himself. We do not receive a new will, a new nature, from God, and then go on of ourselves, having got all that He can give. We are compelled by our cleaving sin to press on into close and permanent communion. "My grace is thy sufficiency." It is not simply our ability, but our sufficiency. It is our perfection no less than our power. We end with it as we began. We end with the same forgiving grace as started us. The recipients of grace are much more than the servants of uprightness. The prodigal was more after God's heart than his brother. And the same would have been true had the brother been sinless by a far finer standard than he had, so long as it was sinless self-sufficiency, a self-contained sinlessness. The headlong sin is perhaps a safer thing than the sinless security. All life, it has been said, is the holding down of a dark, wild, elemental nature at our base, which is most useful, like steam, under due pressure. So with sin and its mastery by faith. The pressure from below drives us to God, and the communion with God by faith keeps it always below. The outward pressure of nature, and even of perverted nature, in man develops in him through God, a power which converts, controls, utilises, and exalts nature. It is doubtful if real holiness is quite possible to people who have no "nature" in them, no passion, no flavour of the good brown earth. Take away that elemental rage from below and you make faith a blanched and inept thing. You have no more than quietist piety, passive religion, perfect in sound happy natures as an enjoyment, but very imperfect as a power. Faith, in the true sense, is all-sufficient, because it brings a rest which is itself power, force, will. It is the offspring of God's power and man's; it is not the mere occupation of man by God, which as often means suppression as inspiration.

5. There is another aspect of the collision between faith and the idea of sinlessness as it is often pursued. Sinlessness is a conception in its nature negative and individual. It has often been pointed out how for this reason it tends continually to an ascetic way of life and morals. Faith, on the other hand, is in its nature positive and social. Its spirit and destiny is love. Love, and not sinlessness, is the maturity of faith. There is an egoism about the sinless idea which stamps this order of piety as immature, remote, purist, and pre-occupied. Human fellowship is otiose to it. Men can be done with or without if only "souls" be won. There is a suspicion of want of heart. A man may put away many sins, and cultivate no small devotion, and yet be a loveless self-seeker and a spiritual *aiguille*. There are certain forms of self-edification which run out into self-absorption, and leave men, and especially women, working at

goodness rather than at duty. This is a frequent result of the culture of sinlessness, and it is in its nature anti-social. It becomes indifferent to churches, and finally to the Church. It is inter-denominational, then undenominational, then it ends in a new sect which is not a church so much as a coterie, and lives upon piety more than on faith.

But God's end in Christ is a Church community, apart from which and its faith and love there is no effectual sonship. In the design of God what is sinless is primarily the Church and not the individual. It is the Church and not the individual that is the counterpart of Christ. If we are complete in Christ, we are complete only in a holy and Catholic Church. A Church of sanctified egoisms would be no Church. Its essence would not be faith but moral or spiritual achievement. If the Church in heaven be one with the Church on earth its sanctity co-exists with much sin. Its heavenly perfection is not sinlessness—'That they without us should not be made perfect.' Nor is any fancied sinlessness to which a mortal may attain to be disjoined from the sin of his age and kind. There is more of it in him than he knows. The isolation that he fancies is impossible. And the General Confession misbecomes him no more than it does the poor publican whose mood leaps to its words.

There may be much sin tarrying in a man if there be but the love of God overriding it, and the love of man in God. Love is not a mere reduction of sin as an amount, but it is a life turned in a new way, tuned to a new key, vowed to a new Lord, and lived in a new spirit. The difference (as I have urged) is one of quality, not of quantity. And it is along that qualitative way that our perfection lies—in a heart that loves, and loves not many but much. It has the source of all its love in the faith to which much is forgiven; the source of its faith in the grace that forgives much; and the condition of its holiness in the fellowship of many whose sin is still a sorrow but a sorrow still. The holiness of Christ Himself was a holiness conditioned by the brotherhood of many sinners whom He was not ashamed to call brethren. And it is the holiness of One who is organically united with a Church in large part sinful still.

So much for the contradictions involved by the idea of mere sinlessness, especially for this life, as the form of perfection and holiness.

6. Where does the solution of these contradictions lie? We ought to find it in the same John who presents the problem. A real revelation, and a true apostle of revelation, push forward no problem whose solution they do not carry in the rear. The problem is but the deflection of the light as it enters our denser air.

John himself believes in two kinds of sin, and both of them are possible to the believer. "There is a sin unto death...and there is a sin not unto death" (I John v. 16, 17). It was a distinction current in the Old Testament, and it explains much in the New, where it is deepened. The sin unto death is when a man falls entirely out of communion with God. He loses the life of God from his soul permanently—I do not say eternally. He has not Eternal Life *abiding* in him. The world conquers him. The habit of his mind becomes earthly; and if he has relapsed it is a more inveterate worldliness that holds him, because faithlessness makes his old faith seem a mockery. He is bitter because he is disillusioned. Sin becomes not an attack, an episode, or a lapse, but the principle of his life. I do not mean gross sin, necessarily, but the godless habit. It settles down on him and into him as frost penetrates the ground. He relapses, never to rise again. That is the sin unto death. And the sin not unto death is every transgression which still leaves the habit and sympathy of the soul for God a living thing. There are lapses which a man by vigilance, repentance, prayer, and well-doing can repair. Sin is a region he may visit, but it does not become his element. He falls into sin, but not into godlessness. The chill is thrown off. The frost does not go in upon him. The attack does not reach the heart. Every believer has more or less of this sin in him, and the risk of it always. But it does not cut him off from the divine life. There is a daily confession, a daily forgiveness, a daily cleansing of the channels of the grace of God.

Now the former, the sin unto death, is sin by preeminence. The man becomes identified with it. He loves sin, he does not love God. His life is one act of sin. And it is incompatible with the regenerate life of faith. Whoso is born of God sinneth not in this sense. No man so sinning abides in Christ. Whoso abides in Christ sinneth not this sin. He may commit sins, but he does not live sin like the man who has returned to be a worldling and practically renounced Christ. Sin does not become his world, his element. His sympathies and affinities, his effort and his service, are all to goodness and to God. His life on the whole and at the core is a life of faith and of growing mastery over the world.

7. But John seems to imply that once a man is born of God relapse is impossible: 3: 9, "He cannot sin, because he is born of God." Now, I admit with great reverence that for the modern Christian mind such language is too absolute. Had John written with an eye to modern ways of thinking he would have said something to show on the spot, as he does show elsewhere, that he did know the difference between the ideal and the

actual, between a moral and a natural necessity, between a judgment of experience and a judgment of faith. If we reason from experience we do find that men born of God have fallen into sin, and have sinned even unto death. Men remain free, with the perils of freedom, even as the subjects of divine grace. The compulsions of God are not natural necessities. The "cannot" here does not mean a natural impossibility as if we said, he cannot fly, cannot fall from the earth's surface, if he is born on the earth. There is no such necessity as if, when a man is born of God, all the rest followed of itself by inevitable sequence and a causative chain. It is not as if sinlessness then worked itself out in us without effort. To be born of God means to pass into fellowship with a living will; that is to say, it is to develop into a greater intensity of living will, to be more than ever a doer, a free doer, if we are like God, and a doer of righteousness, of holiness. "Cannot sin" means not that he is not able to sin, but that his principle will not allow him to sin. As the regenerate personality he cannot do it. He may, of course, be at the same time something other than the regenerate personality in his actual condition so far. But in so far as he is the servant of that personality he cannot. "You cannot do it," we say to a man, not denying the physical possibility, as if he were paralyzed or in jail, but denying the moral possibility. "You cannot, consistently with your principles do it; you cannot, with your nature, with all I have known of you, do it; it would not be you if you did it; you simply cannot." Ideally, whoso is born of God cannot sin. That is the *absolute* truth. That is a judgment of faith as distinct from a judgment of experience. It arises from what we know of God, of Christ, not of human life. These texts of John's are all judgments of faith, formed from his knowledge of the absolute holiness and power of Christ. He has forgotten for the moment the actuality of man. He is possessed with the sense of the omnipotence of Christ. That will be *finally* as actual as it is now ideal. It is the ultimate reality. It is the surest thing in existence. John was speaking from the interior of Christ, possessed by the faith of His moral omnipotence. The words were not written by a man who had attained sinlessness, or watched it in others, and then worked out its implications backward to Christ. They came from one who by faith and not experience had grasped this nature, power, and place of Christ. Experience works up from nature to infer God's power and glory; from human love to infer a divine tenderness and fatherhood; from personal history to implications about Christ and God. And that is the method of a subjective, literary, and humanist age like the present. But faith works downward from its grasp of God in Christ alone, from its absolute and eternal certainties, to actual life. And it works not merely with an inference but with an ought; not with implications but with compulsions; with demands absolute in order to be final and effective; not upon thought or truth, but on conduct. Faith does not induce from life what God must be, but it deduces from God what life must be. It does not predicate about God; it prophesies about man. The experimental religion of true faith is not based on experience, but on revelation and faith. It is *realised* by experience, it proceeds in experience; but it does not proceed *from* experience. Experience is its organ, but not its measure, not its principle. What we experience we possess, but faith is our relation not to what we possess, but to what possesses us. Our faith is not in our experience, but in our Saviour. It is not in our experience of our Christianity, but in a Christ Who, while we are yet without experimental strength, both dies and lives for us. John concludes from Christ to man as the normal man in Christ should be, as Christ alone is. It is not a logical but a Christological judgment. To abide in Christ certainly would be to escape sin. It would not be to acquire sanctity as a recompense for faith, but it would be to perfect that life of faith which is the only sanctity. He who sins does so because he hath not seen Christ or known Him, has not seen into Him and understood Him. He has perhaps been thinking of his own sin, and arguing up from that experience that he must be out of Christ, instead of dwelling on the Redeemer and working down with a spirit-compulsion on his own sin. He has not grasped Christ's spiritual omnipotence in temptation, has not gone in upon Christ, but merely hung on Christ. To hang upon Christ, and to do no more than hang, is to be a drag on Christ and a strain on man. To see and know Him is to enter and live in Him, to walk, run, mount, by the communion of His life. The fall of many who once were Christ's is because they took no serious means with themselves to prosecute their life in Him, but were dragged in His wake till they got tired of the strain. There are men to-day who once tasted Christ, but their serious will was not given to their Christian life but to their affairs. And so the world, having monopolised their *will*, submerged their soul. And to be dragged after Christ, submerged in a medium so dense as the world, means a friction and a strain so severe that they took their fatal relief by cutting the cord—and drifting.

8. I wish to lay much stress on the vital difference between the saint's sin and the sinner's sin, as these texts carry it home to us. It has a vital bearing on the question of a sinful and a sinless perfection, the perfection which is faith, and the perfection which has outgrown faith and become

only rarefied character or conduct. Any perfection which does that has become another than Christian perfection, and in leaving faith behind has fallen from faith. .

The difference between the Christian and the world is not that the world sins and the Christian does not. It suits the world to think that it is; because it offers a handy whip to scourge the Church's consistency while resenting its demands. But such a distinction is no part of the Church's claim. Nor does it mark off the Christian's worldly years from his life in Christ. A difference of that kind is merely in quantity—all the sin on the one side, none of it on the other. But the real difference (I must say often) is not in quantity; it is in quality. It is not in the number of sins, but in the attitude toward sin and the things called sin. It is in the man's sympathies, his affinities; it is in his conscience, his verdict on sin, his treatment of it—whether the world's or his own. The world sins and does not trouble; it even delights in it. In sin it is not out of its element it may even be in its element and most at home there. The fear and hate of sin is not in the least its temper. But with the Christian man there is a new spirit, a new taste, bias, conscience, terror, and affection. His leading attitude to sin is fear and hate. His interest, his passion, is all for good and God. He himself is different from himself. He is renewed in the spirit of his mind. He may indeed lapse. The old instinct, the old habit, breaks out, and surprises him off his guard. The old vice fastens on him in a season of weakness. The old indifference may creep back. Mere nervous exhaustion may make him feel for a long time as if the spirit had been taken from him. But these are either interludes, or they are upon the outskirts of his real nature. The loyalty of his person is still true, and his course in the main is right, whatever deviations the storms may cause, or however the calms may detain and irritate him. What is the thing most deep and assertive in him? I mean, what is most continuous in him? I do not ask what asserts itself *oftenest,* but what asserts itself most persistently on the whole, and in the end most powerfully and effectively. What is the real and only *continuity* of his life? Is it a sinful temper and bias, a sinful joy or indifference, broken only occasionally, and ever more rarely, by spasms of goodness, glimpses of holiness, freaks of mercy and truth? Or is it the sympathy and purpose of holiness, clouded at times by drifts of evil, and cleft, to his grief, by flashes of revolt? That is the question. And it is the way the question will be put at the last. It will not be, How many are your sins and how many your sacrifices? but, On which side have you stood and striven, under which King have you served or died? A man may abide in the many-mansioned, myriad-minded Christ, even if the robber sometimes break into his room, or if he go out and lose his way in a fog. You stay in a house, or in a town, which all the same you occasionally leave for good or for ill. The question is, What is your home to which your heart returns, either in repentance or in joy? Where is your heart? What is the bent of your will on the whole, the direction and service of your total life? It is not a question settled in a quantitative way by inquiry as to the occupation of every moment. God judges by totals, by unities not units, by wholes and souls, not sections. What is the dominant and advancing spirit of your life, the total allegiance of your person? Beethoven was not troubled when a performer struck a wrong note, but he was angry when he failed with the spirit and idea of the piece. So with the Great Judge and Artist of life. He is not a schoolmaster, but a critic; and a critic of the great sort, who works by sympathy, insight, large ranges, and results on the whole. Perfection is not sinlessness, but the loyalty of the soul by faith to Christ when all is said and done. The final judgment is not whether we have at every moment stood, but whether having done all we stand—stand at the end, stand as a whole.

Perfection is wholeness. In our perfection there is a permanent element of repentance. The final symphony of praise has a deep bass of penitence. God may forgive us, but we do not forgive ourselves. It is always a Saviour, and not merely an Ideal, that we confess. Repentance belongs to our abiding in Christ, and so to any true holiness.

We may be essentially parted from our sin while yet it hangs about us. The constitution is renewed, but the disease recurs in abating force. The new nature asserts itself over the head of reactions. We lust for the fleshpots of Egypt, and we return upon our tracks and move in a circle; but it is, after all, but a loop upon our larger line of onward march. The enemy is beaten, though he makes guerilla raids and carries off something we deplore. Our progress is a series of victories over receding attacks which sometimes inflict loss. And the issue turns on the whole campaign, not on a few lost battles. We sin, but we are not of sin. We are its master, though at times the convict seizes the warder and gets him down. But it does not *reign* in us. It is not our life-principle, though it may get expression in our life. We sin, but not unto death. We still have and still use the Advocate with the Father. Against our sin we plant ourselves on God's side. There is that strange power in us to be two yet one, to be a seventh of Romans, to face ourselves, yea to face a divided self, as if we were three in one, and to say No with the total man to a sin which extorts a partial or occasional Yes. Every act of faith is saying No to a sin which says Yes in us. And sometimes the Yes drowns the No, while on the whole the life in faith says Yes to God. We lose on items, but we gain on the whole account. We are free from sin before we are rid of it, and of *all* its effects we are never rid. To all eternity we are what our sin has made us, by God's grace to it either as taken or refused. At our eternal best we are what redemption has made us, and not sanctification alone. We enter heaven by a decisive change, and not merely by a progressive purification. And this is the very marrow of Protestant divinity and Evangelical faith.

9. I should not like to be thought to mean that if the regenerate sin, it is not really they who sin but the flesh in them, the old man still surviving but not affecting their will. If the will were not affected the struggle would not be so severe, nor the tragedy of the conflict so intense. The passion and pity of Romans 7 would not be the classic and searching thing it is and always has been if it were only a will at war with a tendency. It is two wills at war. It is at least a divided will. "It is no more I that do it, but sin that dwelleth in me" cannot mean that the will is wholly on the right side, but that in some slumber of it the dark unholy element wakes to seize the helm and give the course. That would be sad and mad, but not so bad as the awful situation whose despair calls for the redeeming intervention of the Son of God. The sin dwelling in the man is a sinful will, sinful volitions. It is not as if he *had* sin, but did not *do* sin. Sin is essentially an act of the will. And our acts cannot be severed from our central will in the way that these extenuations suppose. There is nothing in a man deeper than his source of action. There is no central something which can be the subject of sinlessness, a holy *Ding an sich,* while the casing of it is spotted with transgression which is not fatal because it is peripheral. Such psychology is mediæval, Catholic, and outgrown. There is nothing at the core which is unaffected by the, act of sin. When sin is done, it is the man that sins. In each act which is not a mere occurrence it is the personality that is involved. Anything done in us, to us, or through us, is not an act, and is not sin, however damnable the sin is that may be the source of it outside us. There comes to my mind Shelley's *Cenci* and its preface.

In the sinful act it is the personality that is involved at its centre, but it need not be involved in a fatal and final way. It is very rarely that any single act embodies and exhausts the *entire* personality. That were the sin unto death, or else the divine act that as decisively redeems. And in either case the act is the compendium of a whole series of acts, which expresses the character of the personality. Acts may be done by the will, good or evil which involve the personality from its centre, and affect it, but do not seal and decide it for ever. Thus will may sin, but the personality, the *series* of volitions, the ruling habit and character of the will, is not given up to evil, and has not chosen it as its good. There may be sinful volitions in us, and yet the sinful principle does not really own us, but the good. "It is no more I that do it" does not mean that it is not his will; for it is. But it does mean that it is not his total, ruling, and distinctive personality that does it. Sin captures certain volitions, but not the whole personality that exerts the volition. The sin comes from the centre, but it has not its home in the centre. Each sin comes from the central will, but not from the focus of the personality. It is a case of two sets of volitions, one of which is a chain, and the other a mere series. The evil volitions do not cohere in habit and affection. The man may put his whole force at any mad moment into a simple volition, but not his whole personality. As the new and regenerate personality he does not sin; and he cannot, in this sense, till the frequency of the sinful volitions, and their neglect, forge them into a chain, and bind the personality under them. It is not sin in the final sense till the sinful volitions are multiplied and spread through his personality, giving it its habit and affection, and dyeing it to the colour of evil. Passion becomes vice, and vice becomes his element.

10. The coherent and continuous line in our Christian life is the line of faith. The sins make a certain series, but broken, scattered, irregular. They emerge, but they do not make the continuity. They may bend the continuous line, or bury it, but they do not break it. They are foreign to us and not germane. What is germane is Christ and faith. Our prevailing habit of soul and bent of will is Christ's. And our falling out may even be (by His grace and our serious treatment of it) but the renewal of love. The fellowship is interrupted, but the base of the character is unchanged. The soul is not subverted. A cable still connects the two shores—Christ's and ours. If it break at a place it can be mended by pains, and connection restored. But the habit of sin, the worldly mind, takes the cable away. While it is there, defect is not destruction. "A sectary," says the Apostle to Titus, "after the first and second warning reject, knowing that he is subverted and sinneth, being judged by himself." There was no subversion, no sin unto death, in his sinful acts, till, in the face of light and warning, they became inveterate, a second nature, the ruling, perverse, crusted habit of his life. It is not sins that damn, but the sin into which sins settle down. Good and evil coexist in the believer as in the redeemed world. But they coexist in a very different way; the currents set

differently; the proportions are different; and it makes all the difference whether they are at the centre or the circumference of the soul, whether they are in its citadel or its suburbs. There is sin as the principle of a soul and sin as an incident, sin which stays and sin which visits. Visitations of sin may cleave indefinitely to the new life, and the freedom to sin and the risk are always there. The great justification does not dispense with the daily forgiveness. There is the great forgiveness once for all, when the man passes from death to life, to a new relation with God; and there is the daily forgiveness which renews it in detail and keeps the channel of grace clean, once it has been cut, and prevents it from silting up. There is the great forgiveness from sin which we ask in Christ's name alone, and there is its detail in the daily forgiveness which depends also on our forgiving daily. There is the bathing of the whole man into the regeneration in which he is born of God, and there is the washing, which is the cleansing of the feet daily exposed and daily soiled. There is all the difference between the pardoned sinner and the pardoned saint, between the step out of the world and the steps up to God. We have to work out into practice what we are in principle, to become what we are and are not, to fight sins because we are freed from sin. And failures in practice, however dangerous, are not the same as the great failure to place ourselves on the side of righteousness and holiness all our days.

It is easy to see the moral value of these great spiritual truths, the greatness, amplitude, magnanimity, freedom, they lend to life. It is always thus with the great spiritual realities. Apart from their direct and conscious power over us, they have an indirect power in us which we but partly know. We acquire their habit. We take life nobly. We escape from moral or mental scrupulism. We teach mere accuracy its true place, and we rescue veracity from the pedagogue for the seer, from Fröbel for Carlyle. We rise above the bondage of the small moralities and punctilios of life, to a noble carelessness which is the truest duty to details and the condition of doing them justice, and no more (which would be less). We walk in the spirit, and escape the importunities of the flesh. It is only so that we are fair to both flesh and spirit. To treat life as a whole is the only justice to the parts of life. And this wholeness of vision, this totality of soul, it is not given even to Art to create, but to Jesus Christ. There have been certainly more magnanimous and patient Christians, in proportion, than artists. To see life most steadily and whole is, after all, the gift of Christ, as it was the power of Christ. He saw the soul from its centre and from its height. And the bane and travail of the world-soul was His, and only His, in the most real and effective sense. The true, sound, and steady view of life does not belong to man's criticism of life, even when the phrase means poetry; it belongs to the judgment of God, Who judges the world in Christ. He judges best who judges last. It is the final judgment that is the soundest. And that is the judgment of Christ, and of those whose moral and spiritual discrimination are cultivated with Him. Thus we are at once saved and judged. Salvation is quite as much judgment as privilege. And being judged, we sit secure upon the world. There is no fear or favour to deflect our own judgment. We are united with Him Who is Himself the final, and therefore faultless, Judge. Know ye not that the saints shall judge the world? The final sanity is complete sanctity. And the Holiest is the Key to the whole.

II

SANCTITY AND FAITH

"Every man perfect in Christ Jesus."—Col. 1:28.
"Complete in Him."—Col 2: 10.

Christianity is the perfect religion because it is the religion of perfection. It holds up a perfect ideal, it calls us *incessantly* to this ideal, and it calls *all* to this ideal. *Each* man is called, and each man *is always* called, to it. It is a religion that issues from the perfect One, and returns to His perfection. But it returns through a far country and a dread. It returns by way of Redemption, so that the means of reaching this perfection for us sinners is not achievement but faith.

Christianity is not the perfect religion in the sense of being revealed as a finished, rounded, symmetrical whole. It is not perfect in the sense of a closed circle, or a plastic form, which can be altered in nothing without being spoiled. It is not a perfection of proportion, of harmony, of symmetry. That is the Greek, pagan idea of perfection; whereas in Christianity we enter the perfect life maimed. The pagan idea of perfection is balance, or harmony of parts with each other. It is self-contained and self-poised. The Christian idea is faith, or harmony of relations with the will and grace of God. It is self-devoted, complete in Him; the perfection not of finish but of faith. It is perfect, not because it presents us with perfection, but because it puts us in a perfect attitude to perfection. Our perfection is not some integrity which we *possess,* in the sense in which the Vatican possesses the faultless Venus, or Christ's infallible Vicar. The one is as pagan in its idea of perfection as the other. It is the æsthetic idea of mere consistency, flawlessness, symmetry of thought and order, external, palpable, and unspiritual. But Christian perfection is something which we are put in the perfect way to *realize,* in the sense that we realize a living, moving ideal of character and life. It is not something with which we are presented; it is not even something we are to *believe;* but it is something into which we are *redeemed.* The perfection of Christianity is not even in the *ideal* of perfection it offers, but in the *power* of perfection it implants; not in its ideal of a Son of God, but in the power it gives, with *the* Son of God, to become sons of God by believing in His name.

Moreover, the perfection of God in Christ is not only a universal demand, but an instant; it is something which we can and must enter on in this life. We cannot exhaust it in this or any life, but we can and must be among the perfect in this life. "Be ye perfect" does not mean, Aim at a perfection in eternity, many lives and cycles away: the idea of cycles of development however true, is foreign to the New Testament. It means, Enter here and now on the perfection of God.

There are two notions of perfection which are wrong, and a third which is right. But all three are right compared with the notion that we are to wait for perfection till some indefinite time in the infinite future. All three urge that Christian perfection is a condition of actual, living people in this world. It is a religion, a faith; it is not merely a hope.

The first idea is Pietist; the second is Popish; the third is Protestant, Apostolic, Christian.

1. The Pietist idea pursues perfection as mere quietist sinlessness with a tendency to ecstasy. Its advocates are people sometimes of great grace and beauty; but it represents a one-sided, narrow, and negative spirituality. Its religion is largely emotional, mystical, and introspective. Its adherents are apt to be the victims of visions and moods. They seek perfection in a state of sinlessness. It is a condition largely subjective, ascetic, anæmic, feminine. It prescribes an *arbitrary* withdrawal from the interests, pursuits, and passions of life. It is a cloistered virtue. It is *distrait,* not actual. There is an absence of true humility. In its stead there may be either a laboured counterfeit, as painfully sincere as it is unsimple; or there is a precise self-righteousness which cannot veil a quiet air of superiority. It is certain that the perfect man will be the last to know how perfect he is. It is not a thing that can be worked at. For essential to all

perfection is humility, and it is too humble to know how humble it is. In its choicer forms this pietism is devoted to love and prayer; but it seldom escapes the tinge of self-consciousness in their culture. In too many cases the prayer is superficial, mindless, without searching insight or passionate worship; while its love is limited, placid, and pale. Its holiness is to the great and classic sainthood, whether Roman or Protestant, as the drawing-room song is to music.

Moreover, this perfectionism is too individualist to feel how the single soul is tainted with the sin of its kind, and its possible achievement lamed by the slow progress of the race. The kind of perfection it aims at is made impossible by the ties that bind us to the part of mankind which is still unregenerate. And with all its introspection, it is too unpsychological to realise how the traces of sin live on in the sin-tainted will. Its self-examination is too mindless, too little mordant, for the individual, as it is too individual for the race. It knows of the exceeding sinfulness of sin, but its moral imagination is too poor to *realize* it. And there are some advocates of this sinless perfection who are of pensive not only to the world, but also to the best of the Church. Their dulness of moral perception, commonness of fibre, and poverty of ideal breed a self-satisfaction which is little removed from Pharisaism. And for public life they are of little worth. They may belong to the National Church, but for want of spiritual freedom they show little interest in the crucial issues of national Christianity. Their treatment of Scripture is accordingly childish. But they abound in devoted philanthropy. They have done much to quicken missionary zeal. And it is a service to insist on the idea of perfection as a present demand and an unworldly call. Their chief error is the identification of perfection with sinlessness. It is not the will of God that in this life we should be sinless, lest we should find a perfection apart from forgiveness.

2. The Popish idea of perfection has much in common with the Pietist. It is unworldly in the negative sense; it flees from the world, it does not master it. It is embodied in the monk and the nun. In the Roman system the monk is the ideal man, the nun the ideal woman. These stand on the summit of moral and spiritual greatness. They are likest Christ. They obey Christ most perfectly. Well, you have Gospels in your hands. You have what Rome has—the Bible and the Holy Ghost. Do you find it so? Was Christ the Divine Monk? Did He recommend the cloister? Were His chief commands poverty, celibacy, and obedience to ecclesiastical superiors? To Rome the last of these is the greatest. Never forget that

perversion. Was it so with Christ, with Paul?

The whole Roman system rests on the double morality involved in this distinction. It is a religion by double entry. It teaches that only some are called to perfection, while for the majority the demands made are much more ordinary. Rome succeeds, like certain governments, by lowering the educational standard for the masses, by not being too hard on the natural man. But it canonises a starved and non-natural man, on whom it is very exacting. It compounds for its laxity with its adherents by its severity with its devotees. There are *precepts,* it says, which all must obey, and there are *counsels* which are only for those few destined to perfection. There are the commandments of the moral law for all, and there are the counsels distinctive of the Gospel, like loving your enemies, or voluntary poverty, which are not commanded, but only advised for those who are set on perfection. The Roman Church reckons twelve of these. There are thus two grades of morality, two classes of men, two moral standards set up inside Christianity and inside the race. All are not alike before God. And all are not called to perfection in Jesus Christ; only a minority, only an aristocracy of Christians are. It is not said that only a minority attain, you will note; nor that those who respond to Christ are the true aristocracy of life amid a common world; but that only a minority of believers are *called* or intended by God for perfection in Christ. And these are not active but contemplative people, monks and nuns. *They* are the ideal Christian men and women. Whereas perfection in Christ is the essential call and badge of all Christians, and must be defined in harmony with that principle.

If the history of the monastic orders do not effectively destroy for us that idea of perfection, we must plunge, with Luther, into the principle and gospel of the New Testament again. I am not saying that human nature rises up against that kind of manhood. That would not be fatal. For there are choice forms of Christian manhood, such as I Corinthians 13, which are not very welcome to mere human nature, and not in its power. If I hear a mere lusty athlete, a lazy libertine, or a keen worldling laughing at monks and nuns, my Christian sympathies for the occasion go to the cloister. I become for the hour a pervert to Rome. Mere natural manhood is not the criterion of such things. The Cross is against human nature. But what does rise up against that kind of perfection is the spirit and principle of the Gospel, the faith and freedom that broke forth from the Cross, first in St. Paul, and then in the Reformation, which is our great Christian legacy and trust. These Pietist and Papist ideas of perfection are Catholic more than Evangelical, and thus are destroyed by the vital, free, final,

sufficient, and perfect principle of Christian faith.[1] The true perfection is
the perfection which is of God in faith. The perfect obedience is not the
obedience which is *associated with* faith or from it, but the obedience of
the soul which is faith, and which is the saving power and perfection for
all. To be perfect is to be in Christ Jesus by faith. It is the right relation to
God in Christ, not the complete achievement of Christian character.

3. The Protestant idea of perfection is the possession of the
righteousness of God. And the righteousness of God, in the New
Testament idea, is something which is a gift of God to us and no
achievement of ours before Him. It is a justification of us, a righting of us,
effected by Him, and on our side appropriated by the obedience not of
conduct but of faith. On the human side, indeed, it is faith, which is held
by God to be our righteousness, our true adjustment to the ultimate moral
reality, which is Christ. In faith we are in the right and perfect relation to
God. But God's justification of us is a perfect and complete thing. In faith,
therefore, we possess the perfect will of God concerning us. We enter on a
full salvation. We have as ours the fulness of Christ. The Roman theology
knows only of a perfection, a righteousness, which is an acquisition,
which is always growing and never there, which is not complete in the act
of union by living faith, but must always be eked out by the sacraments
and the obedience of the Church. There is, indeed, a true sense in which
the perfection even of faith grows. It becomes actual in life and practice;
but that adds nothing to the perfection which is ours in the incredible
salvation which we take home by supernatural faith. Faith is implicit;
what is explicit is experience. We but unfold a perfection which is in God
s sight *there,* we do not accumulate a perfection which we are always
striving to place there. The queen and mother of all the virtues is not our
subjection and obedience to the Church. Implicit faith in anything
institutional is usurped faith. The true faith is implicit in Christ, in Whom
are hid all the treasures of wisdom and knowledge. Faith is in its nature
obedience, but it is the will's obedience to Christ. This is the root and
mother of virtue; this is the new life with the promise and potency in it of
all the perfection which may become actual in us by any sanctification.
Our sanctification only unfolds in actual life the ideal perfection in which
we really stand by faith in Christ. And yet this ideal perfection, being of
pure and free grace, is not the vision foreseen by God of our moral effort's

---

1. It is remarkable how Rome has been fed by a debased Evangelicalism. The early life of Newman is
but one case of many.

final success. But it is the finished and foregone gift of God in Christ through our faith, and the thing which alone promises the final success of any moral efforts. In giving Christ He gave us all things—*i.e.* perfection. It is not our moral success that is presented as perfection to God even in anticipation; it is God's present to us of perfection that makes moral success possible. And this is the whole issue in the Roman controversy which the public on its cycles, newspapers, and political campaigns vainly thinks it has outgrown. The public thinks, but its soul does not. And so it thinks to little forward purpose and to little ultimate success. And it does not discern the most grave dangers to its own security and peace; which serious thought spiritually discerns in subtle and inchoate stages that need generations to work out their evil doom.

I cannot stop to trace how these popish ideas came in to distort the Gospel, how they rose in part from the old Stoic paganism and its mortifications. It could be shown you how Plato and Aristotle had much more to do with them than St. Paul. Almost everything wrong in Romanism is a case of pagan malaria, which crept in on the pure gospel of the New Testament, and which is so hard to get out of the Christian system. The sacerdotalism of Rome, for instance, is much more pagan than Jewish in its origin and nature. So is the connection of Church and State. But I do ask leave to point out the root error that underlies these perversions, and a good many more, at this hour. Because I am not waging a polemic against Romanists; but as preaching to Protestants exposed to the like paganism to-day, I wish to point out how these wrong practices rise out of pagan errors which many Protestants share, and especially out of a supreme belief in the natural man and his morality as the Christian ideal. As soon as you part with the idea that our perfection is in our faith and not in our conduct, you have taken the train for Rome; and I urge you to get out at the first stop and go back to another platform.

The error at the root of all false ideas of perfection is this: it is rating our behaviour *before* God higher than our relation *to* God—putting conduct before faith, deeds before trust, work before worship. That is the root of all pharisaism, Romanism, paganism, and natural and worldly morality. It is the same tendency at bottom which puts the sacraments above simple faith, which neglects the worship of the sanctuary for work in a mission, or replaces the gospel by ethical culture. "I do not care about a man's belief," you say; "show me what he does." Do you mean that? Now, I care comparatively little about what you do, but I care infinitely about whom you believe in. I know if you believe in Christ your conduct will be seen to; but I have no guarantee that it you behave well you will believe in Christ. You may only admire Him as the greatest moral success in your own moral line, a master in your own art, the victor in a conflict, which after all you regard as the same for Him and for you. And all that is something different in kind from trusting Him as your Redeemer through victory in a conflict different in its purpose from yours or all men's. Our Redeemer is not simply a master in a region where we are all amateurs, as a great painter is the idol of his craft. But do you quite mean what you were saying? Do you mean that, if a man is good to the poor and kind to his family, honest in business, and active in humane politics, it is no matter what he thinks about Christ, whether he has to do with Him at all, or how he stands to the Cross? Do examine these phrases which make a flattering appeal to common sense. I suspect every creed which in the name of religion appeals to common sense. Do you really mean that a man's relation to God and to Christ is of little moment so long as he is self-denying, generous, public-spirited? If you do, you are popish and pagan in principle. And if a majority were of your way of thinking, we should have the Roman Church re-established in this country in a few generations. We should have the ethical soil for it. It is because that way of thinking and speaking is so common among Protestants, in the spirit of the age, that Romish principles have got so far with us as they have. It is because Christianity becomes identified with behaviour, with man's treatment of man, with humanism, philanthropy, humanity, with kindness and pity instead of *grace*. Humanity! Why, as Ibsen says, God was not humane to His own Son. We are not saved by the love we exercise, but by the Love we trust. The whole Protestant issue lies in that; and it is surrendered by none more than by the philanthropic liberals in popular theology. Their sympathies have taken the reins from their principles into their spiritual logic. They have never *approfondi leur sentiment.* We have no phrase for that admirable expression more elegant than that they have never sounded their own sentiments, or realized their practical sequel on a long historic scale. If the perfection of a Christian man is in the morals or the mercy he exhibits and not in the Grace he trusts, if it is doing first and believing second, then the Romish form of Christianity is the sole and inevitable. It does not matter whether the doing is moral or ceremonial, behaviour or ritual.

The apotheosis of conduct has become a popular cult through the teaching of Matthew Arnold, so congenial to the British philistine and the semi-Roman Englishman. It is surely more accurate to call British philistinism Arnold's ally rather than his enemy when we remember that the Philistine was not the enemy of an Israel of ideas, as he said, but of an Israel of faith. It is Arnold's despised Non-conformity that represents the prophetic element in religion, which was the soul of the chosen people and the butt of Philistine mockery. And one may call the average Englishman semi-Roman, not only because in temperament he is the Roman of the modern world, but because, ecclesiastically, his moral culture and type have been so largely moulded by the half-reformed Church which he still tolerates, and which he prizes more as an organization of energy and society than of faith. It is a premiated institution of law and works. Well, for Arnold religion was a branch of culture. It was ethical culture, aided by the spiritual imagination. And the Church was to be supported, even by the agnostic, as the great society for the promotion of goodness or conduct, which he memorably defined as "threefourths of life". Like most worship of culture and of the orderly æsthetic idea of perfection, Arnold's work makes ultimately for Rome. Rome is the refuge from his intellectual doubt. Rome is the home of his imaginative religion. Rome realizes his idolatry of good form. And Rome is the soil congenial to his ethical nomism, his moral ritual, his religion of morality inged with emotion, of flushed conduct and blanched belief. All agnostic culture leads to clericalism by lay indifference, and then to Rome by desperation. It does not lead to atheism, because the feminine side of human nature will not endure that; it prefers large and definite error to narrow vague truth, positive peril to negative ruin.

But Christian perfection is not a perfection of culture. It is not a thing of ideas or of finish. Such perfection is for the select few, for a natural elect. It is the perfection of the *élite*. This is so even with ethical culture. Its fine programme is yet no gospel. The soul's true and universal perfection is of faith. It is a perfection of attitude rather than of achievement, of relation more than of realization, of trust more than of behaviour. Conduct may occupy three-fourths of our time, but it is not three-fourths of life. To say that it is, is to return from the qualitative to the quantitative way of thinking, from which culture was expected to deliver us. The greatest element in life is not what occupies most of its time, else sleep would stand high in the scale. Nor is it even what engrosses most of its thought, else money would be very high. It is what exerts intrinsically the most power over life. The two or three hours of worship and preaching weekly has perhaps been the greatest single influence on English life. Half an hour of prayer, morning or evening, every day, may be a greater element in shaping our course than all our conduct and all our thought; for it guides them both. And a touch or a blow which falls on the heart in a moment may affect the whole of life in a way that no amount of business or of design can do. Conduct is not the main thing. To say that it is, is but the pardonable extravagance which gives force to a necessary protest. Look to the faith and the conduct must come. True faith has all ideal conduct in its heart and, what is more, in its power. And it is the only thing that has it. Yea, the main thing is not conduct; and it is not even character. Action may shape character But what shapes action? And it is not action alone that shapes character. It is something more akin to faith that shapes both. There are forms of Christianity which preach character—character, as if that were the saving thing, the thing to work at, as if it were healthy to work at it. It is no more the saving thing than conduct. It is not the soul's perfect state. It is a thing of greatest moment, but it is the fruit of salvation, the expression of our perfection, not its condition. It is the result of being accepted by God; it is not what makes us acceptable. A person of no character may by faith be more acceptable to God than one whose soulless character is in universal esteem. Else what is the meaning of the penitent thief, of publicans and harlots going into the kingdom of heaven before decent Pharisees? Do you think that Pharisees there meant only the rascals of the party, the quacks, the impostors, the conscious hypocrites and pious frauds? Did it need the moral insight and the spiritual authority of Jesus to tell us that a penitent outcast was preferred before these? No. Anybody could see that. He meant that the reprobate, in his act of faith, with his character not only lost but ruined and all to be built up again— that that reprobate was, in the passion of his penitence and trust, inside the kingdom of heaven; while the reputable Pharisee, the esteemed and estimable member of the national party and the national church, whose uprightness and respectability had been such as never to rouse the need of repentance, was without. Yea, the hard, placid matron whose family was well brought up and floated out, who was a patron of society, a sponsor for all new-comers, a chaperon with whom you could go anywhere, she was outside the Kingdom; and poor Magdalene, poor Gretchen, the poor slayer of her unwelcome child, might be in. If that was not Christ's view, what does the story of the prodigal and his brother mean? The prodigal had no character at all; and his brother's character was fit to be held up to all the young farmers of the country-side. But the prodigal had faith and repentance. And in these he had a perfection before God denied to ninety-and-nine too admirable to need repentance. It is not a question of the sinless being postponed to the sinful and repentant. It is not a case of premium on sin and evil-doing that good may come. It is a case of a sinful race, whose one true attitude to God is penitence, and which is more worthily represented in God's sight by the repentant prodigal than by the (lives so charming to our social and friendly associations) to which personal sin seems as strange as the sting of it is unknown. I am not impugning social position, or our persona affinities, affections, and admirations. Society has its rules, which must be recognized; and our natural love and esteem have their own place. They are wholesome on the whole. They are based on merit, on character; and they should be. They must rest on something of which men and women can take cognisance. It is men and women that are the judges. The vice of Pharisaism (as it was Israel's ruin) is that it makes the divine standard the same in its nature; it puts merit everywhere and grace nowhere; it makes the divine ideal to be a matter of our achievement, the divine favour a reward for our goodness; it makes the divine welcome to turn on what we have done, or on what we have grown to be, instead of on faith in the grace which delights to make new men out of our worthlessness and our impotence to grow at all. The saints, in the New Testament, are not the saintly but the believing. What Christ always demanded of those who came to Him was not character, not achievement, but faith, trust. His standard was not *conduct,* it was not *character,* it was not *creed.* It was faith in Himself as God's Grace. It was trust, and trust not in His manner but in His message, His gospel. That was the one demand of God; and to answer it is perfection. Obedience to God's one comprehensive demand must be perfection. "This is His commandment, that ye should believe in Jesus Christ." That is to say, *perfection is not sanctity but faith.* It is the obedience which is faith. Do not miss the real point. Perfection is obedience. Good. Rome says that. It is the obedience of faith. Rome says that too. She says it is that obedience to the Church which grows out of belief in the Church. No! The obedience of faith is not the obedience which grows out of faith, but the obedience which faith is, which constitutes the act of faith, in which it consists. It is that surrender of the *will* which is involved in the act of personal faith in the living, saving Person of Jesus Christ. That is Christian perfection. All other excellence flows from that. All ideal perfection is latent in that. All moral character, all sanctity, is in its germ in that. The man of faith is perfect before God because his will and person is in the relation to God which is God's will for him. And he has the germ and the conditions which will work out in sanctifying time to ethical perfection as well. But that holy perfection, that perfection of character, is there already to the eye of God, Who sees the end in the beginning, and the saint in the penitent.

Let no mistake linger, then, in your minds. Christian perfection is the perfection not of conduct, character, or creed, but of faith. It is not a matter of our behaviour before God the Judge, but of our relation to God the Saviour. Whatever lays the first stress on behaviour or achievement; on orthodoxy, theological, moral, or social; on conformity to a system, a church, a moral type, or a code of conduct; on mere sinlessness, blamelessness, propriety, piety, or sanctity of an unearthly type,—that is a departure from the Gospel idea of perfection; which is completeness of trust, and the definite self-assignment of faith amid much imperfection. To put these things, which are of second and third rank, into the first place, as we have been doing, is to get the soil ready for all the crop that Rome can so skilfully rear. It is the Catholic debris left in Protestantism. It is a nomistic, synergistic survival from mediæval theology. It is the Protestant contribution to the Catholic reaction of the day. Once grant Rome's premises, and her use of them is masterly. Once place religious perfection outside of personal faith in God's grace in Christ, and Rome is master of the situation and of the world. In a word, Christian perfection is the faith which justifies, puts you right with God; it is not culture and sanctification by effort. Sanctification is not a perfection added to justification. It is the spirit of it drawn out, that perfection which is all there latent (and to God's eye patent) in justifying faith. The faith that seizes Christ and makes Him its own already holds perfection.

Faith! Hold, understand, define it well. It is the condition of the Church's salvation and the State's. Do not waste your antagonism upon inferior dangers and false opposites. Some of us, perhaps, are easily excited about ritual. We dread its incoming as the stealing in of Rome. The grand old warfare of our fathers (who really understood the case), in the name of faith against *works,* has dwindled into a squabble among us about Protestantism and *ritual,* as if ritualism were the great peril to Protestantism. That is being led by the eye, not by the mind and not by the soul, by sight and not by insight. All worship, however Protestant, must have some ritual. It is ritual to stand to sing, and bend, or kneel, to pray. It is ritual to have a fixed order of service. The question of a little more ritual or a little less is a small one. A greater question is what is *meant* by the ritual, be it less or more. Is it the ritual of a minister or of a priest? That is the point. It is not: ritual or no ritual. To have a minister at all is to have a ritual. The real question is as to the place of ritual, small or great, in salvation. Does salvation depend on the acts done either by the congregation or in its name—upon sacraments? And the subtlest question of all is about a kind of ritual which seldom strikes the anti-ritualists as the great peril—I mean the ethical ritual of life, conduct, human acts, and achievements of any kind, however good, offered to God as our hope of salvation and ground of welcome. Paul, Luther, the Puritans, saw this real, large, subtle meaning of ritual. The ritual question was to them a mere phase of the great battle of grace and merit, faith and works. When Paul condemned salvation by works, perfection by the law, was he only thinking of the ceremonial law? No. It was all one law for him. The law was a unity, including the Decalogue as well as the priestly code. He found no more salvation in the Ten Commandments than in circumcision. His protest was against salvation by conduct, salvation by doing things, perfection by character, welcome by merit, by anything except absolute trust in the work of Christ as the grace of God. Our chief danger to-day is not the ceremonial ritual, but the moral and social ritual. It is the idea that men are to be saved by well-doing, by integrity, by purity, by generosity, by philanthropy, by doing as Christ did rather than trusting what Christ did, by loving instead of trusting love. We object to the mass because Christ's sacrifice cannot be repeated. But self-sacrifice, which *only imitates* Christ instead of sacrificing the self to Christ, which would die *with* Him before it has died to Him, is the same spirit as Rome lives on. It asks what Christ would do rather than what He is doing. It is doing as Christ did without appropriating what He did. It is ethical ritualism rather than spiritual service, copying the Lord's death Who has gone rather than showing it forth till He come. That is the frame of mind which is in *spirit* so akin to Rome, even while its antagonism may be bitter against Rome; whose presence in the air develops all the Roman germs in our semi-Reformation. Wherever you find the idea that the first condition or the true response to God's grace is *doing something,* there you have the habit of mind from which Rome has everything to gain and Christianity at last everything to lose. The "Christian Agnosticism" which we are assured is the religious tone of the Universities offers more to Rome than to faith. And the way in which the public mind has become misled and trivialised in this question may be seen thus. You will find that some who are most ready to say, "A fig for belief! give me character and conduct," are the very people who are most suspicious about ritual in church, even when it only contributes to the decencies of worship. It is the old story of boggling at a midge and swallowing a camel. And what is the hope for Protestantism when the spiritual sense is so perverted, so externalized, so lost to the real and relative value of things? Such ethical ritualism is really more dangerous to the Protestant principle of Faith than much ceremonial.

Most ministers will know that what I say is true. And many laymen may complain that they do not know what I mean. So much has the rejection of theology destroyed the sense of the real situation in the *haute politique* of the Spirit, and the great issues of the Kingdom.

Your faith (that is, your soul) may be perfected when everything else is very crude and fragmentary. Your attainments even in grace may be very poor, but your faith may be perfect. You may utterly trust Him Who saves to the uttermost. You may perfectly trust your perfect Lord, and charge Him with the responsibility both for your sin and your sanctification. The perfectness of their trust is the only perfect thing about some; but it gives them a perfection which people envy who are far richer in attainment and repute. Perfect faith is possible to some who, with many excellences, have no other perfection whatever. There are imperfect human beings whom we perfectly trust and love. There are faulty wives and husbands, parents and children, lovers and friends, who perfectly trust and love each other. There is no faculty so universal as this of perfect trust. How common it is I do not say; but it is the most universal in its nature. It is possible to those who can do nothing else. The child can exercise it. You can win it from many who are the despair of every other means of culture. The savage can learn it towards his missionary, and still more towards Christ, when he is too low in the scale to acquire much from civilisation beyond its vices. The perfection of faith is the hope of a universal religion. It is the great faculty of manhood. It is the great beauty of manhood and womanhood. It is the divine thing in love. It is the soul of marriage, whether of man and woman, or of mankind to Christ. Faith is the marriage of God's perfection and man's. It is the union of the perfection which is absolute and eternal with the perfection which is relative and perfectly *grows*. It is the human ideal, the supreme exercise of human faculty. It is an incessant demand on us, and it is an opportunity not for an elect but for all, not for a caste but for the soul.

P.S.—I regret that space does not allow me to enlarge the point, so grave and subtle now. As I have dwelt on the effects of religious ethicism, so I should like to have drawn explicit attention to the Catholicising effect of a pietism which practically makes sanctity the first thing and faith only second, and would think more of Faber than say, Livingstone. This quietism is a pax Romana in its inner nature and long result. There is a thirst for "consecration" which is not the true way to holiness; and a worship of saintlinesss which impairs the great sanctity.

III

GROWTH AND PERFECTION

"Not as though I were already *perfected*"— Phil. 3:12.
"Let us who are *perfect* be thus minded."—Phil. 3:15.

A distinguished Frenchman has said that the idea of perfection is more to men than examples of it, and that this is equally so in art and morals.

In religion, it might be added, what we need more than either the idea or the example is the guarantee of perfection

In morals, in character, the aphorism is certainly true. The love of perfection is more precious than the sight of it. An *example* of perfection often ties us down to a literal imitation of his manner of life, instead of kindling us to a fellowship of his spirit. This has happened with Christ Himself. He has been so treated as our perfect Example that His outward fashion of life has been copied at the cost of His inward principle. His poverty, celibacy, and freedom from civic duties—such things have been copied as if they were divine ends for every man, instead of means for a particular man's particular work. And the monks, thinking more of imitating Christ than of trusting Christ, lost the way of life in Christ's mere way of living. They lost the mind of Christ, and the true sense of Christ's unique saving work, till the Reformers set things mightily right. The *idea* of perfection, on the contrary, is a constant call to escape, through all the ascending forms in which perfection has been expressed, into sympathy with the principle that struggled in them to light. Every finite perfection is outgrown as the infinite is more fully revealed. The very Christ after the flesh becomes inadequate to the Christ according to the Spirit. He had to be broken and die for His full scope. He entered maimed into His eternal life. The earthly life of Christ was perfect in this sense, that it was perfectly ruled and ordered by His task, it was perfectly adapted at each stage to carry out *His* purpose in the world, and to finish the work given Him to do. The same manner of life would not be perfect, or even useful, for you or me, to whom His work of Redemption is not given. But there is a sense in which Christ lives more perfectly in His Church to-day than He did in the form of His thirty years on earth. He is more universal, more free from limitations of time and space, more invisible in His action, less exposed to the risks of Messianic misconception. We are less tempted to do exactly as He did, and we are better taught to trust what He did, and then let our faith take a free, spontaneous, and individual form in our social life to His praise. What a thinker in art or morals may call the idea of perfection, that *we* call the Spirit of faith and fellowship. And our faith and fellowship in Christ is worth far more for our perfection than any effort to live up to Him as our example—useful as that may be. We are complete in Him, not merely by His help but by His indwelling. We are organized into Him. It is better, of course, to imitate the example of Christ than to be conformed to the world. But it is better to trust Christ and His work than even to imitate Him. He is worth infinitely more to the world as its Saviour than as its model, as God's promise than as man's ideal. He is more to be admired than copied, more to be loved than to be admired, and He is to be trusted more than all. This trust of Christ is the highest doing a man can do. Trust become habitual is our new nature, our perfection made perfect, our life and abiding in Him.

When Christ bids us be perfect as our Father in heaven is perfect, He does not tell us to do what the Father does. The Father makes His sun to rise on the evil and the good, and sends rain on just and unjust. We cannot do that. We cannot affect sun or rain. We cannot copy God. He is Almighty as we are not. He is, to our great blessing, unseen. To our great blessing Christ is now unseen also. If we could see them we might be copying them, or trying and failing. What they do we know not now. Their method of procedure in the world we cannot trace, else we might ruin their plans by poor imitations of them which would be no more than parodies, like Sheldon's tales.[1] We are not told to do *what* God does, but *as* He does. It is sympathy that is wanted more than imitation. What we are to imitate is the love and grace of God. And there is only one way of imitating that, only one way of learning it. It is by trusting Him. Love is learned by faith in the case of the unseen. With our visible lovers faith may come by love. With the Lover of our souls love comes by faith. Love of the unseen is the girdle of perfectness which is put on over the other garments of faith and hope and all the virtues, and after them, as the last touch which keeps them all in form and place. The art of loving God is that perfection of educated *character,* that actual righteousness which is the result of long *sanctification.* But faith is that perfection of soul attitude

---

1. The Rev. Charles Sheldon, of Kansas, U.S.A., author of *In His Steps, circa* 1900.

to God, of rightness in relation to Him, which is *our justification, our ideal righteousness,* what used to be called an imputed righteousness. There is a perfection of faith before the character has grown up under it, and that is justification. This is the perfection that makes the Church. The saints in the New Testament are not the fully sanctified, but the believers. The Church to-day is not a company of the sanctified, but of the justified. They have only entered on their Christian manhood, they have not fully developed it. They are but spiritual adults, not spiritual heroes. And in the main, when the New Testament speaks of the perfect, it means not the complete but the spiritually adult; not the fully sanctified but the duly justified. They are not people who perfectly love, but who truly trust. They may be defective as yet in many points of character, or relations to each other. But they have entered on the right relation to Christ. They are not all ideal characters. Some are not even beautiful. But they will become so in time or eternity. They have started on that career. They have come to spiritual adultness by faith in Christ, as I say. They have entered on their spiritual vocation. But they have not yet reached spiritual distinction, when faith has its perfect work in love. Faith, therefore, in a sense is more than character because it makes character; and it is perfect before it makes character. But it is less than character, in the sense that the character may be only latent in it and not yet made.

The perfect, then, are those who by faith have settled into their divine place in the perfect Christ and become spiritually of age. You know the difference between a youth and an adult. There is a step taken in life, a step hard to describe and various in its ways, by which the boy passes into the man, the girl into the woman. They are held fit for a share in things to which they were not admitted before. They become initiates in life where before they had been novices. They cease, as it were, to be catechumens of Humanity and become members. They graduate. They are held fit to begin their real education. They are admitted to new circles, to new responsibilities, new rights even in law. Things are discussed with them which are not discussed with boys and girls. They acquire more or less common sense. They become capable of learning from life, instead of fluttering about in it, or drifting. They stand on a new footing, they are ready for burdens, they are expected to cease being carried and to begin to carry. The soul, as it were, comes to itself, settles into being itself. Its organism becomes complete even if faculty is not. The natural character reveals itself in a distinct way. I do not mean that all this takes place just when people become legally of age—at eighteen or twenty-one. With some it may be about then, with some later. I only mean that there is a time when the natural character passes out of the condition of crudity, and rawness, and comparative imperfection, and enters a stage of firmness, setness, and comparative perfection. It is true of the body, of the stature, and it is true of the character and the will. They become knit, compact, individual, characteristic. That is becoming adult. It is a step which is never repeated in life. And yet it is not a final step by any means. It is a perfecting of the organism—the bodily organism or the psychical, the moral, organism, —but it is not the perfecting of the character. It is the end of an age, but it is also the beginning of an age. Perfecting though it be, it is more of a start than a close—like marriage, which only in comedies ends all, but in reality begins all, the serious part of life. We become not so much perfect in the ordinary sense as *habiles,* capable, possible. When St. Paul says, "We speak wisdom among the perfect," he meant that he was talking as he would to spiritual *men* and not to hobbledehoys. He cast himself on their spiritual adultness, common sense, wisdom. It is as when Christ said, "I speak as unto wise men; judge ye what I say." What Paul meant was that, as he was not addressing the celestial and sanctified intelligences, so neither was he providing milk for babes, but speaking as a man to men in Christ Jesus.

Now it is a corresponding thing that takes place in the soul by faith. It is well to get rid of the idea that faith is a matter of spiritual *heroism,* only for a few select spirits. There are heroes of faith, but faith is not only for heroes. It is a matter of spiritual manhood. It is a matter of maturity. I have not used the word maturity, because it is ambiguous. It might be taken to mean the final fulness of power as well as the initial adequacy of power. Faith is the condition of spiritual maturity in the sense of adultness, of entering on the real heritage of the soul. It is the soul coming to itself, coming of age, feeling its feet, entering on its native powers. Faith is perfection in this sense. It is not ceasing to grow, but entering on the real and normal region of growth. It is starting on a progress through the scale of perfections. It is going on from strength to strength. Growth is then progress, not to Christ, but *in* Christ.

I have not said that in *every* case in the New Testament this adultness, this coming of age, is the meaning of the word perfection. There are cases where it does have reference to some comparatively final stage of sanctification which is the goal of infinite hope in Jesus Christ. It means, sometimes, the state in which faith has worked out into love of God and man, into spiritual blessing and beauty, the abiding in Christ. Spiritual adultness and sanctification are not two perfections, but two aspects of the same perfection, which is the faithful soul's progress in faith to love. There is a bold passage in St. Paul (Phil. 3:12), which makes this very clear. The two aspects of perfection meet in a point. He says he is not yet perfect, but in the next breath (v.15) he says he is perfect: "as many of you as are perfect be like me." That is saved from being vanity by the fact that perfection is as conscious of what it is not as of what it is. If you are in the right and perfect relation to Christ, go on to be perfected in Christ. If you are in the way of Christ, let Christ have His way with you. It is your perfection to be in a position in which you are always being perfected. You are perfect when you feel that Christ has everything to do to perfect you. *To believe* in Christ, to *be* in Christ, and to *abide* in Christ, are three stages of the same perfection—which you may call the Petrine, the Pauline and the Johannine stages if you will. A man is perfect when he comes to belong to Christ instead of himself. But he has for his goal, as Christ's property, a perfection in which perfection itself is perfected. A man as a Christian has entered on perfect manhood, but he must always become more and more so. Boys have amused themselves with the puzzle—how can the adjective perfect be compared? If a thing is perfect, can it be more perfect, or most? Well, if we were all circles, I suppose there would be no improvement possible. We should be complete—and empty. A perfect circle is done with. There could be no comparative degree. We should all be then what some believe themselves to be now— incomparable. But dead and done with. Unless, indeed, some ambitious circle had its life poisoned by the passion to rotate on its diameter and become a sphere. But if we were all perfect spheres we should be capable, I suppose, of no more perfection. We should be finished futilities. But as living souls our great perfection is the power of continually becoming what we are, coming to our true selves. As Christian souls, our perfection is in coming to ourselves in Christ. We are perfect in Christ, and in Him continually more so. In Christ we are what we are to be—not in the sense in which a closed figure is all it can be, but in the sense in which the perfect seed has the promise and power of the perfect tree. Eternity is packed in our small souls. It is set in our heart. We are what we have to become. That is what gives faith its power and peace. In faith we are not panting and straining, and minding ourselves after a perfection only ideal possible, remote, and ever receding. We are not toiling to put achievement on the head of achievement, or mortification on the back of mortification, to reach heaven. That is a war of godless giants, which ends in failure, defeat, and chagrin. But we are unfolding a perfection which we already have in fee. We are appropriating what is already ours. We are sure that it is ours before it is ours. It is in us before it is on us. We have it with Christ before we have it with men. We are complete in Him before He completes Himself in us. We are perfect, and yet we are not perfect. We are as having nothing and yet possessing all things. We are in Christ, therefore we are complete; but we are in the world too, therefore we are not complete, but only on the way to completion. Our perfection, therefore, is not to be flawless, but to be in tune with our redeemed destiny in Christ. We are perfect, if not sinless. We are in Christ, even if we do not yet abide in Him. We are in the only relation which is capable of being perfected—the relation of faith. Faith as perfection is conformity to our high calling, which is also an upward calling. It is a perfection which both is and *grows*. True perfection is the power of perfect growth. But that does not mean unbroken growth. There are times when we lie becalmed, times when we have to tack, times when the current carries us astern, times when we are buffeted out of the straight course—when it is much if only we can keep at sea and not go to pieces on the rocks. Ignorance misleads us. Our charts fail us. Our crew mutinies, our passions take command, for a time. But, on the whole, we are on the living way. The master passion and bias of the soul is to Christ. The ruling will is the will of God, however certain impulses escape its control. We may still sin, but we are not sinners. Sin clings, soils, and may sometimes master. There are lapses, repentances, renewed forgivenesses. True perfection is not the power of unbroken growth, but of growing unto perfection, growing on the whole. The judgment is passed on our life-work as a whole. God does not judge us in pieces. He sees our life steadily, and sees it whole. The ship may be battered, but it comes to port, even though scarcely saved.

This note of growth is the most remarkable thing about Christian perfection. It has to sound so paradoxical, in order to be true. But, it is asked, does the perfect God grow? We are bidden to be perfect as He is perfect; is His perfection a thing of growth? No, indeed. The absolute God has all perfection in Him in actual completeness from first to last. We do not read that we are bidden to aim at any of the absolute qualities of God. That would be the old temptation, "Ye shall be as gods." How near the devilish suggestion lies to the divine, temptation to inspiration, "Be as gods" to "Be ye perfect." Our perfection is not to be rival absolutes, but to love and trust the absolute. Be as perfect in your relative way as God is in His absolute way, which contains all relatives. Be as perfect men as He is perfect God. Meet God's will about you in Christ as fully as God meets His own will about Himself *in* Christ. And the union of will and nature in God is by love. It is not, Be perfect fathers, but, Be sons worthy of a perfect Father. But is it such a strange and foolish thing, this perfection which is and is not, but only is to be? It is a mystery, but must it be a folly? It is noble to strive. But would it be so noble if there were not a perfection in our striving as well as by it, if we were not perfect while striving as well as while attaining? Is a perfect quest not part of our perfect good? If there were only perfection in attaining by striving, would not striving, effort, be outside the perfect life, or all perfection removed to another life? Is our striving not a part of our perfection? Is our perfection not, by the very nature and sanctity of effort, a growing thing?

Take an illustration also from your own personality. Go back ten, twenty years. Were you the same person as you are to-day? Yes, and no. Yes. For it was you then, as it is you now. There is something continuous. There is an identity which nothing can destroy. We do not believe that even death can destroy it. But also, No. You are not the same. A great deal has come and gone, and you are changed. You have grown better or worse, but you have changed. Every day has changed you, and made you not the man you were; you are either more worthy of your personality, or less. *There* is a case, apart from the life of faith, a case from mere natural life, of the same mystery of at once being and not being, of being the same yet not the same. You are a perfect personality in the sense that you are distinct from all others, adult, complete in yourself, continuous in your history, and so far consistent with yourself that you are the same person now as long ago. Yet this perfection to which personality has come in you is quite compatible with a constant change and growth. So much so, indeed, that if you had ceased to change and grow it could only have been by the dissolution of your personality itself. You only *are* because of your power to *become* what you are, to *grow*. Incessant growth is a condition of perfect living personality.

Again, take goodness. If a man say, "I am now good, my moral education is finished," it means that he gives up effort, gives up pursuing goodness. And that means that he ceases to be good. He has lost in the boast of possessing it the very thing he had. He has it only by a deep sense that he has it not but must always pursue it, win it, enlarge it, let it grow. That is true in the region of natural morality. It is still more true in Christ. We are only perfect in Him as we are in a condition to grow in Him.

Take, again, happiness. If you arrive at a condition in which you settle down and say, "I will fix this day for ever so," your happiness is doomed. "Stay thus for ever, for thou art so fair." The soul that says that to any earthly state has stood still with all the spiritual world moving. And the meaning of that must soon be that he is out of harmony with the world, and so happiness is gone. Happiness is a power of the soul to find its joy amid the constant change of experience, and to grow in mastery of a growing world.

So with culture and its love of the perfect. If it do not feel with the living time and grow to it, all its acquisitions become mere lore, mere pedantry.

So with character. If you freeze at the perfection of twenty or thirty, your character ceases to live and becomes mere mechanism, mere habit, prejudice, set grey life, moral death, and apathetic end.

You may ascend with the illustration to the character of Christ Himself. In what did His perfection consist? Those three years that we know—were they no more than the dramatic display of a perfection which was all finished before they began? Were they only like a photograph enlarged and thrown on a screen for the world to see—enlarged from a completed perfection existing in small in the Saviour's own soul? Or were they the perfection of real growth, the perfection of the growing life? In doing what He did for us, was He not doing something real for Himself? Surely His manifestation had in it nothing mechanical, nothing stagey. He was perfect at every point. That is, at every stage He was in perfect tune with the will of God. He was perfectly equal to His unique work and the call of the hour. But it was the perfection of an ever-deepening note. Neither omnipotence nor omniscience was among His perfections. They were only those that pertained to His redeeming work. At every point He was completely obedient, but it was an obedience never completed till the Cross. He was perfectly obedient from the first, but He learned obedience by the things He suffered. His problem grew deeper on His gaze, his task grew more solemn as He moved into the deadly antagonisms of His time and the upper reaches of spiritual wickedness. He saw on the paschal night a cross He did not see in the rapture of His baptism, and He accepted then a work which He did not at first realize in its full form and fear. He was not more perfect in His obedience at the end than at the beginning; but it was a more perfect perfection that He obeyed. Always perfect by faith, He was always being perfected in holiness. Always in the right relation to God, His realization of God's will and purpose with Him ever deepened, and it was ever fully met.

And take as a last illustration the Great Redemption itself which His obedience wrought. It was completed in His death. It was finished. Having died unto sin once, it was once for all. That death and conquest needs no repetition. The sacrifice of the mass is an impeachment of Christ's finished work. It needs no supplement. The whole work was in principle done, the everlasting victory was in spirit won. In the spiritual world the Cross is one long indubitable triumph of conclusive bliss; and it would be so were every mass priest paralyzed at the altar. What Christ did was a thing for ever complete and sufficient. Redemption is the condition of the world in God's eternal sight, and with it the perfect God is well pleased. With the world in the Cross, with the travail of the Redeemer's soul, He is satisfied.

But in *your* sight, actually, historically, is it a redeemed world? To your *faith* it is; viewed from this house, from this day, from this worship, from this pulpit, it is. It is so really, but is it actually? To your *sight* is it a redeemed world? Where is the perfection of Christ's work in yesterday's newspaper, in tomorrow's business, in the actual condition to which your soul has attained today, in the degree of sanctification reached by those who bow with you in the faith of the Cross, and put all their faith there? Where is Redemption in current affairs, in the course of past history, in the record even of the Church itself? It is so hard to see, that if we look away from the Cross we may not perceive it at all. "And is the thing we see Salvation?" So hard to see, that even if we look at the Cross with the historian's eye alone, and not with the insight of faith, we mostly miss it. So hard to see, that even the Cross, even to faith's eye, might be ambiguous were its divine meaning not verified by the Resurrection. Yea, so hard to see, that Cross and Resurrection together might be dumb for us as to eternal issues were faith not fed by the witness of the Holy Ghost, and the Kingdom not assured by the perpetual working of its immortal King. For all the eternal and spiritual completeness of our Redemption, it is at the same time an imperfect thing, to many powerful spirits a thing denied. It is in history still, and for long must be, incomplete. It is in our experience very incomplete. An infinite perfection of Redemption is ours, and yet our Redemption is so imperfect. The work is finished, yet how unfinished are we, its products! That seems a strange and impossible thing; and the logicians might make great mirth of it were they not more than logicians—spiritual thinkers. The work is finished, not simply in the sense of being ended, but in the sense of being completed. The work is finished, not simply in the sense that the great Workman closed His day, and did His best, but in the sense that the task was completed, the end achieved, and He brought in eternal Redemption. The work is finished; but what unfinished things are we, in whom the work must take effect! Yes, Redemption is finished and unfinished, complete in heaven, incomplete on earth. Incomplete on earth, with eternal promise and power. Imperfect but no fiasco. We are complete in Him in whom His own work is always complete. He grasps us by the Eternity within us—and by the sin—to pluck out the sin and develop the eternity. Our one perfection is to be in Him. He will perfect Himself in us in His time. Our perfection is the growing perfection of faith in His absolute redeeming perfection. We have a perfect Redemption, however imperfectly redeemed we are at any one stage. In faith we are what we can never feel ourselves perfectly to be. We are by faith what we are not, but are ever growing by grace to be.

IV

PRACTICAL RÉSUMÉ

I would end by resuming the more practical and experimental features of perfection.

Christian perfection cannot be thought of as an external thing, a formal thing, a thing completed and closed.

And yet our perfection must be a limited one. It is not possible for any Christian at any one time to fulfil all possible duties and realize all possible excellences. Your perfection lies in what is possible to you with *your* character and position, in what you are called to be and do, in what lies on *your* conscience, in what concerns the situation in which you find yourself in life. Duty is duty for A as for B. But A's duty is not B's. A's ideal of happiness is not B's. A's love is not B's. A's idiosyncrasy is not B's. A's call is not B's. There are limitations for each soul; and in those limitations lies his freedom, his perfection. An unlimited perfection is not possible. Even God is limited, though it is by Himself. But were it possible it would be a great burden on us. An unchartered freedom would only tire us. Our freedom is *our* freedom. It has the stamp of *our* character. It has a charter in our individuality, a specification, definite features, inalienable qualities, distinctive of each one of us. In our worst misery we dread parting with ourselves and ceasing to be. Our freedom and our perfection is not to be as gods but to find our place in God. And that we find by faith in Jesus Christ and growth in Him. Individual perfection is not possible, apart from the perfection of all, especially as that is antedated in Christ. And the perfection of all is that each should be a member of the other in the Kingdom of God in the faith, service, and communion of Jesus Christ. Perfection makes his soul a whole; but it is a whole which is only perfected in *the* whole, in the Kingdom of God, under its conditions, its limitations. The most free and universal of all perfections was that of Jesus Christ. And in what narrow limits that perfection moved and grew! How it was perfected in the most awful agony and pressure of limitation the world ever knew—the weight and bondage of the Cross! In His death He was crushed under all the sorrow and sin of the world. Every master finds his opportunity and realizes his mastery in his limitations. It was the Cross of Christ that gave Him the world, the future, eternity, perfection, for a prey.

The features of Christian perfection are these. First, *faith,* as I have said. But I wish to define more Christianly the *kind* of faith. By faith I do not mean only that utterly inward transaction in which the soul forgets the world and deals with God, committing itself to Him in a high, spiritual, mystic, rapturous act. It is not the fine frenzy of religious emotion, the glow of exalted adoration and surrender. That may be in it, but that is not necessarily of it; it is not its test. There is a better test of faith than rapture. It is confidence, patience, and humility. Faith is not best expressed in boisterous assertions of assurance, however honest at the time, but in those forms of life and character. St. Paul's life-faith was greater than any of the finest expressions of it in his writings—partly because he never felt carried so high but that he might become a castaway if he did not take care. "He that endureth to the end shall be saved." Tune down your heroics to that; it is really tuning them up. Faith does not make you an angel cleaving the blue sky remote from the world. It makes you a son with the Father. It is not wings it gives you, but hands and feet to grasp and to go. Look at the extremes it avoids. At one extreme you may have incessant worry and care; at the other you have a carelessness about all the world so long as you are shut in with your religious dreams. Or at one end you have indifference, weak, spiritless, or desperate; at the other you have Stoic indifference, strong and proud. Faith is none of these things. It is filial trust in God's love, redemption, and providence amidst the duties, affections, pleasures, enterprises, perils, fears, guilts, gains, losses of active life. I do not say it is simple trust. It is not so simple, in the sense of being easy. You know well enough it is not easy to rise up out of those cares, absorptions, perplexities, impotences of yesterday's work to a simple faith to-day. The greatest simplicities are not easy. And the simplicity of faith embodies all the difficulty of Christ with the modern world. And faith is not a piece of self-control. Nor is it a particular experience of life, or insight into life, like a genius's. It rests on an experience of Jesus Christ and God's grace in Him. It rests in God amid much ignorance; though we do not know the future, and do not understand the past. It saves us from being victims of the world. It gives us mastery over it. It is the soul of sonship. It consists more of obedience and quiet confidence than of visions. And at the last it approves itself better (as I say) in *humility* and *patience* than in ecstasies. It is more faith to cleave to God in the dark hour of life and the dull commonness of duty than to throw ties, duties, services away, and seek a religion principally of sweet seasons and uplifted states. It is better to trust God in humiliated repentance than to revel in the sense of sinlessness. It is better to bear the chastening of the Lord as sons than to feel in the angelic mood of those who know they need no repentance. It is better to come home weeping than to stay at home self-satisfied.

It is not very often, comparatively, that the New Testament writers offer Christ as our example. But when they do, it is almost always in connection with His humility and patience and self-sacrificing love. It is His spirit, His faith and love, that are our example, not His conduct, not His way of life.

Humility is a frame of perfect mind not possible except to faith. It is no more depression and poverty of spirit than it is loud self-depreciation. It rests on our deep sense of God's unspeakable gift, on a deep sense of our sin as mastered by God, on a deep sense of the Cross as the power which won that victory. It is not possible where the central value of the Cross is forgotten, where the Cross is only the glorification of self-sacrifice instead of the atonement for sin. A faith that lives outside the atonement must lose humility, as so much Christian faith in a day like this has lost it, as so much worship has lost awe. It is very hard, unless we are really and only broken with Christ on the Cross, to keep from making our self the centre and measure of all the world. This happens even in our well-doing. We may escape from selfishness, but it is hard to escape from a subtle egotism which it is not quite fair to call selfish. This personal masterfulness of ours needs mastering. In many respects it is very useful, but it must go ere God in Christ is done with us. And it is mastered only by the Cross as the one atonement for sin.

Humility is a great mystery to itself. It is the amazement of the redeemed soul before itself, or rather before Christ in itself. It may take the shape of modesty before men, or it may not; humility is not anything which we have in the sight or thought of other men at all. It is the soul's attitude before God. "Hast thou that faith? Have it unto thyself" before God. It can take very active, assertive, and even fiery shape in dealing with men. It is not timidity or nervousness. It is not shy, not embarrassed, not hesitant, not self-conscious, not ill at ease, not a seeker of back seats or a mien of low shoulders and drooping head. Yet it is not self-sufficient in a proud and Stoic reserve, nor self-assertive in a public Pharisee fashion. It can never be had either by imitating the humble or by mortifying the flesh. Devotion is not humility, though humility is devout. It is only to be had by the mastery of the Cross which taketh away the self-wrapt guilt of the world.

With humility goes *patience* as a supreme confession of faith. Do not think that patience is a way of bearing trouble only. It is a way of doing work—especially the true secret of not doing too much work. It is a way of carrying success. It is not renouncing will and becoming careless. It is an act of will. It is a piece of manhood. To part with will is to become a *thing*. It is not mere resignation or indifference—which often goes with despair and not faith. It is a form of energy, even when it curbs energy. It is Christian form of bravery, and it has the valour often to be called cowardice. It is the form of energy that converts suffering, and even helplessness, into action.

> *"I am ready not to do*
> *At last, at last."*

It is the intense form of action which made the power of the Cross, and stamped the example of Christ in the deepest way on the mind and heart of the first Church.

Both humility and patience are only Christian in the spirit of *thankfulness*. Faith is for the Christian enveloped in praise. It is no gloomy humility, no sombre patience, no dull endurance, no resentful submission. It is all clothed with hope. It is the faith and submission of a soul that knows itself both immortal and redeemed, and owes all to God's purely marvellous grace. Its atmosphere is glad hope. Christian public worship begins much more fitly with thanksgiving than confession; it should open as well as close with a doxology. And the central act of

Christian worship is the Eucharist—which is thanksgiving. The spirit of Christian life and worship is thanks and praise. Whatever we offer to God, were it life and health itself, is offered in the name of Christ, in sequel to His Cross, as the joyful response to our redemption there. You can never doubt, when you actually see the thankfulness and sweetness in some life-long martyrs and sufferers, that that is the true Christian victory, whatever the failures of their life may have been. *There* is a perfection never won by culture, art, or any success.

The next feature of perfection is *prayer*—prayer as a habit, joy, and prize of life. Humility takes the form of reverence and yet communion. The heart converses with God in Christ. It offers thanks, it confesses sin, it makes its petitions, but it above all converses with God. That is the inmost energy of faith—prayer. It is faith's habit of heart. All *acts* of prayer become but expressions of this *habit.* Work goes to this tune. Everything rises to God's throne. Everything the child does has a reference to the father, direct or indirect. Every form of prayer is speech with God the Father and Redeemer. "Praise is the speech of faith, petition is the speech of hope, intercession is the speech of love, confession is the speech of repentance."

A further feature of Christian perfection is *duty.* Humility takes shape as devotion to the will of God in the natural and social order that holds us. It is daily duty in our relations and calling. If it is a calling God cannot bless, it is not for you. If He can bless it, it is a contribution to Him. And it is duty in the wide sense. It is the duty, not of your business or family only, but of your social and civic position. Distrust the religion that makes you careless of social duties, public rights, and civic faithfulness. How is society to be converted if conversion take men out of society? How is the Kingdom to come if all the good are only "saints", if the "saint" is a ruling caste among believers, and piety is more than faith? A man's duty to the public does not justify him in neglecting his wife; but his duties to his family do not justify him in neglecting the public. A man's religious duties are only partly met by the observances of his religion. All the duties of his position are religious. And it is a perfection of another than the Christian kind that makes the Church the one field of God's perfect will for him. That carries us back to Romanism, and monkhood, and the double morality of the religious and the lay. What is called Church work may be sacred enough; but it is not in its nature more sacred than the Christian's doing of the world's work in his place and calling unto God in Christ.

And the last feature of Christian perfection is *love,* and especially love to man. I have spoken of love to God. That may be a passion. "Thou shalt love the Lord thy God with all thy heart, soul, strength, and mind." But the love of man is less so. It is at least less of an emotion than a principle, and especially a principle of action. "Thou shalt love thy neighbour as thyself." But self-love is not an emotion so much as a principle, a habit of mind and action. So with the love of men. When will the public learn that that is not necessarily a tenderness of mood or manner? These have been lacking in some of the great lovers of their kind, and the dutiful assumption of them is a fertile source of Pharisaism. Love is not mere natural benevolence. It is not easy compliance. It does not consist in giving alms or gifts. Its type is rather the family love that grows up unmarked as a part of us than the passionate love of man and woman, which we fall into, and which seizes us with a mighty hand. It is a principle and habit of heart and conscience, a frame or temper of life which steadily desires the welfare of men, and especially their salvation, as if it were our own. It is anxious and considerate justice at the least, especially in the public form. And it rises to be much more. Love's desire is not to please but to bless. It can be loud, and even sharp, when needful, as well as kind and easily entreated. It shines through our behaviour to men even when we seek to do no more for them than is involved in our daily calling. It lurks in our words, our acts, our look, our whole way of intercourse. It does not always appear at first. It comes home to you sometimes only when you have known the man for years; whereas the false thing takes at the outset, and then wears thin. It does not come and go with men's behaviour. It is not easily offended. It is fed from another source than men's appreciation—at the Cross of the misprized Christ. It is there prepared for being misunderstood, uncomprehended—and still going on. When men have ceased to be lovable for their own sake, it finds a new Humanity welling up in Christ, and keeping the heart sweet at that eternal spring.

It is this love that is the perfection of Christ. We do not really know Christ till we find it in Him and toward Him. It is inimitable in Him, yet communicable. It cannot be copied, but it can be conveyed. It cannot be presented to us, yet it can be learned. You cannot feel it in Him without its tending to make itself felt in you to others. You cannot trust His love and righteousness without gaining the disposition to trust love and justice above all things everywhere. Why do so few people in Christendom really trust love as the ruling power in mankind? Because Christ is not for them a real personality, loving and loved; because they have been taught to seek

Christian perfection in the completeness of some institution, or the maintenance of some law, or the fever about some conviction. Something Christian is the object of their enthusiasm more than Christ. Something Christian more than Christ is the object of their faith. A conviction about Christ or His Church, held with great warmth, is not the love of Christ. Nor is it really the faith of Christ. These things are more the work of men than the free gift of God. And they cannot act on men as the free grace and love-charm of God only can. All these things belong to a lower stage of religion than Christ, to some kind of law religion, some kind of salvation by doing something some kind of self-redemption or salvation by character or achievement. What we need is the personal impression of Christ, the personal sense of His cross, the fresh, renewing, vitalizing, sweetening contact of His soul in its wisdom, its tenderness, its action for us—and all so freely for us, so mercifully, so persistently, so thoroughly. What we need is the touch, the communion of that kind of perfection. We need to realize how in the Cross the defeat of that sort of goodness is really its victory, its ascent to the throne of the world. The Ruler of the world must be the consummation of the world. The Judge of *all* the earth must be the Law of all the earth. And the law of all must be the secret of all its harmony and perfection.

You must let that come home to *you*, to your own peculiar case. To be perfect with God you must have Christ come *home,* come HOME, to you and sit by your central fire—come home to you, to YOU, as if for the moment mankind were centred in the burning point of your soul, and you touched the burning point of God's. You must court and haunt His presence till it break forth on you, and it becomes as impossible not to believe as to believe is hard now. Then we realize what we were made for, made to be redeemed; we lay hold by faith of our destiny of perfection in another; we are already in spirit what it is latent in redemption that we shall be—what some curse in our nature seemed before to forbid and thwart our being. Our dry rod blossoms. We put forth buds one after another along the line of life. We grow into a stately, seemly tree, whose boughs are for shelter and whose leaves are for healing. Our pinched hearts expand, our parched nature grows green. The fever of life is cooled. Its fret is soothed. Its powers stand to their feet. Its hopes live again. Its charities grow rich. We feel in that hour that this is what we were made for, and we are sure that we are greater than we know. We find ourselves. We lose our load. We are delivered from our plague. Our weakness is made strong. Our enemies flee before us. Our promised land is round us.

Life beckons where it used to appal. And all things with us are returning, through Christ, to the perfection of God from whom they came.❦

THE TASTE OF DEATH AND THE LIFE OF GRACE

1901

"That he by the grace of God should taste death for everyman."
                                            -HEBREWS 2:9

In this great verse I would enforce these three points:

I. HE TASTED DEATH.
II. IT WAS A UNIVERSAL DEATH.
III. IT WAS A GRACE AND GIFT OF GOD TO HIM.

I. Jesus Christ not only died, but He tasted death as incredible bitterness and penury of soul. I would dwell on the psychology even more than on the theology of it.

II. He did so because He died for every man. He experienced in a Divine life the universal death.

III. Yet this desertion and agony of death was a gift and grace of God, not only to us, but to Him. And He knew it was so. And that faith was His victory and our redemption.

I.—THE TASTE OF DEATH

Christ not only died, but He tasted death. He gauged its bitterness, meanness, and dismal woe.

1. The Taste Of Death To-day

The Englishman is an optimist. He has little sympathy with the pessimistic systems which lay such hold of other lands. He puts them down to disordered digestion; he is like an ancient haruspice; he is too much influenced by the viscera, and too ready to read events in the state of the liver. His optimism is based quite as much upon ignorance as upon faith; he succeeds, so far as success is attainable by underrating what he has to contend with. In the spiritual region this is especially so. He preserves his piety rather by going on as if there were no spiritual foes, than by recognising and defeating them. He lacks the spiritual imagination; his faith, therefore, is not very relevant in its form to the spiritual situation of the hour. He does not grasp the world-problem; he does not master it with the world-soul. He may call his Christianity Catholic, but it is not really ecumenical. It meets *his* needs rather than those of the race. It reflects a temporary situation rather than the eternal problem of the soul. It handles some form of death or phase of life, rather than the race's life or the race's doom. He does not readily apprehend the human problem or make the soul's last stand. And, therefore, he does not draw upon the last resources of his creed, or elicit the deepest powers of his Church, his Saviour, or his God. We cannot realize the riches of Christ till we have well-sounded the need of Him.

If we try to look at the matter with larger and other eyes than our own, we may come to perceive that in the death and misery which we are too healthy to dwell on, there are spiritual opportunities far richer than the mere chance of wiping them out or alleviating them. And a true diagnosis of the time may show that the modern difficulty is not death so much as pain. Such is the case in other lands of Europe if not in our own. I speak more of the old civilization than of the New World. Life grows more and more severe. Pain becomes more inward—more in the nature of care, fear, or despair. It is, therefore, more intractable and taxing. Zymotic diseases abate, and nervous increase. Grief and strain advance along with physical security and comfort. Civilization only internalizes the trouble. We have fewer wounds, but more weariness. We are better cared for, but we have more care. There is less agony, perhaps, but, perhaps also, more misery; less that we see, more that we divine.

Besides, we grow more sensitive. The nervous organisation grows more susceptible. Or if our nerves feel no more our sympathies do. The old pain is more felt, more impatiently borne. For this the gospel itself is in some measure responsible. We very properly hear much of the gospel as amelioration; but we ought to hear more of it as aggravation. It makes men worse on the way to make them better. At least, it carries home and brings out the evil that is in them. Its law enters that sin may be shown to be sin, and the soul be shut up unto mercy by being cornered into despair.

And it is another phase of the same action in the gospel when its ideals turn our achievements to dust, and put us out of all conceit with our actual state. Its promises make us more impatient of the slow payment we receive, and its hopes make us resent more keenly the small instalments that arrive. The gospel has fixed in the race, even of its deniers, a deeper conviction of destined bliss, and, therefore, pain is felt to be more of an intrusion. It is more of an intrusion into the ideal order of things. More people than ever before feel their right to happiness and resent its destruction. There is more anger at pain, and at the order of things including it. The mind of Europe is a magnified Job. We are rent asunder by a progressive culture and an arrested ethic, by an imagination that grows faster than the practical conditions of realizing it. Reality seems several lives beyond intuition. We dream a dream of good, but the Agnostics will not let us identify it with the ultimate reality of God. And for want of God our practical progress limps and halts far in the wake of our great surmise. And of the moral energy that we do have so much is engrossed with healing or preventing pain, that it is withdrawn from the noble enduring of it, from the conversion and sanctification of wounds incurable.

Many would welcome euthanasia as release from fruitless, hopeless suffering. An increasing number, especially abroad, end by suicide a life of moral confusion, and many more would do so if they had the courage, or if they could get rid of the hereditary arrest. Death is less regarded with supernatural awe, and men quail more at the earthly misery before or after, at the poverty and helplessness it may entail on those who are left.

From thinking more of pain than of death people are passing on to think of death itself as a form of pain rather than as a supernatural mystery or a spiritual experience. It comes not so much as a ghost, but as a torturer. Men used to pray for delivery from sudden death; now they pray for delivery by it—for sudden death, to cheat the pain which they dread more.

Death affects the person of the man less and his sense more. He does not think of it in relation to what he is, but to what he feels. And he feels it as the dissolution of all personal relations, sympathies, and helps. Faith views it as the deepening of the personality by a new intimacy of personal relation to God in Christ, but it is not so that it is felt by this age. It is an ache rather than an experience. We are passive in it and not active. It is the loss of all we have been gaining, and not the gain of all we have been hoping. It scatters our wrath, wilts our affection, and turns the love we clung to into wretched regrets. We do not count on a future for ourselves, and when we think of the future of our dear ones we are prone to wish we had not had a past. Death ceases to be a personal act and becomes a mere inevitable fact, and it sinks to the commonness of all mere facts when severed from acts. In a word, we just die with the rest instead of dying with Christ.

So we taste death more than our fathers did. It rankles more. It lingers on the palate. It is taken by many with the daily food. It is a present misery rather than an imaginative fear. It is a tale of mud flats and wan struggles rather than anything with the dignity of the unseen and the majesty of spiritual fear. Death becomes a natural enemy more than a supernatural mystery, a moral irritant rather than a spectral dread. It becomes a moral problem where it used to be a moral penalty. It does not so much terrify as a ghost, but intrudes like a Satan to accuse the goodness of God and impugn the reality of His moral order. It does not so much bring another world near as it increases the pain and terror of this. Men do not pine to be immortal, but to escape pain and avert it from those they love.

What is the *taste* of death?

That is something horrible—below the power of any art to convey. Art may try expression by sight or sound. But taste! No art speaks to the sense of taste. So the horror of the deathliest death cannot be mitigated or dignified by the treatment of art. Death in its lees is bitter and ashy. It is nauseous and sordid when we really taste its last touch on life. The more we live and the greater our vitality the more acrid and squalid is that subtle, stealthy death which thwarts, poisons, corrodes and erases life. It is grey, leprous, and slow.

The worst and worldliest pain of death is something which cannot be medicined by the resources of art.

> To know the change and feel it,
> With none at hand to heal it,
> Nor numbed sense to steal it,
> Was never told in rhyme.

For death, if thorough, is not sheer oblivion and Nirvana, but it does extinguish those ennobling resources and imaginations by which our higher senses conquer sense. And so we take the pain of a lower and unimaginative sense, like taste, to express the utter deathliness of death. If we are *to feel* death, realise the deadliness of it, and yet master it, it must be by *Faith*, for we are beyond the help of imagination. Imagination, thank God, may carry us through death if it supply visions of heaven and glory vivid enough to submerge its most hideous fears. But it is only faith in God that can master it in its ultimate form, its most desolate, squalid, benumbing and panic form, death in a moral waste, in spiritual solitude, impotence and failure, death with just enough feeling left to feel itself dead.

2. The Taste Of Death For Christ

Now, Christ tasted death (I press this from the fact, not from my text, which does not intend to emphasize the word as I do); He did not simply die like most. The whole efficacy of His death lay in that. He experienced the worst of it, touched the bottom of it, nay, went under that. He felt the horror, the sordid horror of it, the Godforsakenness of it, the earthiness, the deadness of it. No poetry of it helped him. He did not flush to anticipate the scene. There was no enthusiasm of battle, no sympathy of comrades, no shouting for a cause. There was no ideal beauty or power in it at the worst moment. It was the pain symbolized by one of the lower senses, such as taste; a pain which could borrow no relief from imaginative aspects of the case. It was death with a past of failure, a lonely present, and a dark future. It was a dreary hell, a dismal swamp, an icy grave. It was like the death of an explorer, with broken nerve and evil memories, in the Arctic fog. If Christ sounded and tasted death to the uttermost, He conquered by principle a death like that. He knew "despair", as Calvin says of the cry on the cross; He knew for a space the modern malady of despair. And it makes nothing against this that it was a broken-hearted and resigned despair, and not a furious. Despair on the heroic scale is not furious. It certainly is not so in the modern mind. The worst despair is that which has sapped energy, so much that there is no vigour for fury. It has worn down the soul so that it cannot rage. It may be bitter, but it is not frantic. It may even settle down, as in Matthew Arnold, into a wistful regret, whose foot falls soft upon the carpets of Anglican culture, and whose language is tuned to the Dorian mode of flutes and soft recorders. The despair of our day is not frantic, but it may be all the more desperate. It may be the despair of souls too underfed for vigorous hopelessness, and too pruned and trimmed for flat denial. There was much more pathos than frenzy in the Godforsakenness of it; and there was so much the more contact with the quiet hopelessness that blights the spiritual outlook of an overbusy age.

There is no sign that Christ was sustained in the crisis of that black hour by thoughts or visions of the long future. "Instead of the joy set before Him, He endured the cross." He was not supported by foreseeing what coming blessing His death or agony would bring. That would have been an imaginative glory in whose wealth He might well have forgotten the horror of the hour. And, on the other hand, the pain of death was not for Him a dread or prevision of the future fires of hell. Heaven did not mitigate death, and hell did not sharpen it. The pain and horror were, as in our modern case, in death itself. If He was the death of death, it was because He tasted the death in death, and visited the caverns of horror that underlie the soul, and are seldom entered even by the dying man. He tasted the death of the universal soul—death eternal. It was the horror of the holy when He "became sin". And this suggests another point where His death touches our modern attitude to it. We feel the pain and disappointment of death as impugning the moral goodness of God. To us pain and death seem a moral outrage, a violent injustice done to the good. And it was moral outrage on the holy that gave the sting and the mean misery of death for Him. Only a great difference remains. The taste of death makes us think that it is a moral outrage on us—a tyranny; whereas He tasted it as the fruit of a moral outrage by us—a treason. And how prompt we are to accept Christ as a sympathizer with our oppressions, and how slow to take Him as the accuser of our sins!

The Moral Or Second Death

He tasted death as it can only be tasted by the moral delicacy of the High and Holy One, who feels Himself in the atmosphere of base, revolting sin, of moral atheism, ashiness, mustiness, torpor, dust. He bruised the serpent—a thing of the slime. The last sin He met was ignoble, devoid of that heroic rebellion which robs some evil of its grossness and gives a Redeemer at least a worthy foe. A satyr may conquer at last the soul that once withstood a Satan. The enemy that Christ met in death had nothing of greatness, perhaps, to nerve him and aid his valour. I am speaking only of the last form of evil that He faced. His conflict with evil did not begin with the passion week. At the outset, in the temptation, and during His strenuous ministry, Christ did feel that He was coping with the great Satan, a world-power, wickedness in high places. But him He vanquished, and saw him fall like lightning from heaven. It was a Satan falling even from his first fall—deformed by it, earthy and debased, that He met last. At the end there is no sign of that first grand antagonism; evil assails Him in a deadlier, more inveterate, even subtler form— yea, a form more inaccessible to Him because meaner, less Satanic, less Miltonic, more modern and Mephistophelian. There is nothing in moral art more fine and true than the debasement which in "Paradise Lost" passes upon the sublime Satan after his rout, changing him, as he persists in his Satanism, from his noble form to the serpent shape, and turning his eloquence to a hiss. Base sin may be hard to destroy just in proportion as it is easy to resist. The noble heart cannot stoop to its plane. It is hard to slay what it is hard to meet. There is a sense in which it is hardest to cope with that which cometh and findeth nothing in you. There are evils to be destroyed for the world, and they are the hardest if they offer no temptation to ourselves. They cost us nothing to resist when they come to us, but it is all the more loathsome for us to go to them and destroy them. The trials that come are light beside those we go to. Therefore we pray, "lead us not into temptation", rather lead temptation up to us. The more we abhor them the more sickening it is to exterminate them, to seek their lair, breathe their air, kill them in their nest. There is sin which a Universal Redeemer cannot leave unslain, which yet does not so much break the sword of the Spirit as corrode it, like Grendel's blood, in Beowulf. It uses the dagger instead of the sword, so to say. It poisons the wells, but does not take the field. It poisons the murky air, obscures the issue, and unnerves the arm. It is mephitic, the prince of the power of the air. It does not encounter, it envelopes. Its hideousness, like the sea monster, couches in the blinding cloud it makes. Satan himself, if he be still the arch-foe, is a sorry Satan, a demoralized, vulgarised Satan, a Satan of the latter days, whether Christ's or ours, the Satan of the sneer and the everlasting No. We might speculate how far Judas gave Christ the final type of the last enemy to be destroyed. With us, at least, this is the hardest kind of foe. The deadliest Satan is an ignoble Satan. It is the ignoble adversary, the base conflict, that steals most of the warrior's strength. The loathing of filth may be so great, says Nietzsche, that it prevents us from washing, i.e., from justifying ourselves. It is a universe of petty evil, an infinity of moral meanness, that wears down his faith and puts him to the sorest test. It is the mean, petty fighter that the true protagonists most dread, the enemy too low for their sword, who lurks in the long grass with a nimble knife, with cunning, silence, innuendo and contempt, who buys your recruits with a bribe, meets your arguments by imputing motives, and damns your cause by smirching your character. The king of terrors is the old serpent, the spirit of the slime, the great dragon, the wrinkled elder of the snakes. And within ourselves the worst enemy, a Saviour's despair, is that troop of base, cunning, almost impish, often reptile, temptations which make the conflict so mean that we have no stimulus to our moral best, nor vigilance enough to cope with the slow, sleepless microbic perdition. So general and so fatal is this form of evil today that a great living genius[1] has enthroned in the moral world of his art a power whose vast, but impish, providence is well served by the base passions and tendencies that thwart in all his characters the good and pure.

All sin runs out at last to mean sin. And it is the mean sinners that are the hardest to save, the last tax on a Redeemer, perhaps hopeless, intractable, in the end, even to his death. Their element is death at its deadliest. They haunt a miry suburb in the soul's black country, of mean houses, half built and then deserted, "bog, clay and rubble, sand and stark black death". To encounter that, to enter such benumbing, belittling, inert, penurious air is to taste the death in death. It is the very atmosphere of suicide. It is the region of moral and spiritual nausea.

Now, this is faith's opportunity. There is no living through that death but by faith, as force flags and vision fails. It is a Protestant salvation—by faith alone. Faith's last victory is not over a majestic foe, but over a shifty, sordid, stifling, paralyzing foe. That is the last death to be destroyed in death. Your heroism is not in encountering the great temptations with the elation of strength but in meeting the mean, incessant, wearing temptations through moral habit bred from past elations; when you have to drag yourself to the conflict, benumbed in vitality, and alive only in trained faith to the grace and goodness of a darkling God.

II.—DEATH FOR THE MILLION

It was thus He tasted the death of the million, death "for every man", the death which is the death of all of us. He tasted the average man's death, not the hero's alone, the death of the little man, the failure and collapse of the man in a mean way of moral business, the cave-dwellers of the conscience. He tasted that in our moral death which is most universal, the commonness of it, the sorriness of it, what gives it access to all doors, and entrance at the very cracks and chinks in the rear of our nature. He tasted death from a generation of vipers. It was death by sickly candlelight in a little house in a back street among miles of them. It was

---

1. Thomas Hardy.

death made cheap, death for the million.

1. A World Of Death

"For every man!" universal death. I have spoken of its meanness. I speak now of the universality of its meanness. And I will risk the charge of ambition by dwelling on the *vastness* of that death and of its results. The tone of much of our culture is robbing us of our sense of the *greatness* of Christ and His gospel. There is an affectation of subduedness and a modesty of mere good form, which clips the wings of faith lest preaching should pass beyond good talk or piety quit the region of sisterly affection.

How should a man feel who was alive, alone, in a world of the dead? It is beyond imagination desolate. To be alone on the earth with none but the dead, go where you might! It would be dreary and appalling enough for most men to be frozen up with one or two companions only in the Arctic Circle. To be there alone in a world of monotonous thick-ribbed ice, in the darkness of a long night, in driving snowstorms—what could be more desolate and awful? One thing, perhaps; to know, while there, that you were the only living soul on the earth, that if you returned to warmer suns you would find everyone dead, that the whole earth was one vast cemetery in which you were the only man alive. That would be what Shelley calls "desolation deified." Your mind could not bear this strain; you would go mad in the awful dreariness of such death. The taste of it would kill you physically. Is this imagery more awful or less awful than what Christ felt? Was Christ's agony below imagination or above it, beyond it? too trifling or too solemn for it? His solitude was that of *the Life* amidst the dead world. The more He was the life the more power He had to feel death. Poverty means more to a man used to plenty. For Him the soul of man was dead—in principle at least. I do not say the death was *total* as yet; there was still greatness and goodness among men, even among some who failed to see His. But it was *universal;* all were infected by it. There were none wholly great. And all were moving to death, only give the generations time. Every soul was dead compared with Him. It was a world of the dead so far as His life and purpose were concerned. Of the people there were none with Him. Morally, spiritually, He was the only soul truly alive. He had no man like-minded to care for their state. The light shone in the darkness and the darkness comprehended it not. He came unto His own and His own received Him not. He was Life Eternal, and all men refused Him. They were therefore dead. As a living man would be to a world of dead or dying men, so was Christ to the world of living men. With all the energy and culture of the then world, it was yet dead in trespasses and sins, and the more dead that it did not know it. Christ stood alone, amid all the sunshine indeed that there is now, but amid universal moral death. To an eye like His this must be more awful than physical death. And the spectacle of the dead spiritual world around Him must be more awful than our imagination of any lonely survivor on the graveyard of the earth. That survivor would taste the bitterness of death as he could not if there were but one other living soul beside him. We can imagine, but he would realise. We can imagine a world of the dead, and see a certain grandeur in the solitary figure surviving in such a vast and ghastly desert. But there is a certain grandeur in such an imagination: and our shudder is not the actual chill of death, but an æsthetic effect of something which is called before our mind's eye, yet outside of us and our reality. We are there with our poetry; and the survivor is not absolutely alone. But with Christ is was not imagination. He did not view a pictorial world of the dead. He was the life of men, and so He realized it. He died that death. It was not in imagination that He passed through such an experience. What He felt was not an æsthetic chill, nor a mere spectator's fear. He realized this moral death. It was less than actual sin in Him, but more than sympathy. He tasted it as really universal. This death of the million He died for the million. As it was universal, He was involved in it—involved, though not diseased, not captured. His life as Man was a real life, and He was bound to feel the last reality of man's deadness. And He alone could feel it. They were too dead in sin. Alone He fulfilled the condition of feeling a moral death utterly universal, and therefore dreary, cold, loathsome, to such a soul as His. He so went down with His more than sympathy into the reality of our moral death that He was unsustained by any sense of the grandeur and sublimity of the situation. Æsthetic sympathy is but a parable of the moral sympathy of Christ. If He was to taste human death He must forgo that imaginative vision of it in which its very universality seems grand. He did not simply behold death as being in every man; He tasted death for every man. He lived, died, that death. Universality when beheld with the eye of genius has a grandeur. But to enter this universal was to lose the sense of its universality in its deadness. It was to be caught in the chill of its mortality. He experienced the eclipse which made imaginative vision as impossible as men have felt it to be in extreme stages of exhaustion and depression. He felt the universal blight. He "poured out His soul unto death". What a phrase! As if the limpid water which transfigured every pebble ran off and left but the muddy bed and debris of death. He parted with what men call "soul", or fine insight, and took the state of the commonest, dreariest man or woman who has been robbed of everything—fortune, faculty, and feeling— except faith.

Dying for every man means that He shared in soul (though not in conscience) a universal moral death. And to enter *universal* death is to *taste its* reality and become its prey, to shudder and *dwindle* in a sense, to feel the fog and sick poison of that dismal world on the scale of His own great soul, to feel on Him the curse of that sin which His soul loathed, which embraced Him, but found in Him no consent. The death for all men was a death *from* all men. And He survived this world of death, and He conquered for every man by nothing imaginative, but by the quenchless power and vitality of the one thing left Him—of His faith in God. The taste of universal death means all the world-pessimism which either ends downwards in universal suicide, or, mounting by faith, obtains universal Redemption. If Christ had not gained that victory human history would simply have evolved universal destruction. It was the final, absolute, universal dilemma of the human soul—if you will think to the bottom of things.

2. *Our Fatal Avoidance Of Death*

I anticipate the complaint that I linger too long and insist too much upon the dull, mean misery of soul involved in the taste of universal death. I may be told that it is not well to dwell on such terror—that the saving work is done, and we are now in the realm of the Holy Ghost and the joy of salvation. May I say, in reply, first this, that we could not possibly dwell there in the way of habitual residence. We may dwell on it without dwelling in it. Next, that Christ Himself only tasted this death. He did not pass His life, or any large portion of it, in it. He certainly did realize its awful quality. He did not merely contemplate or imagine it. But as to quantity, or extent, it did not cover His life. He descended into this hell, but He did not dwell there. It was but a taste, though it was a taste and not a sip.

But let me say this also, that I think by our avoidance of such subjects we are losing in spiritual sensibility, spiritual experience, and so in spiritual power. I am sure that the attention so freely given by the Church to-day to grace in the Greek sense, to the beauty of Christ, the beauty of the Cross, the beauty of holiness, has done something to impair real spiritual feeling, to produce, not levity, but religious mediocrity and inadequacy. It is too æsthetic in its nature. It does not search, harrow, and elicit the soul enough. It does not plough deep enough for the true crop of the Cross and the fruits of the Spirit. Not to realize hell is not to prize the Cross. Am I right in thinking that specific and profound Christian experience is growing rarer even where Christian sensibility is by no means dull? Are we parting with soul in the race for souls? We do seem too much accustomed to-day to translate the love of Christ into the terms of human affection, and the Cross of Christ into the terms of human surrender, or into the law of philosophic reconciliation. We treat all love as God's love by a certain juggle with the word divine. We seek the perfection of love in sacrifice instead of in redemption, in sacrifice for the beloved's good instead of sacrifice for the rebel's salvation. We identify renouncing love with redeeming love. We idealize reciprocal love, and call it divine, instead of reading God's revelation of His love as dying for the ungodly. This is love original and absolute. Hereby know we love at its source. If we translate let us translate from that. Let us translate from the original, and not back from a translation. Let us work downward from Love's own account of itself in Christ. Let us begin at the beginning, or, however we translate, at least let us interpret man by God, love by grace. The real revelation is not in the cradle, but in the Cross; not in the home, but in the Church. We should interpret our human affection by the love of God who first loved us, our life's afflictions by the sufferings of Christ, and the eternal process by His awful conflict. It would do more for our spiritual sensibility itself. Have not the tenderest men you knew, the men of real moral tenderness, been sterner than most of the merely gentle and kind? It would certainly do more for our Christian strength and character. With a great price we obtained our freedom. I know it is useless and mischievous to paint horrors, to dwell on suffering as suffering, just as it is morally worthless to make sacrifices merely for the sake of sacrifice. But it is quite necessary that we should be recalled time after time to a true sense of the sufferings of Christ, and detained upon the nature of His death.

And by a true sense I mean a sense germane to the real spiritual situation of our age, and to its mental dialect, a sense relevant to its moral tone, and to its idea of death, not in our own circle or communion or country, but in Europe, say. There was a time when it was more congenial to the condition of society to dwell much on the physical sufferings of Christ. It is the case still in the Romance races, and in Catholic lands. It was the habit of that middle age when it was a rude and full-blooded Europe, of incessant bloodshed and coarseness and cruelty. And the custom survived even into Protestant times. Now we must always worship and preach the precious blood of Christ. But there is a way of speaking about the blood of Christ and dwelling on it which is not only distasteful but, what is worse, is meaningless to our time. Few of us see bloodshed, as the Jews did in sacrifices, and the Middle Ages in war. If the pavement is stained by an accident, it is the business of society to cleanse it from sight at once. The language of blood does not come home to us as it did once. But the horror of death does, though it is in other forms, in other terms. I do not think the old preachers overdid the dark and awful side of the death of Christ. I do not think it is overdone in the attention of the Churches who keep a rigid Lent and a solemn Good Friday. I only say they are apt to seek the horror and the solemnity in the wrong place. They pursue it on its physical side, and the world has moved away from physical terror to psychical. It is the moral horror of death that comes home to us to-day. It is not writhing agony, for we have hospitals and anaesthetics; but it is the mute, lonely, soulless misery of a faithless, hopeless, loveless round of drudgery, failure, and lacerated life. It is not the grief of broken limbs in a struggle with executioners, but of broken hearts in the struggle for existence. Or it is (as in France) the moral nausea of sated lust, of love idolized, then debased, then a scourge, then the madness of spiritual thirst, and national, universal death. It is not the horror of a bleeding frame, of a crucifixion, but the horror of a "grey, void, lampless, deep, unpeopled world". Yes, the colour of death to our modern mind is not red, but grey. It is death in a desert, not a battle. It is the death horror of an age familiar with shaking creeds, iron laws, and the struggle for existence, with tales of shabby streets, mirthless laughter, and the *ennui* of coarse wealth. It is the horror of an age whose chief trouble is not pain but the fear of it, not acute agony but dull and stony woe, not furious despair but incurable melancholy amid unexampled resource. It is a Hamlet age, with

> *Power to transmute all elements, but lack*
> *Of any power to sway that fatal skill.*

It may be good for us, good for our spiritual sensibility, good for our Christian heart, that we should apprehend the reality of Christ's death in terms of the spiritual dialect of our time. We refuse to bow to the spirit of the age, but we ought at least to speak the language of that age, and address it from the Cross in the tone of its too familiar sorrow. It is a mean death that dominates the day, closing much grim and sombre life. The very Titans are tired. The gloom of the pessimist is but the shadow of this weary age, the exhibition of its secret grief He reveals the thoughts of many hearts, except of course those who resolutely turn away from such things in a hearty optimism which is temperament rather than faith. Many who wait on the Lord only maintain their strength. They do not renew it. They do not run, nor soar. Has the death of Christ nothing in common with that dim vexation, sheer exhaustion, and spiritual dreariness which is our modern death? It is not the death of wrong faith, but of no faith. Was His not a spiritual ebb, a spiritual death, far more than a physical? Was it not the curse, though not the experience, of unfaith that fell on His faithful soul? The physical death only showed forth the spiritual. It was there that the value lay. And a spiritual death, in absolute obedience, amid an atmosphere of unfaith, when it is really tasted and not merely sipped, means fog and gloom sour and chill, formless fears and failing force—no visions, no raptures, no triumphs, no flush of energy, no heroic glow. That was the blood of Christ. And you cannot dwell too much on the blood of Christ so long as you are sure it was Christ's blood, the Lamb of God carrying the sin of the world. You cannot dwell too long on the death of Christ, however you conceive it, so long as you see it through the resurrection light as the grace of God. You cannot think too much of the universality of death so long as it reveals the infinite universality of grace. Where death abounds there does grace much more abound. A worn and pessimist Europe may be nearer the Kingdom of God than the cruel, lusty, military Europe that creates it. The gloom of to-day may also be nearer the Cross than the pitiless faith of the "Ages of Faith". The blindness when things have been too much for faith is better than the blindness of a faith which will not see at all. Nay, I am not sure that it is not nearer to it than the amateur optimism of mere temperament, or of what is called sound British sense; nearer, too, than a reconciliation which is only philosophic and rational, and does not feel the tragedy enter its soul at all.

He tasted, then, universal death. The wide empire of death went deep into His soul. His soul itself died. It is very tragic, very terrible; as a historic spectacle awful, as a psychological spectacle profound and unique.

But where is the religion of it? Where is its Gospel? That a man should die for men, die in spiritual horror—it is fine, great; but how does it help us, who are dying too, to see the greatest of the sons of men caught and crushed in the whirl of the same wheel as rolls us into mean dust? So we are led to the real Gospel and glory of the situation.

III.-DEATH AS GRACE

By the grace of God He tasted universal death. There is a death which is a grace of God. The last mystery of death is the mystery of grace. Behind it is not only the awe of a world unseen, but the depth and wonder of the riches of the wisdom and love of all men's God. Death as the expression of the grace of God becomes neither a penalty nor a problem, but a promise. It is, therefore, the centre, not of a philosophy, but of a religion, a faith.

1. The Exegesis

You may suggest, perhaps, that the allusion to the grace of God refers not to Christ's bitter taste of death, but to the fact that it was for every man. But there are two things in the passage itself which show that the grace to Christ in His death is here meant: first, the text goes back on the previous phrase, "the suffering of death", picks that up, and enlarges it. It is the death of Christ, His suffering and the glory and perfection of it that is the theme; that is what is being traced to the grace of God, not the vicarious nature of it. It is the blessing of Christ's death to Himself, as the path to His perfecting as Redeemer—it is that which is the theme, and not the blessing of it to us. And then, in the second place, this word grace is taken up in turn in the following verse, (it is all woven music, phrase issuing from phrase) where it says, "For it became Him, the Lord of all, to make the Redeemer perfect by suffering." It became, it befitted, a gracious God, not to bring many sons to glory, not to make the Son the Saviour, but to make the Saviour a perfect Saviour by the extremity of suffering. He gave the Saviour the last grace, the perfection of death. The mystery to a Jew was that God should not only permit, but require, His Messiah, His favourite, His King, to suffer and die. The writer (of Hebrews) has learnt enough of Paul to say boldly that this was not the lack of grace, but the supreme grace, gift and privilege. It was reserved by God for His Son, nay, by God for Himself. It became the Lord of all to die for all. In conferring death on Christ the Father took the Son into His own unapproachable grace and perfection of giving Himself for the world to the uttermost. The death of Christ was a function, and not merely a commission, of the supreme power, grace and glory. It was an act of God, and not merely of God's agent. God did not send the Son, He came as the Son. What reconciled the world was God in Christ. God does not suffer by deputy, or sacrifice by substitute. It is not His prerogative to receive sacrifices greater than any He makes. He does not delegate redemption; He redeems in the Son with whom He is one. It is no Christian God who sits steamed by the incense of heroic woe or filled with an æsthetic delight in the tragedy of men. The God of Jesus Christ is more of a giver than a receiver. When He gave His Son He gave more, and at more cost, than any but the Son could repay. His blessedness is not to be self-contained, and in Himself enough, but it is to seek and to save. It is more Godlike to give than to receive even life.

2. Death As The Gift And Grace Of God

It was by the grace of God He tasted death. And I mean death was there in God's grace to Christ Himself, and not simply to us. You do not suppose that the grace of God only came *through* Christ and was not *to* Christ, that it was ever withdrawn from Christ for our sakes? The face was withdrawn, but never the grace. How could it ever save us if it failed Him? This bitter, dismal taste of death, it was God's grace to Christ. When He tasted death He tasted how gracious the Lord was. "God gave me blindness," said Dr. Moon, "as a talent to be used for His service, that I might see the needs of those who could not see." So to Christ God gave the grace of a universal death. "This is my beloved Son," was said to Him in the exaltation of His Baptism; and immediately the Spirit drove Him into the wilderness to be tempted of the devil. That was the immediate effect and sign of the Father's good pleasure and total trust. The Father could trust Him in the worst desert of the soul. And amid all Christ knew that and held to it. He knew that when He knew nothing else. All thought of the grandeur of death, the heroism of dying, the beauty of sacrifice, the sweetness of loving devotion, all that fell from His darkened mind. Moral imagination failed, but moral fidelity did not. Obedience stood. He obeyed the Father even when His love of His brethren had received the shock of desertion. He was never much dependent on visions, but if ever He was they failed Him now. Death blanched them, and they died. But one thing death did not master or quench; it was His faith in the grace of God amid this moral mephitis, the fixed obedience of His will amid the stupefying contagion of universal sin, and the failure of hopes and powers. Death never got the better of Christ's faith in the grace of God. The eclipse of feeling never unhinged His loving will, or His obedience to that grace whatever its form. There was a value and a grace in death which He did not feel, but for which He trusted God; He did not see, but He knew, that He could do nothing of such worth for the kingdom as to succumb and die. The Father would have taken Him from the cross had He asked it—though that would have lost all at the moment which turned all. But He did not ask it. His faith and will held sure when His heart was dim and broken. Death could hide the Father or remove Him, but could not change Him. He did not ask it. He could not ask it. He honoured in His faithfulness unto death a holy law and judgment which were as precious to God as His Holy Son or His unholy prodigal. God would not be God if He loved His own holy nature less than man. Then the Divine death might have been an act of pity, but not of grace. It was by the grace of God that Christ died. It was by the grace of God He tasted death, emptied the cup, realised a world of death. Such at least was Christ's own faith. The darkness was the shadow of the Almighty wing. It was the grace of God that put the cross there—the cross as a state of soul and act of will— together with all the glory that only the cross could win. It is a hard saying, but is it not true? The soul's death and agony of Christ was a grace bestowed on Him by God. He was the captain of all those that have the grace of dying "Ye know *the* grace of our Lord Jesus Christ, that though He was rich yet for our sakes He became poor." Being rich in life yet He became poor unto death. Like all His graces that, too, was God's gift to Him, God's grace. The humiliation of the Cross was the Father's greatest gift to His Son, save one—His resurrection; and that was but its completion. Do not doubt that it was a grace of God to Him. It was a gift that He alone could carry.

3. The Fascination Of Death

Heaven was peopled with millions, who would have vied with each other for a grace from their King like this—to be sent to die for men—had any death but the Son of God availed. But none of them could by any means redeem, nor give a ransom. The redemption of the soul is costly, and must be let alone by them for ever. It was the grace of our Lord Jesus Christ.

"Death cannot be an evil," says Schiller, "being so universal." That is a poet's optimism—the optimism of a philosophic poet who did not live with the miserable many. It is a fine saying. There are stages of culture to which it comes broad, profound, and beautiful; yet it is not true. It is hardly even a half truth. It is not true of pain. It is not true to the moral sense of the race; it is not true to its most universal experience, nor to the experience of those most to be regarded. It was not true to the moral soul of that Hebrew race which produced the living conscience of mankind; it was not true to the experience of Buddhism; it is not true to the philosophy which at least has a heart for the world's sorrow and a conscience not to be smoothed by the dialectic of pure reason, or the process of the pure idea. I mean the humane and hopeless philosophy of Pessimism, so gloomy because so much more full of heart and insight than of faith. And it is not true to the faith and experience of the Christian Church. The universality of death is an aggravation of its evil; the commonness of death is but the increase of its bitterness. There is but one condition in which death is not an evil. It is when it becomes the supreme organ of revelation; then it is more than revelation; it delivers men from itself. It is redemption. Death is the last evil and enemy till it become the supreme organ of the grace of God in the cross of Christ. The death of Christ has redeemed death itself. It has immortalised mortality. The last enemy becomes the greatest vassal. Saul turns Paul. And man's extremity is God's opportunity.

To many of the greatest there has been a fascination, yea, even a distinction, about death, as the *locus* of the great secret, as the final problem whose answer answers all. Where the carcase was there were eagles ever. Even if they could not solve it they had an instinct that the solution of humanity lay there in what seemed its dissolution. It is our weakness, not our strength, that consents to the agnosticism of the grave, to death as complete erasure. Faith and philosophy, as well as valour, feel this spell, this call to wring power from death, and wrest meat from the eater. To take the philosophies only, it is those that feel its fascination, yea, its misery, most that are most akin in feeling to the sympathies of faith. I have referred to systematic pessimism. Christianity is not pessimist. But it has attachments in pessimism which it has not in optimism. There is more sympathetic affinity. To grapple with death is at least to shake the door of grace. The optimist philosophy, whose watchwords are reason and reconciliation, does not seize the public need like that whose note is will and its process Redemption. There is a realism and a humanity in the latter, pessimist though it be, which savours more of the true Cross. The way to the soul's final greatness lies through its misery rather than through its success. The grace of God comes home most mightily to those who have looked to it through the desperations, and not only the contradictions of life. The misery of the soul never seemed so terrible and hopeless as it did to the eye of grace. It was the pessimism of

God that moved Him to redeem. "When there was no eye to pity and no arm to save, then His own eye pitied and His own arm brought salvation." The light that saved was the light that best showed the hell it saved from. For this reason Christianity can never be pessimist; because we never see the very worst until we have been saved from it into the best, and view it with the eyes of its Saviour. None can realise hell but a redeemer, however many may suffer it. The pity of the Saviour is more than all pity of Buddha, or the ingenious self-pity of the modern soul. It pities from its height of holiness a sinfulness which is much more pitiful than the sorrow felt by the humane heart of a sympathetic man. He who emerges above man feels man more than he who is immersed in himself. Must he not also feel more than a total humanity could feel with nothing but itself to be immersed in?

> *Unless above himself he can*
> *Erect himself how poor a thing is man.*[1]

To be lost in self—is it not to be lost to self? And if this occur on the scale of the whole race great must be the fall thereof.

Yes, there is a fascination in death—else there were no heroes and no martyrs—and it does not exist for the human soul alone. For even to the Divine mind itself there was this attraction of the Cross, this invitation, this challenge from death, this insight of death's resources under compulsion, this power to pluck the jewel life from the jaws of death. For God Himself there was this sense of opportunity, of capability in death to be the organ of grace, the way of glory, and the perfecting of the soul. But the resources were not in death itself, but in the use Godhead could make of it. The universal Grace, seeking its opening, seized on the thing in man most universal— more universal even than love. And that was death. For there are some who love not, but none who do not die. Death and grace made one salvation. The evening and the morning are one day. Darkness and light are both alike to God, and together involve the revolution of the world. The universality of death was the only experience adequate to the universality of grace. It was the only experience wide and solemn enough. That it was a universal enemy was but another fascination to a divine and holy love that felt in itself all power to cope with human ill. If evil was to be destroyed it should be mastered in its great stronghold, its most paralysing form, its fortress in the dismal fen. The wages of sin should

---

1. Wordsworth: *The Excursion* (Preface)

become the seed of holiness, and what sin dreaded most faith should trust and use still more. Love, to appear exceeding lovely, dared to die. It consented to weakness and horror as the condition of all might. All! "All things are delivered to me of My Father." And at the bottom of this Pandora gift was death. His greatness was a doom. He was buffeted in kindness. Love tasted death that it might overpass love and be worshipped as grace. The depth of need was sounded by the fulness of power. And the range of universal death should be at least no less than the realm of universal grace. Nothing the heart could experience should be beyond the Saviour whose triumph the heart should trust.

4. Death And Grace As Experience And Trust

Experience and trust, death and grace—can they be co-equal powers?

The trouble of the time is this—that we are more universal in our thought and experience than we are in our faith. Our experience is wider than our faith. Death is wider than grace. Our ideas are wider than our real religion. Our culture is wider than our actual creed. Our crises overwhelm our Christ. Men range the world with ships, trains, and wires. They range the universe with microscope, telescope, and spectrum. They explore human nature with the aid of genius, and they go far in that knowledge of the soul which comes of culture. History and geography, science and literature, serve us as they never did before. We are cosmopolitan, but are we really universal? We go far, but do we go deep? We have more experience than we have faith to carry. If masses are under-educated, masses are over-educated. Their resources submerge their conscience. And their conscience itself outruns their ethics. Men see a right which they cannot make a habit, or pass into public use. Their knowledge of the world is so great that it actually belittles their world. The more they know of it the less they think of it. Prosperity brings leanness of soul and meanness of ideal. The more they know of men the less they respect man. The more they see the less they believe. The more their experience the less their faith in the great faiths, hopes and gospels. They like broad views, often because these seem to make less demand on their bankrupt souls.

Men come, for instance, to know the dark races as a colonist might. They have dealings with them. And the experience is too much for faith many a time. The black man who tries their English patience, they say, is incurable. Christianity only makes him more intractable and more insufferable. He is not the man for whom Christ died. Missions are a mistake. They must make way for politics. The apostle shall go no further than the diplomatist allows. And it would simplify trade much if he did not go at all. Let him practice philanthropy and so reduce the rates at home. Christianity is a gospel only for the superior races. Well, that is the universality of mere experience conquering the universalism of faith. And in this respect the villager of faith and love with his missionary-box is more universal than the travelled peer, the colonial colossus, the imperialist millionaire.

Another man goes sympathetically into the dark places of Europe, of England. He finds rascality and suffering such as he had never dreamed of. He is filled with impotent rage against the order of society. It is oppression, misery and death everywhere, except among the prosperous. And even among them it is only a worse and more heartless death. His faith was only enthusiasm, and it fails him. It was only sympathy, milk of human kindness, and it goes sour. His experience is too much for his faith. For him the grace of God is not upon sorrow and death. The cross weighs down the very Redeemer. The cross is on the Redeemer; the Redeemer is not upon the cross. The cross is crushing the Redeemer; He does not rise from His cross.

Or another man, ardent for well-doing, falls into disease. He is powerless to help in any good. He lingers in the misery of impatience and impotence. His depression deepens. He feels but earth's sorrow. He tastes death daily, but he never assimilates it. He is never reconciled to it. It is because he is not reconciled by it. He lies on a mattress-grave. He is not transfigured on a mountain apart. Christ even seems to him to die in the common martyrdom, not in the universal Redemption. Death is not surmounted by grace. It is not the organ of grace. His experience has mastered his faith. His ideas are more universal than his creed. His heart is greater than his God. He carries in his sympathy a larger world than he lives in by his faith. And there is more curse for him in this world than grace, just in proportion as he is in earnest. And it is all because he has taken everything more in earnest than he has taken Christ. He despises the theologians, it may be, but he lets them rule him and even enslave him. Because he rejects their christ he lets himself be without a christ, or he consents to an ineffectual christ. The theologians have, at least, this advantage as yet, that they have the effectual Christ—the Christ that works. The non-theological christ is popular; he wins votes; but he is not mighty; he does not win souls; he does not break men into small pieces and create them anew. The martyrdom of Christ was never so respected as it is to-day. The name of Jesus, they say, is cheered in the East-end, and is no bad passport in the West. The clergy are socially welcome. The religion of suffering has even literary patronage; there is money in it at the theatres under the sign of the Cross; and the Church, as a branch of the public service and the social order, is treated with some deference in the writers' clubs. But it is a spectacular Christ throughout. And His kingdom is not spectacular. It cometh not with observation. It is within you. Nor is the spectacle of Christ on His cross in itself enough to lift men from their misery, break them of self, or release them from the malady of their time. The crucifix, as the apotheosis of sorrow, may even be but the greatest of earth's burdens. It is possible so to view the Cross as to carry more of the world's woe into it than we receive from it of redeeming grace. Nay, it is natural to do so. It is the natural thing to recognize in the dying Christ but a fellow-sufferer (even if He be the classic one), a fellow-victim of the death we die. Death is wider to include Christ than Christ is to include death. We see easily the misery of the world upon the Cross of Christ. What it is not easy to see is the Cross of Christ upon the misery, and upon the misery of *the world*. It is no natural vision that sees that.

ROMANTIC RELIGION AND TRAGIC

I speak of the misery of the world. I have spoken throughout of the misery of the world. I have heard the whole creation groan. I have presumed on an instructed sympathy which does not measure human life by our own lot, or pronounce upon destiny just by our own experience, or our friends'. Who does not know the fatal trivialist who makes every discussion of principles or ideas vanish in the sand as he narrates a series of petty incidents from his petty career; or smothers it in a dust storm of his relatives ground fine. The relevant thing is not this and that man's groping. The great Scripture is not of private interpretation. I have been speaking of the soul as the human soul, not as this or that man's experience. And if I have spoken of a misery which is not in this land organized into a creed, of a squalor which has only partially infected our literature from other lands, why is it otherwise among us? Why, because of a freedom to worship, think, act, and combine, chiefly due to the Free Churches and their witness of free grace. When I picture the world-woe as it comes home to Church-ridden lands, or to the genius of unfaith, I say that it is not easy to see the Cross of Christ upon the misery and sin of the world—it is not natural, it is entirely supernatural, it is not human, it is quite superhuman. It is a miraculous vision that sees in that Martyr more than a martyr—a Healer; and in the Healer more—the Redeemer. To see sin, sorrow, and death continually under the Cross, to see the grace of God triumphing over them in it, is the very soul and victory of faith. It is possible to see a beauty in sacrifice which draws the young imagination that way bent into a certain enthusiasm and imitation of the Cross. The high, but hollow, naturalism of George Eliot had room for the action on Maggie Tulliver of Thomas á Kempis. But that is a faith too æsthetic or too subjective for the stay and victory of the thorough-going soul over the last moral horrors of the world. In London, in one twenty-four hours, there is more, if we knew it, than a faith like that could bear. And even when we come to very close quarters with Christ crucified the saviour of the Cross may but deepen the sad tone of many a morbid soul; it may fix the hue and habit of eclipse upon the pious heart, in spite of fitful gleams of cheer and joy. There is much more in the Cross than such a darkling faith has fathomed. The infinite, ultimate love of God is there. The gift and grace of God for the whole world is there. It is not simply nor chiefly the love of Christ for His brethren that is in the Cross. That was indeed uppermost in Christ's life, but in His death that is not direct but indirect; and the primary thing is Christ's obedience to God, and His action, therefore, as the channel of God's redeeming love. It is the love of God for the godless, loveless, hating world that is there. And it is there, not simply expressed but effected, not exhibited but enforced and infused, not in manifestation merely, but in judgment and decision. The last judgment, in the sense of the ultimate Divine verdict on sin, is already by. It was passed in the Cross of Christ, where sin was condemned once for all. All future judgment is but the working out of this. The prince of this world is already judged. He acts to-day as a power, indeed, but only as a doomed power. His sentence went out in the Cross. And he knows it. Humanity was rescued from him there. The crisis of man's spiritual destiny is there. The *opus operatum* of history is there. It is not simply revelation, but revelation as redemption. It does not *show*, it *does*. It is not displayed for refining effect upon our moral nature, it is in action for our spiritual recreation and regeneration. Do not empty such words as these of their fundamental and searching significance. Beware of the watering of the Christian stock. Do not let the litterateurs and poets capture, pare, and monopolise them to fit their range of experiences; as if renunciation were the Cross, sacrifice were faith, and purification were the Holy Ghost. The Christ is He who came by water and by blood; not by water only but by water and by blood; not for purification so much as for salvation, nor for refinement so much as for redemption. When we read of the rowdy American hero that

> *Christ isn't going to be too hard*
> *On a man that died for men,*[1]

it is clever poetry, but it is mawkish piety; it has the blight of affectation and unreality upon it, like much literary heroism. Faith does not lend itself to literature except with geniuses of the very first rank, like Dante or Milton, to whose commanding intellects theology is the envisagement of the things most gracious, searching, and sublime. Redemption by the grace of God in the Cross of Christ, regeneration by the Spirit of God in His Church— these are things deeper than literature can go or philosophy expound. There are few dangers threatening the religious future more serious than the slow shallowing of the religious mind towards the literary shore, the stranding of faith, and the bleaching of its ribs—the desiccation, by even religious culture, of words which won their wealth from experiences stirred by the New Testament when it was not viewed as literature at all, but as the very Word of God. *Tendimus in altum.* Our safety is in the deep. The lazy cry for simplicity is a great danger. It indicates a frame of mind which is only appalled at the great things of God, and a senility of faith which fears that which is high. Men complain that they are jaded and cannot rise to such matters. That may mean that the matters of the world absorb all the energies of the great side of the soul, that Divine things are no more than a comfort. And if so, it means much for the future of religion, and much that is ominous. And the poverty of our worship amid its very refinements, its lack of solemnity, poorly compensated by an excess of tenderness and taste, is the fatal index of the peril. We do need more reverence in our prayer, more beauty in our praise, less dread of tried and consecrated form. But still more do we want the breathless awe, and the stammering tongue, and the solemn wonder, and the passionate gratitude, which are the true note of grace, and the worship of a soul plucked from the burning and snatched by a miracle from the abyss. We want the new song of those who stand upon the rock, taken from the fearful pit and the miry clay, with the trembling still upon them and the slime still moist. We want the devotion of men whom grace found, and scarcely saved, in the jaws of death, and took from the belly of

---

1. *Jim Bludso:* Pike Country Ballads, John Hay, Boston, 1886.

hell. We want more joy, but more of the joy of men who have tasted death either in their own conscience or in the communion of their Redeemer's. We need it to make Faith what in some of its popular forms it is ceasing in any imperial way to be—a power and a passion in authority among the passions and powers of the race. We want a Gospel to give conscience might, where it is owned to have right. We could dispense with some of its pathos if we changed it for more of its power. There is no persuasiveness like that of men who have known the terror of the Lord. There is no reason so authoritative as supernatural grace—amazing and incomprehensible.

5. The Mystery Of Iniquity And The Miracle Of Mercy

The mystery of iniquity who can understand? Sin is utterly irrational. Death none can comprehend, for we can question none who have returned from the grave. Sorrow is hard to bear, and harder still to explain; for the good and pure have an ache of their own in a world like this when all the common sources of pain are stilled. But to comprehend is not to forgive, to explain is not to redeem. The grace of God is not only unaccountable, but if it could be accounted for it would cease to be sovereign grace. Faith is in its very nature faith in a miracle. To challenge miracle without leaving in the net result a profounder sense of the essential miracle of grace and fate is poor service to the Gospel or the soul. It is miracle far more than reason that feeds the soul. No treatment of the miracles should ignore that; no fate of theirs can alter that. It is the evangelical nerve of Christianity and the marrow of the Gospel. To give up miracle is to leave the field to magic. God's attitude to such as we are is an eternal anomaly, and the Christian life is miraculous or it is nothing. Atonement ceases to be religious when it is offered as explanation. The justifier can never justify himself at any human bar. Nothing can justify justifying grace. Sin, grief, death, and grace make a standing rebuke to our lust of lucidity, our rational religion, and our passion to explain. The Lord of death and grace does not explain till we are inexplicably blessed in Him; and then our thought is for ever far in the wake of our faith and our worshipping love.

EVOLUTION AND REVOLUTION

Do not turn, then, from the awful horror of the Cross, or you will lose the solemn power of it. Do not say it is morbid to look so much on the Cross in its contact with human despair. It is the one death which is charged with more grace and power for the human soul than all the blithe and vigorous enterprise of the world. It is the one death which has taken control of human life; as, indeed, it is the ruling and interpreting point for the life of Christ Himself. It has made the whole of human history simply an ante-chamber of the spiritual world; and the grace of God revealed in the Cross contains more of His nature and purpose than all our inductions from the experience of the race. It has graven upon the soul the conviction not only that the Cross is for man, but that man is for the Cross. The grace of God in the death of Christ has, indeed, revealed the principle of sacrifice as an essential, or even supreme, factor in human progress. The Cross is there for man in that sense. It is the classic case of the sacrifice that makes human greatness. But it is much more than that, and has done more. It has changed the nature of man's greatness. It has changed the spiritual centre of gravity, and moved it outside of humanity altogether. It has changed man's own spiritual place. It has made man a contributor to the Cross even more than the Cross a contributor to man. It has made man owe himself, and not merely his religious progress, to the Cross and God's grace in it. Man belongs by right to the Cross even more than the Cross to man. The whole question of the time as to a spiritual world concerns not so much its existence, but its place. The day is over when materialism could challenge its existence, except among those scientists who are not thinkers, but only the skilled artisans of the intellect or the chief clerks of mind. The better culture of the age has outgrown the negation of a spiritual realm, and the question is as to its place. Does it belong to man, or does man belong to it? Is humanity its king or its subject? Is it to glorify man, or man to glorify it? Is it a department of human culture, swelling the triumph of a humanity still on the summit of things? Or is it a world which holds man, and which all his culture obeys? We raise that question to a higher place, and we make it more definite, when we ask it about the Cross of Christ and its grace of God. But it is the same question. It is always the chief question of the age that is put and answered by the Cross. Does the Cross belong to man, or does man belong to the Cross? Is the grace of God only a factor in human evolution, or is it the condition of all evolution, and its destiny as well, its source and goal in one? Is the Cross a grace or *the* grace? Is faith in Christ a department of the soul, or is it the total energy of the soul? Does it serve the soul, or is it the soul in service? Is the Church but one of the public services? Is Christ a sectional interest, or is He the soul's new world? Did He die to promote human welfare on the noblest of natural lines, or to redeem us to a new nature?

Did the Cross mean a new departure or a new creature? Evolution or Revolution? Is the Cross the spiritualizing of the old man or the creation of a new man? Is grace the transfiguration of nature, or the foundation of a kingdom on the ruins of nature? Yea, within the Church itself, within the Christianity of the time, the question must arise. Among those who believe the gospel the issue must be sharpened, and put thus: Does the gospel carry the Cross, or the Cross carry the gospel? In the beginning was—what? the Word or the Deed? Is it the gospel of love that carries in its hand the act of grace, or is it the act of grace that carries for the soul the gospel of love? Is the prime object of faith Fatherly love or Redeeming grace?

To questions like these there is but one answer when we come to the core of faith. Man belongs to the Cross much more than the Cross belongs to man. Christ did not die to exhibit, but to act, nay, to create. He did not die to show how deep and fine the Cross was in human nature, if we would be true to ourselves; but to effect in human nature a total change and bring to pass its death into a new life, its life into a new lord. The new master made a new man, and not a reformed man. The Cross has far more claim upon man than man upon the Cross. The poetry of man uses the Cross for man; for its chief interest is man. But the religion of man uses man for the Cross, for its ruling interest is the grace of God, the holy God, the Redeemer. And in the grace of God there lies a destiny for the soul through faith which, as it was achieved by faith when all high imagination had failed and died, so transcends all that imagination can surmise, art body forth, or imperious wills achieve. It is the Cross which carries the gospel, not the gospel the Cross. In the beginning was the Word as eternal Deed. There is no real revelation of the gospel of Fatherly love but in the grace of forgiveness by the Cross. Revelation to such as us is impossible, except as Redemption. The sense for it has to be created. It is not revelation that redeems so much as redemption that reveals. The soul realizes its greatness less in what is shown it of the love of God than in what is done for it by the grace of God.

6. The Greatness Of Human Nature And Of Its Redemption

Oh, we are shut up into a greatness which is not of us at all!

Life is great, and death is great, and love is stronger than death; but great beyond all is the grace which is eternal life to us from the dead, and a new self beyond ourselves.

The world is great and the soul is great, and great is the soul's mastery of the world; but greater than soul can say is the grace that masters the soul and recreates the will for a life beyond life.

We inherit greatness and breathe it. Earth and sky and day and night; stars in the naked heavens, breathings of wind, and the coming of spring; hill and plain, rolling tracts, and river and sea; the mist on the long, wet moor, and above it the black, baleful cloud; fleets and camps, cities and realms; valour and power, science, trade, churches, causes, arts, charities; the fidelities of peace and the heroisms of war, the rhythm of order and the stream of progress; the generations that go under and the civilizations that survive; the energies unseen, the vanished past, the forgotten and the unforgettable brave the majesty of the moral hero and the splendour of the public saint; agonies, love, and man's unconquerable mind—oh, we have a great world, great glories, great records, great prospects and great allies! We inherit greatness, and we inhabit promise. The capitalized legacies of the past and the condensed suffering of the many become in us an instinct of greatness which moves us to an unapprehended destiny. The brave possess the earth, and the noble are at home in the glorious natural world.

> *Winds blow and waters roll*
> *Strength to the brave, and power, and deity.*

But as our sun rises there is a rising cloud. In the moving soul there is a frail seam, an old wound, a tender sore. The stout human heart has a wearing ache and a haunting fear. There is a hollow in the soul's centre, in its last hold no fortress, and in its sanctuary no abiding God. A vanity blights the glory of time, a lameness falls on the strenuous wing, our sinew shrinks at certain touches, and we halt on our thigh; pride falters, and the high seems low, and the hour is short, and the brief candle is out, and what is man that he is accounted of? There is a day of the Lord upon all that is haughty, on lofty tower, and tall cedar, and upon all pleasant imagery. And misery, sin, and death grow great as all our triumph dwindles on the sight. They baffle the wisdom of the wise, and they are stronger than the valour of the brave. The City heroes are feasted in the morning, and the City streets are a hell at night. And the heart's cheer fails, and love yields to death, and we cannot, cannot bear it. Memory turns to terror—not only for lost love but lost purity. Conscience belittles all greatness, and submerges it all by the greatness of its law, evermore saying, Holy, Holy, Holy is the Lord God of Hosts; and by the greatness of its cry, My wound, my wound! My grievous sin and my desolate end.

The greatness of the soul is more apparent in the greatness of its misery than in the triumph of its powers. Our spiritual failure is more than all our mighty doings. We achieve at last—oblivion and a grave; at the most a progress never realised; because each generation bequeaths to the next more hope than peace—if even hope. Then cometh the end.

And the end—what is it?

It is the Christ of God, the Saviour. We taste death, we feel decay, we face judgment. And what is the judgment of God on human guilt and woe? Lift up your eyes, lift up your hearts. Behold the Lamb of God! It is the Saviour. Christ is God's judgment on the world. Our judgment is our salvation. His chastisement is our peace. We deserved death, and death He gave us—the death of the cross. The end of all is the grace unspeakable, the fulness of glory—all the old splendour fixed, with never a one lost good; all the spent toil garnered, all the fragments gathered up, all the lost love found for ever, all the lost purity transfigured in holiness, all the promises of the travailing soul now yea and amen; all progress already possessed, all works immortalised in faith, all sin turned to salvation, all the labour and sorrow hallowed, the tears and gore of the ages flowing as the saving water and blood.

> For all the blood that's shed upon earth
> Runs through the springs o' that countrie.[1]

All things are for our sakes, that the abundant grace might turn to the glory of God.

And, even now, eternal thanks be unto God, who hath given us the victory through Jesus Christ our Lord, and by His grace, the taste of life for every man.

---

1.   Scottish Ballad, Thomas the Rhymer.

THE SOUL OF PRAYER

1916

Chapter One

THE INWARDNESS OF PRAYER

It is a difficult and even formidable thing to write on prayer, and one fears to touch the Ark. Perhaps no one ought to undertake it unless he has spent more toil in the practice of prayer than on its principle. But perhaps also the effort to look into its principle may be graciously regarded by Him who ever liveth to make intercession as itself a prayer to know better how to pray. All progress in prayer is an answer to prayer—our own or another's. And all true prayer promotes its own progress and increases our power to pray.

The worst sin is prayerlessness. Overt sin, or crime, or the glaring inconsistencies which often surprise us in Christian people are the effect of this, or its punishment. We are left by God for lack of seeking Him. The history of the saints shows often that their lapses were the fruit and nemesis of slackness or neglect in prayer. Their life, at seasons, also tended to become inhuman by their spiritual solitude. They left men, and were left by men, because they did not in their contemplation find God; they found but the thought or the atmosphere of God. Only living prayer keeps loneliness humane. It is the great producer of sympathy. Trusting the God of Christ, and transacting with Him, we come into tune with men. Our egoism retires before the coming of God, and into the clearance there comes with our Father our brother. We realize man as he is in God and for God, his Lover. When God fills our heart He makes more room for man than the humanist heart can find. Prayer is an act, indeed *the* act, of fellowship. We cannot truly pray even for ourselves without passing beyond ourselves, and our individual experience. If we should begin with these the nature of prayer carries us beyond them, both to God and to man. Even private prayer is common prayer—the more so, possibly, as it retires from being public prayer.

Not to want to pray, then, is the sin behind sin. And it ends in not being able to pray. That is its punishment—spiritual dumbness, or at least aphasia, and starvation. We do not take our spiritual food, and so we falter, dwindle, and die. "In the sweat of your brow ye shall eat your bread." That has been said to be true both of physical and spiritual labour. It is true both of the life of bread and of the bread of life.

Prayer brings with it, as food does, a new sense of power and health. We are driven to it by hunger, and, having eaten, we are refreshed and strengthened for the battle which even our physical life involves. For heart and *flesh* cry out for the living God. God's gift is free; it is, therefore, a gift to our freedom, *i.e.* renewal to our moral strength, to what makes men of us. Without this gift always renewed our very freedom can enslave us. The life of every organism is but the constant victory of a higher energy, constantly fed, over lower and more elementary forces. Prayer is the assimilation of a holy God's moral strength.

We must work for this living. To feed the soul we must toil at prayer. And what a labour it is! "He prayed in an agony." We must pray even to tears if need be. Our cooperation with God is our receptivity; but it is an active, a laborious receptivity, an importunity that drains our strength away if it does not tap the sources of the Strength Eternal. We work, we slave, at receiving. To him that hath this laborious expectancy it shall be given. Prayer is the powerful appropriation of power, of divine power. It is therefore creative.

Prayer is not mere wishing. It is asking—with a will. Our will goes into it. It is energy. *Orare est laborare.* We turn to an active Giver; therefore we go into action. For we could not pray without knowing and meeting Him in kind. If God has a controversy with Israel, Israel must wrestle with God. Moreover, He is the Giver not only of the answer, but first of the prayer itself. His gift provokes ours. He beseeches us, which makes us beseech Him. And what we ask for chiefly is the power to ask more and to ask better. We pray for more prayer. The true "gift of prayer" is God's grace before it is our facility.

Thus prayer is, for us, paradoxically, both a gift and a conquest, a grace and a duty. But does that not mean, is it not a special case of the truth, that all duty is a gift, every call on us a blessing, and that the task we often find a burden is really a boon? When we look up from under it it is a load, but those who look down to it from God's side see it as a blessing. It is like great wings—they increase the weight but also the flight. If we have no duty to do God has shut Himself up from us. To be denied duty is to be denied God. No cross no Christ. "When pain ends gain ends too."

We are so egotistically engrossed about God's giving of the answer that we forget His gift of the prayer itself. But it is not a question simply of willing to pray, but of accepting and using as God's will the gift and the power to pray. In every act of prayer we have already begun to do God's will, for which above all things we pray. The prayer within all prayer is

"Thy will be done." And has that petition not a special significance here? "My prayer is Thy Will. Thou didst create it in me. It is Thine more than mine. Perfect Thine own will"—all that is the paraphrase, from this viewpoint, of "Hear my prayer." "The will to pray," we say, "is Thy will. Let that be done both in my petition and in Thy perfecting of it." The petition is half God's will. It is God's will inchoate. "Thy will" (in my prayer) "be done (in Thy answer). It is Thine both to will and to do. Thy will be done in heaven—in the answer, as it is done upon earth—in the asking."

Prayer has its great end when it lifts us to be more conscious and more sure of the gift than the need, of the grace than the sin. As petition rises out of need or sin, in our first prayer it comes first; but it may fall into a subordinate place when, at the end and height of our worship, we are filled with the fullness of God. "In that day ye shall ask me nothing." Inward sorrow is fulfilled in the prayer of petition; inward joy in the prayer of thanksgiving. And this thought helps to deal with the question as to the hearing of prayer, and especially its answer. Or rather as to the place and kind of answer. We shall come one day to a heaven where we shall gratefully know that God's great refusals were sometimes the true answers to our truest prayer. Our soul is fulfilled if our petition is not.

When we begin to pray we may catch and surprise ourselves in a position like this. We feel to be facing God from a position of independence. If He start from His end we do from ours. We are his *vis-a-vis;* He is ours. He is an object so far as we are concerned; and we are the like to Him. Of course, He is an object of *worship.* We do not start on equal terms, march up to Him, as it were, and put our case. We do more than approach Him erect, with courteous self-respect shining through our poverty. We bow down to Him. We worship. But still it is a voluntary, an independent, submission and tribute, so to say. It is a reverence which we make and offer. We present something which is ours to give. If we ask Him to give we feel that we begin the giving, in our worship. We are outside each other; and we call, and He graciously comes.

But this is not the Christian idea, it is only a crude stage of it (if the New Testament is to guide us). We are there taught that only those things are perfected in God which He begins, that we seek only because He found, we beseech Him because he first besought us (2 Cor. v. 20). If our prayer reach or move Him it is because He first reached and moved us to pray. The prayer that reached heaven began there, when Christ went forth. It began when God turned to beseech us in Christ—in the appealing Lamb slain before the foundation of the world. The Spirit went out with the power and function in it to return with our soul. Our prayer is the answer to God's. Herein is prayer, not that we prayed Him, but that He first prayed us, giving His Son to be a propitiation for us. The heart of the Atonement is prayer—Christ's great self-offering to God in the Eternal Spirit. The whole rhythm of Christ's soul, so to say, was Godhead going out and returning on itself. And so God stirs and inspires all prayer which finds and moves Him. His love provokes our sacred forwardness. He does not compel us, but we cannot help it after that look, that tone, that turn of His. All say, "I am yours if you will"; and when we will it is prayer. Any final glory of human success or destiny rises from man being God's continual creation, and destined by Him for Him. So we pray because we were made for prayer, and God draws us out by breathing Himself in.

We feel this especially as prayer passes upwards into praise. When the mercy we besought comes home to us its movement is reversed in us, and it returns upon itself as thanksgiving. "Great blessings which are won with prayer are worn with thankfulness." Praise is the converted consecration of the egoism that may have moved our prayer. Prayer may spring from self-love, and be so far natural; for nature is all of the craving and taking kind. But praise is supernatural. It is of pure grace. And it is a sign that the payer was more than natural at heart. Spare some leisure, therefore, from petition for thanksgiving. If the Spirit move conspicuously to praise, it shows that He also moved latently the prayer, and that within nature is that which is above it. "Prayer and thanks are like the double motion of the lungs, the air that is drawn in by prayer is breathed forth again by thanks."

Prayer is turning our will on God either in the way of resignation or of impetration. We yield to His Will or He to ours. Hence religion is above all things prayer, according as it is a religion of will and conscience, as it is an ethical religion. It is will and Will. To be religious is to pray. Bad prayer is false religion. Not to pray is to be irreligious. "The battle for religion is the battle for prayer; the theory of religion is the philosophy of prayer." In prayer we do not think out God; we draw Him out. Prayer is where our thought of God passes into action, and becomes more certain than thought. In all thought which is not mere dreaming or brooding there is an element of will; and in earnest (which is intelligent) prayer we give this element the upper hand. We do not simply spread our thought out before God, but we *offer* it to Him, turn it on Him, bring it to bear on Him, press it on Him. This is our great and first sacrifice, and it becomes pressure on God. We can offer God nothing so great and effective as our obedient acceptance of the mind and purpose and work of Christ. It is not easy. It is harder than any idealism. But then it is very mighty. And it is a power that grows by exercise. At first it groans, at last it glides. And it comes to this, that, as there are thoughts that seem to think themselves in us, so there are prayers that pray themselves in us. And, as those are the best thoughts, these are the best prayers. For it is the Christ at prayer who lives in us, and we are conduits of the Eternal intercession.

Prayer is often represented as the great means of the Christian life. But it is no mere means, it is the great end of that life. It is, of course, not untrue to call it a means. It is so, especially at first. But at last it is truer to say that we live the Christian life in order to pray than that we pray in order to live the Christian life. It is at least as true. Our prayer prepares for our work and sacrifice, but all our work and sacrifice still more prepare for prayer. And we are, perhaps, oftener wrong in our work, or even our sacrifice, than we are in our prayer—and that for want of its guidance. But to reach this height, to make of prayer our great end, and to order life always in view of such a solemnity, in this sense to pray without ceasing and without pedantry—it is a slow matter. We cannot move fast to such a fine product of piety and feeling. It is a growth in grace. And the whole history of the world shows that nothing grows so slowly as grace, nothing costs as much as free grace; a fact which drives us to all kinds of apologies to explain what seems the absence of God from His world, and especially from His world of souls. If God, to our grief, seems to us far absent from history, how does He view the distance, the absence, of history from Him?

A chief object of all prayer is to bring us to God. But we may attain His presence and come closer to Him by the way we ask Him for other things, concrete things or things of the Kingdom, than by direct prayer for union with Him. The prayer for deliverance from personal trouble, or national calamity, may bring us nearer Him than mere devout aspiration to be lost in Him. The poor woman's prayer to find her lost sovereign may mean more than the prayer of many a cloister. Such distress is often meant by God as the initial means and exercise to His constant end of reunion with Him. His patience is so long and kind that He is willing to begin with us when we are no farther on than to use Him as a means of escape or relief. The holy Father can turn to His own account at last even the exploiting egoism of youth. And He gives us some answer, though the relief does not come, if He keeps us praying, and ever more instant and purified in prayer. Prayer is never rejected so long as we do not cease to pray. The chief failure of prayer is its cessation. Our importunity is a part of God's answer, both of His answer to us and ours to Him. He is sublimating our idea of prayer, and realizing the final purpose in all trouble of driving us farther in on Himself. A homely image has been used. The joiner, when he glues together two boards, keeps them tightly clamped till the cement sets, and the outward pressure is no more needed; then he unscrews. So with the calamities, depressions, and disappointments that crush us into close contact with God. The pressure on us is kept up till the soul's union with God is set. Instant relief would not establish the habit of prayer, though it might make us believe in it with a promptitude too shallow to last or to make it the principle of our soul's life at any depth. A faith which is based chiefly on impetration might become more of a faith in prayer than a faith in God. If we got all we asked for we should soon come to treat Him as a convenience, or the request as a magic. The reason of much bewilderment about prayer is that we are less occupied about faith in God than about faith in prayer. In a like way we are misled about the question of immortality because we become more occupied with the soul than with God, and with its endless duration more than its eternal life, asking if we shall be in eternity more than eternity in us.

In God's eyes the great object of prayer is the opening or restoring of free communion with Himself in a kingdom of Christ, a life communion which may even, amid our duty and service, become as unconscious as the beating of our heart. In this sense every true prayer brings its answer with it; and that not "reflexly" only, in our pacification of soul, but objectively in our obtaining a deeper and closer place in God and His purpose. If prayer is God's great gift, it is one inseparable from the giver; who, after all, is His own great gift, since revelation is His Self-donation. He is actively with us, therefore, as we pray, and we exert His will in praying. And, on the other hand, prayer makes us to realize how far from God we were, *i.e.* it makes us realize our worst trouble and repair it. The outer need kindles the sense of the inner, and we find that the complete answer to prayer is the Answerer, and the hungry soul comes to itself in the fullness of Christ.

Prayer is the highest use to which speech can be put. It is the highest meaning that can be put into words. Indeed, it breaks through language and escapes into action. We could never be told of what passed in Christ's mountain midnights. Words fail us in prayer oftener than anywhere else;

and the Spirit must come in aid of our infirmity, set out our case to God, and give to us an unspoken freedom in prayer, the possession of our central soul, the reality of our inmost personality in organic contact with His. We are taken up from human speech to the region of the divine Word, where Word is deed. We are integrated into the divine consciousness, and into the dual soliloquy of Father and Son, which is the divine give and take that upholds the world. We discover how poor a use of words it is to work them into argument and pursue their dialectic consequences. There is a deeper movement of speech than that, and a more inward mystery, wherein the Word does not spread out to wisdom, nor broods in dream, but gathers to power and condenses to action. The Word becomes Flesh, Soul, Life, the active conquering kingdom of God. Prayer, as it is spoken, follows the principle of the Incarnation with its twofold movement, down and up.[1] It is spirit not in expression only, but in deed and victory. It is speech become not only movement, but moral action and achievement; it is word become work; as the Word from being Spirit became flesh, as Christ from prophet became priest, and then Holy Spirit. It is the principle of the Incarnation, only with the descending movement reversed. "Ye are gods." God became man in His Son's outgoing that man might become divine; and prayer is in the train of the Son's return to the Father, a function of the Ascension and Exaltation, in which (if we may not say man becomes God) we are made partakers of the divine nature, not ontologically, but practically, experimentally. It is the true response, and tribute, and trophy to Christ's humiliation. Man rises to be a coworker with God in the highest sense. For it is only by action, it is not by dream or rapture, far less in essence, that we enter communion with an active being—above all with the eternal Act of God in Christ that upholds the world. As such communion prayer is no mere *rapport,* no mere contact. It is the central act of the soul, organic with Christ's; it is that which brings it into tune with the whole universe as God's act, and answers the beating of its central heart. It is a part and function of the creative, preservative, and consummatory energy of the world.

What is true religion? It is not the religion which contains most truth in the theological sense of the word. It is not the religion most truly thought out, nor that which most closely fits with thought. It is religion which comes to itself most powerfully in prayer. It is the religion in which the soul becomes very sure of God and itself in prayer. Prayer contains the

---

1. See last chapter of my *Person and Place of Christ* (Hodder & Stoughton).

very heart and height of truth, but especially in the Christian sense of truth—reality and action. In prayer the inmost truth of our personal being locks with the inmost reality of things, its energy finds a living Person acting as their unity and life, and we escape the illusions of sense, self, and the world. Prayer, indeed, is the great means for appropriating, out of the amalgam of illusion which means so much for our education, the pure gold of God as He wills, the Spirit as He works, and things as they are. It is the great school both of proficiency and of veracity of soul. (How few court and attain proficiency of soul!) It may often cast us down, for we are reduced by this contact to our true dimensions—but to our great peace.

Prayer, true prayer, does not allow us to deceive ourselves. It relaxes the tension of our self-inflation. It produces a clearness of spiritual vision. Searching with a judgment that begins at the house of God, it ceases not to explore with His light our own soul. If the Lord is our health He may need to act on many men, or many moods, as a lowering medicine. At His coming our self-confidence is shaken. Our robust confidence, even in grace, is destroyed. The pillars of our house tremble, as if they were ivy-covered in a searching wind. Our lusty faith is refined, by what may be a painful process, into a subtler and more penetrating kind; and its outward effect is for the time impaired, though in the end it is increased. The effect of the prayer which admits God into the recesses of the soul is to destroy that spiritual density, not to say stupidity, which made our religion cheery or vigorous because it knew no better, and which was the condition of getting many obvious things done, and producing palpable effect on the order of the day. There are fervent prayers which, by making people feel good, may do no more than foster the delusion that natural vigour or robust religion, when flushed enough, can do the work of the kingdom of God. There is a certain egoist self-confidence which is increased by the more elementary forms of religion, which upholds us in much of our contact with men, and which even secures us an influence with them. But the influence is one of impression rather than permeation, it overbears rather than converts, and it inflames rather than inspires. This is a force which true and close prayer is very apt to undermine, because it saps our self-deception and its Pharisaism. The confidence was due to a lack of spiritual insight which serious prayer plentifully repairs. So by prayer we acquire our true selves. If my prayer is not answered, I am. If my petition is not fulfilled, my person, my soul, is; as the artist comes to himself and his happiness in the exercise of the talent he was made for, in spite of the delay and difficulty of turning his work to money. If the genius is happy who gets scope, the soul is blessed that truly comes to itself in prayer.

Blessed, yet not always happy. For by prayer we are set tasks sometimes which (at first, at least) may add to life's burden. Our eyes being opened, we see problems to which before we were blind, and we hear calls that no more let us alone. And I have said that we are shown ourselves at times in a way to dishearten us, and take effective dogmatism out of us. We lose effect on those people who take others at their own emphatic valuation, who do not try the spirits, and who have acquired no skill to discern the Lord in the apostle. True searching prayer is incompatible with spiritual dullness or self-complacent. And therefore, such stupidity is not a mere defect, but a vice. It grew upon us because we did not court the searching light, nor haunt the vicinity of the great white Throne. We are chargeable with it because of our neglect of what cures it. Faith is a quickening spirit, it has insight; and religious density betrays its absence, being often the victim of the sermon instead of the *alumnus* of the gospel. It is not at all the effect of ignorance. Many ignorant people escape it by the exercise of themselves unto godliness; and they not only show wonderful spiritual acumen, but they turn it upon themselves; with a result, often, of great but vigilant humility, such as is apt to die out of an aggressive religion more eager to bring in a Kingdom coming than to trust a Kingdom come. They are self-sufficient in a godly sort, and can even carry others, in a way which reveals the action of a power in them beyond all natural and unschooled force. We can feel in them the discipline of the Spirit. We can read much habitual prayer between their lines. They have risen far above religion. They are in the Spirit, and live in a long Lord's day. We know that they are not trying to serve Christ with the mere lustiness of natural religion, nor expecting to do the Spirit's work with the force of native temperament turned pious. There are, even amongst the religious, people of a shrewd density or nimble dullness who judge heavenly things with an earthly mind. And, outside the religious, among those who are but interested in religion, there may be a certain gifted stupidity, a witty obtuseness; as among some writers who *sans gene* turn what they judge to be the spirit of the age upon the realities of Eternity, and believe that it dissolves them in spray. Whether we meet this type within the Church or without, we can mostly feel that it reveals the prayerless temper whatever the zeal or vivacity may be. Not to pray is not to discern—not to discern the things that really matter, and the powers that really rule. The mind may see acutely and clearly, but the personality perceives nothing subtle and mighty; and then it comforts and deludes itself by saying it is simple and not sophisticated; and it falls a victim to the Pharisaism of the plain man. The finer (and final) forces, being unfelt, are denied or decried. The eternal motives are misread, the spell of the Eternal disowned. The simplicity in due course becomes merely bald. And all because the natural powers are unschooled, unchastened, and unempowered by the energy of prayer; and yet they are turned, either, in one direction, to do Christian work, active but loveless, or on the other, to discuss and renounce Christian truth. It is not always hard to tell among Christian men those whose thought is matured in prayer, whose theology there becomes a hymn, whose energy is disciplined there, whose work there becomes love poured out, as by many a Salvationist lass, and whose temper is there subdued to that illuminated humility in which a man truly finds his soul. "The secret of the Lord is with them that fear him, and he will show them his covenant." The deeper we go into the things the more do we enter a world where the mastery and the career is not to talent but to prayer.

In prayer we do not ask God to do things contrary to Nature. Rather here ascending Nature takes its true effect and arrives. For the God we invoke is the Lord and Destiny of the whole creation; and in our invocation of Him Nature ends on its own key-note. He created the world at the first with a final and constant reference to the new creation, whose native speech is prayer. The whole creation thus comes home and finds itself in our prayer; and when we ask from the God of the *whole* Creation we neither do nor expect an arbitrary thing. We petition a God in whom all things are fundamentally working together for good to such a congenial cry. So far from crossing Nature, we give it tongue. We lift it to its divinest purpose, function, and glory. Nature excels itself in our prayer. The Creation takes its true effect in personality, which at once resists it, crowns it, and understands it; and personality takes true effect in God— in prayer. If there be a divine teleology in Nature at all, prayer is the telos. The world was made to worship God, for God's glory. And this purpose is the world's providence, the principle of creation. It is an end present all along the line and course of natural evolution; for we deal in prayer most closely with One to whom is no after nor before. We realize the simultaneity of Eternity.

When we are straitened in prayer we are yet not victims of Nature, we are yet free in the grace of God—as His own freedom was straitened in Christ's incarnation, not to say His dereliction, to the finishing of His task. It is hard, it is often impossible, for us to tell whether our hour of constriction or our hour of expansion contributes more to the divine purpose and its career. Both go to make real prayer. They are the systole and diastole of the world's heart. True prayer is the supreme function of the personality which is the world's supreme product. It is personality with this function that God seeks above all to rear—It is neither particular moods of its experience, nor influential relations of it with the world. The praying personality has an eternal value for God as an end in itself. This is the divine fullness of life's time and course, the one achievement that survives with more power in death than in life. The intercession of Christian heaven is the continuity and consummation of His supreme work on earth. To share it is the meaning of praying in the Spirit. And it has more effect on history than civilization has. This is a hard saying, but a Christian can say no otherwise without insofar giving up his Christianity.

"There is a budding morrow in midnight." And every juncture, every relation, and every pressure of life has in it a germ of possibility and promise for our growth in God and grace; which germ to rear is the work of constant and progressive prayer. (For as a soul has a history, prayer has its progress). This germ we do not always see, nor can we tend it as if we did. It is often hidden up under the earthly relations, and may there be lost—our soul is lost. (It can be lost even through love.) But also it may from there be saved—and we escape from the fowler's net. Its growth is often visible only to the Saviour whom we keep near by prayer, whose search we invoke, and for whose action we make room in prayer. Our certainty of Him is girt round with much uncertainty, about His working, about the steps of His process. But in prayer we become more and more sure that He is sure, and knows all things and hesitates or falters never, and commands all things to His end. All along Christ is being darkly formed within us as we pray; and our converse with God goes on rising to become an element of the intercourse of the Father and the Son, whom we overhear, as it were, at converse in us. Yet this does not insulate us from our kind; for other people are then no more alien to us, but near in a Lord who is to them what He is to us. Private prayer may thus become more really common prayer than public prayer is.

And so also with the universe itself as we rise in Christ to prayer. Joined with its Redeemer, we are integrated into its universality. We are made members of its vast whole. We are not detained and cramped in a sectional world. We are not planted in the presence of an outside, alien universe, nor in the midst of a distraught, unreconciled universe, which speaks like a crowd, in many fragments and many voices, and drags us from one relation with it to another, with a Lo, here is Christ, or there. But it is a universe wholly vocal to us, really a universe, and vocal as a whole, one congenial and friendly, as it comes to us in its Christ and ours. It was waiting for us—for such a manifestation of the Son of God as prayer is. This world is not now a desert haunted by demons. And it is more than a vestibule to another; it is its prelude in the drama of all things. We know it in another knowledge now than its own. Nature can never be understood by natural knowledge. We know it as science never can— as a whole, and as reality. We know it as we are known of God—altogether, and not in pieces. Having nothing, and praying for everything, we possess all things. The faith that energizes in Christian prayer sets us at the centre of that whole of which Nature is the overture part. The steps of thought and its processes of law fade away. They do not cease to act, but they retire from notice. We grasp the mobile organization of things deep at its constant and trusty heart. We receive the earnest of our salvation—Christ in us.

> *There, where one centre reconciles all things,*
> *The world's profound heart beats.*

We are planted there. And all the mediation of process becomes immediate in its eternal ground. As we are going there we feel already there. "They were willing to receive him into the boat, and straightway the boat was at the land whither they were going." We grasp that eternal life to which all things work, which gives all the waxing organization its being and meaning—for a real organism only grows because it already is. That is the mark of real life. And soul and person is the greatest organism of all. We apprehend our soul as it is apprehended of God and in God, the timeless God— with all its evolution, past or future, converted into a divine present. We are already all that we are to be. We possess our souls in the prayer which is real communion with God. We enter by faith upon that which to sight and history is but a far future reversion. When He comes to our prayer He brings with Him all that He purposes to make us. We are already the "brave creature" He means us to be. More than our desire is fulfilled—our soul is. In such hour or visitation we realize our soul or person at no one stage of it, but in its fullness, and in the context of its whole and final place in history, the world, and eternity. A phase which has no meaning in itself, yet carries, like the humble mother of a great genius, an eternal meaning in it. And we can seize that meaning in prayer; we can pierce to what we are at our true centre and true destiny, i.e. what we are to God's grace. Laws and injunctions, such as "Love your neighbour," even "Love your enemy," then become life principles, and they are law pressures no more. The yoke is easy. Where all is forgiven to seventy times seven there is no friction and no grief any more. We taste love and joy. All the pressure of life then goes to form the crystals of faith. It is God making up His jewels.

When we are in God's presence by prayer we are *right,* our will is morally right, we are doing His will. However unsure we may be about other acts and efforts to serve Him we know we are right in this. If we ask truly but amiss, it is not a sin, and He will in due course set us right in that respect. We are sure that prayer is according to His will, and that we are just where we ought to be. And that is a great matter for the rightness of our thought, and of the aims and desires proposed by our thought. It means much both as to their form and their passion. If we realize that prayer is the acme of our right relation to God, if we are sure that we are never so right with Him in anything we do as in prayer, then prayer must have the greatest effect and value for our life, both in its purpose and its fashion, in its spirit and its tenor. What puts us right morally, right with a Holy God (as prayer does), must have a great shaping power on every part and every juncture of life. And, of course, especially upon the spirit and tenor of our prayer itself, upon the form and complexion of our petition.

The effect of our awful War will be very different on the prayerful and the prayerless. It will be a sifting judgment. It will turn to prayer those who did not pray, and increase the prayer of those who did. But some, whose belief in God grew up only in fair weather and not at the Cross, it will make more sceptical and prayerless than ever, and it will present them with a world more confused and more destitute of a God than before; which can only lead to renewed outbreaks of the same kind as soon as the nations regain strength. The prayerless spirit saps a people's moral strength because it blunts their thought and conviction of the Holy. It must be so if prayer is such a moral blessing and such a shaping power, if it pass, by its nature, from the vague volume and passion of devotion to formed petition and effort. Prayerlessness is an injustice and a damage to our own soul, and therefore to its history, both in what we do and what we think. The root of all deadly heresy is prayerlessness. Prayer finds our clue in a world otherwise without form and void. And it draws a magic circle round us over which the evil spirits may not pass. "Prayer," says Vente, "is like the air of certain ocean isles, which is so pure that there vermin cannot live. We should surround ourselves with this atmosphere, as the diver shuts himself into his bell ere he descends into the deep."

If there must be in the Church a communion of belief, there must be there also a communion of prayer. For the communion of prayer is the very first form the communion of belief takes. It is in this direction that Church unity lies. It lies behind prayer, in something to which prayer gives effect, in that which is the source and soul of prayer—in our relation with God in Christ, in our new creation. Prayer for Church unity will not bring that unity; but that which stirs, and founds, and wings prayer will. And prayer is its chief exercise. The true Church is just as wide as the community of Christian prayer, *i.e.* of due response to the gospel of our reconcilement and communion with God. And it is a thing almost dreadful that Christians who pray to the same God, Christ, and Saviour should refuse to unite in prayer because of institutional differences.

A prayer is also a promise. Every true prayer carries with it a vow. If it do not, it is not in earnest. It is not of a piece with life. Can we pray in earnest if we do not in the act commit ourselves to do our best to bring about the answer? Can we escape some kind of hypocrisy? This is especially so with intercession. What is the value of praying for the poor if all the rest of our time and interest is given only to becoming rich? Where is the honesty of praying for our country if in our most active hours we are chiefly occupied in making something out of it, if we are strange to all sacrifice for it? Prayer is one form of sacrifice, but if it is the only form it is vain oblation. If we pray for our child that he may have God's blessing, we are really promising that nothing shall be lacking on our part to be a divine blessing to him. And if we have no kind of religious relation to him (as plenty of Christian parents have none), our prayer is quite unreal, and its failure should not be a surprise. To pray for God's kingdom is also to engage ourselves to service and sacrifice for it. To begin our prayer with a petition for the hallowing of God's name and to have no real and prime place for holiness in our life or faith is not sincere. The prayer of the vindictive for forgiveness is mockery, like the prayer for daily bread from a wheat-cornerer. No such man could say the Lord's Prayer but to his judgment. What would happen to the Church if the Lord's Prayer became a test for membership as thoroughly as the Creeds have been? The Lord's Prayer is also a vow to the Lord. None but a Christian can pray it, or should. Great worship of God is also a great engagement of ourselves, a great committal of our action. To begin the day with prayer is but a formality unless it go on in prayer, unless for the rest of it we pray in deed what we began in word. One has said that while prayer is the day's best beginning it must not be like the handsome title-page of a worthless book.

"Thy will be done." Unless that were the spirit of all our prayer, how should we have courage to pray if we know ourselves at all, or if we have come to a time when we can have some retrospect on our prayers and their fate? Without this committal to the wisdom of God, prayer would be a very dangerous weapon in proportion as it was effective. No true God could promise us an answer to our every prayer. No Father of mankind could. The rain that saved my crop might ruin my neighbour's. It would paralyse prayer to be sure that it would prevail as it is offered, certainly and at once. We should be terrified at the power put into our foolish hands. Nothing would do more to cure us of a belief in our own wisdom than the granting of some of our eager prayers. And nothing could humiliate us more than to have God say when the fulfillment of our desire brought leanness to our souls, "Well, you would have it." It is what He has said to many. But He said more, "My grace is sufficient for thee."

Chapter Two

THE NATURALNESS OF PRAYER

We touch the last reality directly in prayer. And we do this not by thought's natural research, yet by a quest not less laborious. Prayer is the atmosphere of revelation, in the strict and central sense of that word. It is the climate in which God's manifestation bursts open into inspiration. All the mediation of nature and of things sinks here to the rear, and we are left with God in Christ as His own Mediator and His own Revealer. He is directly with us and in us. We transcend these two thousand years as if they were but one day. By His Spirit and His Spirit's creative miracle God becomes Himself our new nature, which is yet our own, our destined nature; for we were made with His image for our "doom of greatness." It is no mere case of education or evolution drawing out our best. Prayer has a creative action in its answer. It does more than present us with our true, deep, latent selves. It lays hold on God, and God is not simply our magnified self. Our other self is, in prayer, our Creator still creating. Our maker it is that is our Husband. He is Another. We feel, the more we are united with Him in true prayer, the deep, close difference, the intimate otherness in true love. Otherwise prayer becomes mere dreaming; it is spiritual extemporizing, and not converse. The division runs not simply between us and nature, but it parts us within our spiritual self, where union is most close. It is a spiritual distinction, like the distinction of Father and Son in heaven. But nature itself, our natural selves, are involved in it; because nature for the Christian is implicated in Redemption. It "arrives." It is read in a new script. The soul's conflict is found in a prelude in it. This may disturb our pagan joy. It may quench the consolations of nature. The ancient world could take refuge in nature as we cannot. It could escape there from conscience in a way impossible to us, because for us body runs up into soul, and nature has become organic with spirit, an arena and even (in human nature) an experience of God's will. It groans to come to itself in the sons of God. Redemption is cosmic. We do not evade God's judgment there; and we put questions about His equity there which did not trouble the Greek. If we take the wings of the morning and dwell in the uttermost parts of the earth, God still besets us behind and before. We still feel the collision of past and future, of conduct and conscience. If we try to escape from His presence there, we fail; the winds are His messengers, the fire His ministers, wars and convulsions instruments of His purpose. He is always confronting us, judging us, saving us in a spiritual world, which Nature does not stifle, but only makes it more universal and impressive than our personal strife. In Nature our *vis-a-vis is* still the same power we meet as God in our soul.

> *The voice that rolls the stars along*
> *Speaks all His promises.*

Our own natural instincts turn our scourges, but also our blessings, according as they mock God or serve Him. So Nature becomes our chaperone for Christ, our tutor whose duty is daily to deliver us at Christ's door. It opens out into a Christ whose place and action are not historic only, but also cosmic. The cosmic place of Christ in the later epistles is not apostolic fantasy, extravagant speculation, nor groundless theosophy. It is the ripeness of practical faith, faith which by action comes to itself and to its own.

Especially is this pointed where faith has its most pointed action as prayer. If cosmic Nature runs up into man, man rises up into prayer; which thus fulfills Nature, brings its inner truth to pass, and crowns its bias to spirit. Prayer is seen to be the opening secret of creation, its destiny, that to which it all travails. It is the burthen of evolution. The earnest expectation of the creation waits, and all its onward thrust works, for the manifestation of the sons of God. Nature comes to itself in prayer. Prayer realizes and brings to a head the truth of Nature, which groans, being burdened with the passion of its deliverance, its relief in prayer. *"Magna ars est conversari cum Deo."* "The art of prayer is Nature gone to Heaven." We become in prayer Nature's true artists (if we may so say), the vehicles of its finest and inmost passion. And we are also its true priests, the organs of its inner commerce with God, where the Spirit immanent in the world meets the Spirit transcendent in obedient worship. The sum of things for ever speaking is heard in heaven to pray without ceasing. It is speaking not only to us but in us to God. Soliloquy here is dialogue. In our prayer God returns from His projection in Nature to speak with Himself. When we speak to God it is really the God who lives in us speaking through us to Himself. His Spirit returns to Him who gave it; and returns not void, but bearing our souls with Him. The dialogue of grace is really the monologue of the divine nature in self-communing love. In prayer, therefore, we do true and final justice to the world. We give Nature to itself. We make it say what it was charged to say. We make it find in thought and word its own soul. It comes to itself not in man but in the praying man, the man of Christian prayer. The Christian man at prayer is the secretary of Creation's praise. So prayer is the answer to Nature's quest, as God is the answer to prayer. It is the very nature of nature; which is thus miraculous or nothing at its core.

Here the friction vanishes, therefore, between prayer and natural law. Nature and all its plexus of law is not static, but dynamic. It is not interplay, but evolution. It has not only to move, but to arrive. Its great motive power is not a mere instinct, but a destiny. Its system is not a machine, but a procession. It is dramatic. It has a close. Its ruling power is not what it rises from, but what it moves to. Its impulse is its goal immanent. All its laws are overruled by the comprehensive law of its destination. It tends to prayer. The laws of Nature are not like iron. If they are fixed they are only fixed as the composition is fixed at H_2O of the river which is so fluid and moving that I can use it at any time to bear me to its sea. They are fixed only insofar as makes them reliable, and not fatal, to man's spirit. Their nature is constant, but their function is not stiff. What is fixed in the river is the constancy of its fluidity. "Still glides the stream, and shall for ever glide." The greatest law of Nature is thus its bias to God, its *nisus* to return to His rest. This comes to light chiefly in man's gravitation to Him, when His prodigal comes home to Him. The forwardest creation comes to itself in our passion for God and in our finding of Him in prayer. In prayer, therefore, we do not ask God to do things contrary to Nature, though our request may seem contrary to sections of it which we take for the whole. We ask Him to fulfill Nature's own prayer.

The atmosphere of prayer seems at first to be the direct contrary of all that goes with such words as practical or scientific. But what do we mean by practical at last but that which contributes to the end for which the world and mankind were made? The whole of history, as the practical life of the race, is working out the growth, the emancipation of the soul, the enrichment and fortifying of the human spirit. It is doing on the large scale what every active life is doing on the small —it is growing soul. There is no reality at last except soul, except personality. This alone has eternal meaning, power, and value, since this alone develops or hampers the eternal reality, the will of God. The universe has its being and its truth for a personality, but for one at last which transcends individual limits. To begin with the natural plane, our egoism constructs there a little world with a definite teleology converging on self, one which would subdue everybody and everything to be tributary to our common sensible self. On a more spiritual (yet not on the divine) plane the race does the like with its colossal ego. It views and treats the universe as contributory to itself, to the corporate personality of the race. Nature is here for man, man perhaps for the superman. We are not here for the glory of God, but God is here for the aid and glory of man. But either way all things are there to work together for personality, and to run up into a free soul. Man's practical success is then what makes for the enhancement of this ego, small or great. But, on the Christian plane, man himself, as part of a creation, has a meaning and an end; but it is in God; he does not return on himself. God is his *nisus* and drift. God works in him; he is not just trying to get his own head out. But God is Love. All the higher science of Nature, therefore, is an exposition of its work in the service of souls and their love. It is the science of a nature which is the *milieu* and the machinery that give the soul its bent to love, and turn it out its true self in love All the practice and science of the world is there, therefore; to reveal and realize love and love's communion. It is all a stage, a scenery, a plot, for a *denouement* where beings mingle, and each is enriched by all and all by each. It all goes to the music of that love which binds all things together in the cosmic dance, and which makes each stage of each thing prophetic of its destined fullness only in a world so bound. So science itself is practical if prayer end and round all. It is the theory of a cosmic movement with prayer for its active end. And it is an ethical science at last, it is a theology, if the Christian end is the real end of the whole world. All knowledge serves love and love's communion. For Christian faith a universe is a universe of souls, an organism of persons, which is the expression of an Eternal Will of love. This love is the real presence which gives meaning, and movement, and permanence to a fleeting world of sense. And it is by prayer that we come into close and conscious union with this universe and power of love, this living reality of things. Prayer (however miraculous) is, therefore, the most natural thing in the world. It is the effectuation of all nature, which comes home to roost there, and settles to its rest. It is the last word of all science, giving it contact with a reality which, as science alone, it cannot reach. And it is also the most practical thing in all man's action and history, as doing most to bring to pass the spiritual object for which all men and all things exist and strive.

Those who feel prayer stifled by the organization of law do not consider that law itself, if we take a long enough sweep, keeps passing us on to prayer. Law rises from nature, through history, to heaven. It is integrated historically, *i.e.* by Christ's cross and the Church's history, with the organization of love. But that is the organization of Eternity in God, and it involves the interaction of all souls in a communion of ascending prayer. Prayer is the native movement of the spiritual life that receives its meaning and its soul only in Eternity, that works in the style and scale of Eternity, owns its principles, and speaks its speech. It is the will's congenial surrender to that Redemption and Reconciliation between loving wills which is God's Eternity acting in time. We beseech God because He first besought us.

So not to pray on principle means that thought has got the better of will. The question is whether thought includes will or will thought; and thought wins if prayer is suppressed. Thought and not personality is then in command of the universe. If will is but a function of the idea, then prayer is but a symptom, it is not a power. It belongs to the phenomenology of the Infinite, it is not among its controls.

Prayer is doing God's will. It is letting Him pray in us. We look for answer because His fullness is completely equal to His own prayers. Father and Son are perfectly adequate to each other. That is the Holy Spirit and self-sufficiency of the Godhead.

If God's will is to be done on earth as it is in heaven, prayer begins with *adoration.* Of course, it is thanks and petition; but before we give even our prayer we must first receive. The Answerer provides the very prayer. What we do here rests on what God has done. What we offer is drawn from us by what He offers. Our self-oblation stands on His; and the spirit of prayer flows from the gift of the Holy Ghost, the great Intercessor. Hence praise and adoration of His work in itself comes before even our thanksgiving for blessings to us. At the height of prayer, if not at its beginning, we are preoccupied with the great and glorious thing God has done for His own holy name in Redemption, apart from its immediate and particular blessing to us. We are blind for the time to ourselves. We cover our faces with our wings, and cry "Holy, Holy, Holy is the Lord God of hosts; the fullness of the earth is His glory." Our full hearts glorify. We magnify His name. His perfections take precedence of our occasions. We pray for victory in the present war, for instance, and for deliverance from all war, for the sake of God's kingdom—in a spirit of adoration for the deliverance there that is not destroyed, or foiled, even by a devilry like this. If the kingdom of God not only got over the murder of Christ, but made it its great lever, there is nothing that it cannot get over, and nothing it cannot turn to eternal blessing and to the glory of the holy name. But to the perspective of this faith, and to its vision of values so alien to human standards, we can rise only in prayer.

But it would be unreal prayer which was adoration only, with no reference to special boons or human needs. That would be as if God recognized no life but His own—which is a very undivine egoism, and its collective form is the religion of mere nationalism. In true prayer we do two things. We go out of ourselves, being lost in wonder, love, and praise; but also, and in the same act, we go in upon ourselves. We stir up *all that is within us* to bless and hallow God's name. We examine ourselves keenly in that patient light, and we find ourselves even when our sin finds us out. Our nothingness is not burned and branded into us as if we had above us only the starry irony of heaven. Our heart comes again. Our will is braced and purified. We not only recall our needs, but we discover new ones, of a more and more intimate and spiritual kind. The more spiritual we grow, the more we rise out of the subconscious or the unconscious. We never realize ourselves as we do when we forget ourselves after this godly sort in prayer. Prayer is not falling back upon the abyss below the soul; even as the secret of the Incarnation is sought in vain in that nonmoral zone. Prayer is not what might be called the increased drone or boom of an unspeakable Om. But we rise in it to more conscious and positive relation with God the Holy—the God not abysmal but revealed, in whose revelation the thoughts of many hearts are revealed also, and whose fullness makes need almost as fast as it satisfies it.

After adoration, therefore, prayer is *thanksgiving* and petition. When we thank God our experience "arrives." It finds what it came for. It fulfills the greatest need of experience. It comes to its true self, comes to its own, and has its perfect work. It breathes large, long, and free, *sublimi anhelitu.* The soul runs its true normal course back to God its Creator, who has stamped the destiny of this return upon it, and leaves it no peace till it find its goal in Him. The gift we thank for becomes sacramental because it conveys chiefly the Giver, and is lost in Him and in His praise. It is He that chiefly comes in His saints and His boons. In real revelation we rise far above a mere interpretation of life, a mere explanation of events; we touch their Doer, the Life indeed, and we can dispense with interpretations, having Him. An occurrence thus becomes a revelation. It gives us God, in a sacrament. And where there is real revelation there is thanksgiving, there is eucharist; for God Himself is in the gift, and strikes His own music from the soul. If we think most of the gift, prayer may subtly increase our egoism. We praise for a gift *to us*. We are tempted to treat God as an asset, and to exploit Him. But true prayer, thinking most of the Giver, quells the egoism and dissolves it in praise. What we received came for another end than just to gratify us. It came to carry God to us, and to lift us to Him and to the concent of His glory. The blessing in it transcends the enjoyment of it, and the Spirit of the outgoing God returns to Him not void, but bringing our souls as sheaves with Him.

So also with *the petition* in our prayer. It also is purified by adoration, praise, and thanksgiving. We know better what to pray for as we ought. We do not only bring to God desires that rise apart from Him, and that we present by an act of our own; but our desires, our will, as they are inspired are also *formed* in God's presence, as requests. They get shape. In thanks we spread out before Him and offer Him our past and present, but in petition it is our future.

But has petition a true place in the highest and purest prayer? Is it not lost in adoration and gratitude? Does adoration move as inevitably to petition as petition rises to adoration? In reply we might ask whether the best gratitude and purest thanks are not for answered petitions. Is there not this double movement in all spiritual action which centres in the Incarnation, where man ascends as God comes down? Does not man enlarge in God as God particularizes upon men? But, putting that aside, is the subsidence of petition not due to a wrong idea of God; as if our only relation were dependence, as if, therefore, will-lessness before Him were the devout ideal—as if we but acknowledged Him and could not act on Him? Ritschl, for example, following Schleiermacher, says, "Love to God has no sphere of action outside love to our brother." If that were so, there would be no room for petition, but only for worship of God and service of man without intercession. The position is not unconnected with Ritschl's neglect of the Spirit and His intercession, or with his aversion to the Catholic type of piety. If suffering were the only occasion and promptuary of prayer, then resignation, and not petition, might be the true spirit of prayer. But our desires and wills do not rise out of our suffering only, nor out of our passivity and dependence, but also out of our freedom (viewed both as a power and a peril), and out of our duty and our place in life; and therefore our petition is as due to God and as proper as our life's calling. If we may not will nor love, no doubt petition, especially for others, is a mistake. Of course, also, our egoism, engrossed with our happiness, influences our prayer too often and too much But we can never overcome our self-will by will-lessness, nor our greed of happiness by apathy.

Petitions that are less than pure can only be purified by petition. Prayer is the salvation of prayer. We pray for better prayer. We can rise above our egoism only as we have real dealing with the will of God in petitionary prayer which does change His detailed intentions toward us though not His great Will of Grace and Salvation.

The element of adoration has been missed from worship by many observers of our public prayer. And the defect goes with the individualism of the age just past. Adoration is a power the egoist and individualist loses. He loses also the power both of thanksgiving and of petition, and sinks, through silence before God, to His neglect. For our blessings we are not egoistically meant, nor do they remain blessings if so taken. They contemplate more than ourselves, as in deed does our whole place and work in the gift of life. We must learn to thank God not only for the blessings of others, but for the power to convey to others gifts which make them happier than they make us—as the gifts of genius so often do. One Church should praise Him for the prosperity of other Churches, for that is to the good of the gospel. And, as for petition, how can a man or a Church pray for their own needs to the omission of others? God's fundamental relation to us is one that embraces and blesses all. We are saved in a common salvation. The atmosphere of prayer is communion. Common prayer is the inevitable fruit of a gospel like Christ's.

Public prayer, therefore, should be in the main liturgical, with room for free prayer. The more it really is common prayer, and the more our relations with men extend and deepen (as prayer with and for men does extend them), the more we need forms which proceed from the common and corporate conscience of the Church. Even Christ did. As He rose to the height of His great world-work on the cross His prayer fell back on the liturgy of His people—on the Psalms. It is very hard for the ordinary minister to come home to the spiritual variety of a large congregation without those great forms which arose out of the deep soul of the Church before it spread into sectional boughs or individual twigs.

Common prayer is not necessarily public. To recite the Litany on a sick-bed is common prayer. Christ felt the danger of common prayer as public prayer (Matt. 6: 5, 6). And this is specially so when the public prayer is "extempore." To keep that real calls for an amount of private prayer which perhaps is not for everyone. "Extempore" prayers are apt to be private prayers in public, like the Pharisee's in the temple, with too much idiosyncrasy for public use; or else they lose the spontaneity of private prayer, and turn as formal as a liturgy can be, though in another (and perhaps deadlier) way. The prayers of the same man inevitably fall more or less into the same forms and phrases. But private prayer may be more common in its note than public prayer should be private in its tone. Our private prayer should be common in spirit. We are doing in the act what many are doing. In the retired place we include in sympathy and intercession a world of other men which we exclude in fact. The world of men disappears from around us but not from within. We are not indifferent to its weal or woe in our seclusion. In the act of praying for ourselves we pray for others, for no temptation befalls us but what is common to man; and in praying for others, we pray with them. We pray for their prayers and the success of their prayers. It is an act of union. We can thus be united even with churches that refuse to pray or unite with us.

Moreover, it is common prayer, however solitary, that prevails most, as being most in tune with the great first goal of God's grace—the community. So this union in prayer gives to prayer an ethical note of great power and value. If we really pray with others, it must clear, and consolidate, and exalt our moral relations with them everywhere. Could we best the man with whom and for whom we really pray? There is a great democratic note in common prayer which is also true prayer. "Eloquence and ardour have not done so much for Christ's cause as the humble virtues, the united activity, and the patient prayers of thousands of faithful people whose names are quite unknown." And we are united thus not only to the living but to the long dead. "He who prays is nearer Christ than even the apostles were," certainly than the apostles before the Cross and Resurrection.

We have been warned by a man of genius that the bane of so much religion is that it clings to God with its weakness and not with its strength. This is very true of that supreme act of religion of which our critics know least—of the act of prayer. So many of us pray because we are driven by need rather than kindled by grace. Our prayer is a cry rather than a hymn. It is a quest rather than a tryst. It trembles more than it triumphs. It asks for strength rather than exerts it. How different was the prayer of Christ! All the divine power of the Eternal Son went to it. It was the supreme form taken by His Sonship in its experience and action. Nothing is more striking in Christ's life than His combination of selflessness and power. His consciousness of power was equal to anything, and egoism never entered him. His prayer was accordingly. It was the exercise of His unique power rather than of His extreme need. It came from His uplifting and not His despair. It was less His duty than His joy. It was more full of God's gift of grace than of man's poverty of faith, of a holy love than of a seeking heart. In His prayer He poured out neither His wish nor His longing merely, but His will. And He knew He was heard always. He knew it with such power and certainty that He could distribute His value, bless with His overflow, and promise His disciples they would be heard in His name. It was by His prayer that He countered and foiled the godless power in the world, the kingdom of the devil. "Satan hath desired to have thee—but I have prayed for thee." His prayer means so much for the weak because it arose out of this strength and its exercise. It was chiefly in His prayer that He was the Messiah, and the Revealer and Wielder of the power and kingship of God. His power with God was so great that it made His disciples feel it could only be the power of God; He prayed in the Eternal Spirit whereby He offered Himself to God. And it was so great because it was spent on God alone. So true is it that the kingdom of God comes not with observation that the greatest things Christ did for it were done in the night and not in the day; His prayers meant more than His miracles. And His great triumph was when there were none to see, as they all forsook Him and fled. He was mightiest in His action for men not when he was acting on men but on God. He felt the dangers of the publicity where His work lay, and He knew that they were only to be met in secrecy. He did most for His public in entire solitude; there He put forth all His power. His nights were not always the rest of weakness from the day before, but often the storing of strength for the day to come. Prayer (if we let Christ teach us of it) is mightiest in the mightiest. It is the ether round the throne of the Most High. Its power answers to the omnipotence of grace. And those who feel they owe everything to God's grace need have no difficulty about the range of prayer. They may pray for everything.

A word, as I close this chapter, to the sufferers. We pray for the removal of pain, pray passionately, and then with exhaustion, sick from hope deferred and prayer's failure. But there is a higher prayer than that. It is a greater thing to pray for pain's conversion than for its removal. It is more of grace to pray that God would make a sacrament of it. The sacrament of pain! That we partake not simply, nor perhaps chiefly, when we say, or try to say, with resignation, "thy will be done." It is not always easy for the sufferer, if he remain clear-eyed, to see that it is God's will. It may have been caused by an evil mind, or a light fool, or some stupid greed. But, now it is there, a certain treatment of it is God's will; and that is to capture and exploit it for Him. It is to make it serve the soul and glorify God. It is to consecrate its elements and make it sacramental. It is to convert it into prayer.

God has blessed pain even in causing us to pray for relief from it, or profit. Whatever drives us to Him, and even nearer Him, has a blessing in it. And, if we are to go higher still, it is to turn pain to praise, to thank Him in the fires, to review life and use some of the energy we spend in worrying upon recalling and tracing His goodness, patience, and mercy. If much open up to us in such a review we may be sure there is much more we do not know, and perhaps never may. God is the greatest of all who do good by stealth and do not crave for every benefit to be acknowledged. Or we may see how our pain becomes a blessing to others. And we turn the spirit of heaviness to the garment of praise. We may stop grousing and get our soul into its Sunday clothes. The sacrament of pain becomes then a true Eucharist and giving of thanks.

And if there were a higher stage than all it would be Adoration—when we do not think of favours or mercies to us or ours at all, but of the perfection and glory of the Lord. We feel to His Holy Name what the true artist feels towards an unspeakable beauty. As Wordsworth says:

> *I gazed and gazed,*
> *And did not wish her mine.*[1]

---

1. There was a girl of 15, tall, sweet, distinguished beyond her years. And this is how Heine ran into English at the sight of her:

> *No flower is half so lovely*
> *So dear, and fair, and kind.*
> *A boundless tide of tenderness*
> *Flows over my heart and mind,*
>
> *And I pray. (There is no answer*
> *To beauty unearthly but prayer.)*
> *God answer my prayer, and keep you*
> *So dear, and fine, and fair.*

Chapter Three

THE MORAL REACTIONS OF PRAYER

All religion is founded on prayer, and in prayer it has its test and measure. To be religious is to pray, to be irreligious is to be incapable of prayer. The theory of religion is really the philosophy of prayer; and the best theology is compressed prayer. The true theology is warm and it steams upward into prayer. Prayer is access to whatever we deem God, and if there is no such access there is no religion; for it is not religion to resign ourselves to be crushed by a brute power so that we can no more remonstrate than resist. It is in prayer that our real idea of God appears, and in prayer that our real relation to God shows itself. On the first levels of our religion we go to our God for help and boon in the junctures of our natural life; but, as we rise to supernatural religion, gifts become less to us than the Giver; they are not such as feed our egoism. We forget ourselves in a godly sort; and what we court and what we receive in our prayer is not simply a boon but communion—or if a boon, it is the boon which Christians call the Holy Spirit, and which means, above all else, communion with God. But lest communion subside into mere meditation it must concentrate in prayer. We must keep acquiring by such effort the grace so freely given. There is truly a subconscious communion, and a godliness that forgets God well, in the hourly life of taxing action and duty; but it must rise to seasons of colloquy, when our action is wholly with the Father, and the business even of His kingdom turns into heart converse, where the yoke is easy and the burden light. Duty is then absorbed in love— the deep, active union of souls outwardly distinct. Their connection is not external and (as we might say) inorganic; it is inward, organic, and reciprocal. There is not only action but interplay, not only need and gift but trust and love. The boon is the Giver Himself, and its answer is the self of the receiver. *Cor ad cor loquitur.* All the asking and having goes on in a warm atmosphere, where soul passes into soul without fusion, person is lost in person without losing personality, and thought about prayer becomes thought in prayer. The greatest, deepest, truest thought of God is generated in prayer, where right thought has its essential condition in a right will. The state and act of true prayer contains the very substance and summit of Christian truth, which is always there in solution, and becomes increasingly explicit and conscious. To grow in grace is to become more understanding in prayer. We make for the core of Christian reality and the source of Christian power.

Our atonement with God is the pregnant be-all and end-all of Christian peace and life; and what is that atonement but the head and front of the Saviour's perpetual intercession, of the outpouring of His sin-laden soul unto death? Unto death! That is to say, it is its outpouring utterly. So that His entire self-emptying and His perfect and prevailing prayer are one. In this intercession our best prayer, broken, soiled, and feeble as it is, is caught up and made prayer indeed and power with God. This intercession prays for our very prayer, and atones for the sin in it. This is praying in the Holy Ghost, which is not necessarily a matter either of intensity or elation. This is praying "for Christ's sake." If it be true that the whole Trinity is in the gospel of our salvation, it is also true that all theology lies hidden in the prayer which is our chief answer to the gospel. And the bane of so much theology, old and new, is that it has been denuded of prayer and prepared in a vacuum.

Prayer draws on our whole personality; and not only so, but on the whole God. And it draws on a God who really comes home nowhere else. God is here, not as a mere presence as He is in Nature, nor is He a mere pressure as He closes in upon us in the sobering of life. We do not face Him in mere meditation, nor do we cultivate Him as life's most valuable asset. But He is here as our Lover, our Seeker, our Visitant, our Interlocutor; He is our Saviour, our Truth, our Power, nay, our Spiritual World. In this supreme exercise of our personality He is at once our Respondent and our Spiritual Universe. Nothing but the experience of prayer can solve paradoxes like these. On every other level they are absurd. But here deep answers deep. God becomes the living truth of our most memorable and shaping experience, not its object only but its essence. He who speaks to us also hears in us, because He opens our inward ear (Rom. 8:15; Gal. 4:6). And yet He is Another, who so fully lives in us as to give us but the more fully to ourselves. So that our prayer is a soliloquy with God, a monologue *a deux*.

There is no such engine for the growth and command of the moral soul, single or social, as prayer. Here, above all, he who will do shall know. It is the great organ of Christian knowledge and growth. It plants us at the very centre of our own personality, which gives the soul the true perspective of itself; it sets us also at the very centre of the world in God, which gives us the true hierarchy of things. Nothing, therefore, develops such "inwardness" and yet such self-knowledge and self-control. Private prayer, when it is made a serious business, when it is formed prayer, when we pray audibly in our chamber, or when we write our prayers, guided always by the day's record, the passion of piety, and above all the truths of Scripture, is worth more for our true and grave and individual spirituality than gatherings of greater unction may be. Bible searching and searching prayer go hand in hand. What we receive from God in the Book's message we return to Him with interest in prayer. Nothing puts us in living contact with God but prayer, however facile our mere religion may be, and therefore nothing does so much for our originality, so much to make us our own true selves, to stir up all that it is in us to be, and hallow all we are. In life it is not "dogged that does it" in the last resort, and it is not hard work; it is faculty, insight, gift, talent, genius. And what genius does in the natural world prayer does in the spiritual. Nothing can give us so much power and vision. It opens a fountain perpetual and luminous at the centre of our personality, where we are sustained because we are created anew and not simply refreshed. For here the springs of *life* continually rise. And here also the eye discerns a new world because it has second sight. It sees two worlds at once. Hence the paradoxes I spoke of. Here we learn to read the work of Christ which commands the world unseen. And we learn to read even the strategy of Providence in the affairs of the world. To pray to the Doer must help us to understand what is done. Prayer, as our greatest work, breeds in us the *flair* for the greatest work of God, the instinct of His kingdom, and the sense of His track in Time.

Here, too, we acquire that spiritual veracity which we so constantly tend to lose; because we are in contact with the living and eternal reality. Our very love is preserved from dissimulation, which is a great danger when we love men and court their love. Prayer is a greater school and discipline of divine love than the service of man is. But not if it is cut off from it.

And no less also is it the school of repentance, which so easily can grow morbid. We are taught to be not only true to reality, but sincere with ourselves. We cannot touch God thus without having a light no less searching than saving shed upon our own hearts; and we are thus protected from Pharisaism in our judgment of either self or friend or foe— especially at present of our foe. No companion of God can war in His name against man without much self-searching and self-humiliation, however reserved. But here humility turns into moral strength.

Here we are also regathered in soul from the fancies that bewilder us and the distractions that dissolve us into the dust of the world. We are collected into peace and power and sound judgment, and we have a heart for any fate, because we rest in the Lord whose judgments are salvation. What gives us our true stay gives us our true self; and it protects us from the elations and despairs which alternate in ourselves by bringing home to us a Saviour who is more to us than we are to ourselves. We become patient with ourselves because we realize the patience of God. We get rid of illusions about ourselves and the world because our intimacy is with the real God, and we know that we truly are just what we are before Him. We thus have a great peace, because in prayer, as the crowning act of faith, we lay hold of the grace of God the Saviour. Prayer alone prevents our receiving God's grace in vain. Which means that it establishes the soul of a man or a people, creates the moral personality day by day, spreads outward the new heart through society, and goes to make a new ethos in mankind. We come out with a courage and a humanity we had not when we went in, even though our old earth remove, and our familiar hills are cast into the depth of the sea. The true Church is thus co-extensive with the community of true prayer.

It is another paradox that combines the vast power of prayer both on the lone soul and on the moral life, personal and social, with the soul's shyness and aloofness in prayer. Kant (whose genius in this respect reflected his race) has had an influence upon scientific thought and its efficiency far greater than upon religion, though he is well named the philosopher of Protestantism. He represents (again like his race) intellectual power and a certain stiff moral insight, but not spiritual atmosphere, delicacy, or flexibility, which is rather the Catholic tradition. Intellectualism always tends to more force than finish, and always starves or perverts ethics. And nowhere in Kant's work does this limitation find such expression as in his treatment of prayer, unless it be in his lack of any misgiving about treating it at all with his equipment or the equipment of his age. Even his successors know better now—just as we in England have learned to find in Milton powers and harmonies hidden from the too great sagacity of Dr. Johnson or his time. Kant, then, speaks of prayer thus. If we found a man (he says) given to talking to himself we should begin to suspect him of some tendency to mental aberration. Yet the personality of such a man is a very real thing. It is a thing we can be more sure of than we can of the personality of God, who, if He is more than a conclusion for intellectual thought, is not more than a postulate for moral. No doubt in time of crisis it is an instinct to pray which even cultivated people do not, and need not, lose. But if any such person were surprised even in the attitude of private prayer, to say nothing of its exercise, he would be ashamed. He would think he had been discovered doing something unworthy of his intelligence, and would feel about it as educated people do when found out to be yielding to a superstition about the number thirteen.

A thinker of more sympathy and delicacy would have spoken less bluntly. Practical experience would have taught him discrimination. He would have realized the difference between shame and shyness, between confusion at an unworthy thing and confusion at a thing too fine and sacred for exposure. And had his age allowed him to have more knowledge and taste in history, and especially the history of religion, he would have gone, not to the cowardice of the ordinary cultivated man, but to the power and thoroughness of the great saints or captains of the race—to Paul, to Thomas a Kempis, to Cromwell with his troops, or Gustavus Adolphus with his. I do but humbly allude to Gethsemane. But Kant belonged to a time which had not realized, as even our science does now, the final power of the subtler forces, and the overwhelming effect in the long run of the impalpable and elusive influences of life. Much might be written about the effect of prayer on the great history of the world.

Chapter Four

THE TIMELINESS OF PRAYER

Let him pray now that never prayed before.
And him that prayed before but pray the more.

The nearer we are driven to the God of Christ, the more we are forced on paradox when we begin to speak. I have been led to allude to this more than once. The *magnalia dei* are not those great simplicities of life on which some orders of genius lay a touch so tender and sure; but they are the great reconciliations in which life's tragic collisions come to lie "quiet, happy, and supprest." Such are the peaceful paradoxes (the paradox at last of grace and nature in the Cross) which make the world of prayer such a strange and difficult land to the lucid and rational interpreters of life. It is as miraculous as it is real that the holy and the guilty should live together in such habitual communion as the life of prayer. And it is another paradox that combines the vast power of prayer for the active soul, whether single or social, with the same soul's shyness and aloofness in prayer.

There is a tendency to lose the true balance and adjustment here. When all goes well we are apt to overdo the aloofness that goes with spiritual engagement, and so to sacrifice some of its power and blessing for the soul. Prayer which becomes too private may be too remote, and is apt to become weak. (Just as when it is too intimate it becomes really unworthy, and may become absurd even to spiritual men; it does so in the trivialities associated sometimes with the answer to prayer). It is neither seemly nor healthy to be nothing but shy about the greatest powers in life. If we felt them as we should, and if we had their true vitality in us, we could not be so reserved about them. Some churches suffer much from extempore prayer, but perhaps those suffer more that exclude it. It at least gives a public consecration to prayer private and personal, which prayer, from the nature of it, must be extempore and "occasional." The bane of extempore prayer is that it is confused with prayer unprepared; and the greatest preparation for prayer is to pray. The leader of prayer should be a man of prayer—so long as prayer does not become for him a luxury which really unfits him for liturgy, and private devotion does not indispose him for public worship. Delicacy and propriety in prayer are too dearly bought if they are there at the cost of its ruling power in life, private and public, and of its prevailing power with God.

It is one of the uses of our present dreadful adversity that we are driven to bring the great two-handed engine of prayer frankly to the fore. There is probably a greater volume of personal prayer today than for generations we have had in this somewhat silent people, and there is less embarrassment in owning it. One hears tales of the humour in the trenches, but not so much of the prayer which appears, from accounts to be at least equally and visibly there. And it is not the prayer of fear, either at home or abroad, but of seriousness, of a new moral exaltation, or at least deepening, a new sense of realities which are clouded by the sunshine of normal life. How can we but pray when we send, or our hearts go out to those who send, the dearest to a noble peril, or lose them in a noble death; or when we melt to those who are cast into unspeakable anxiety by the indirect effects of such a war upon mind or estate? We are helpless then unless we can pray. Or how can we but pray as we regain, under the very hand and pressure of God, the sense of judgment which was slipping from our easy and amiable creed? Above the aircraft we hear the wings of the judgment angel; their wind is on our faces; how should we not pray? We now discuss with each other our prayers as we have seldom done before; and we do it for our practical guidance, and not merely our theological satisfaction. We ask our neighbours' judgment if we may pray for victory when we can be so little sure as we are in the increased complexity of modern issues that all the right is on one side; or when our enemy is a great nation to which the Christianity and the culture of the world owe an unspeakable debt, whether for reformation or illumination. And if Christian faith and prayer is a supernatural, and therefore an international, thing, should it be exploited in the interest of national rivalries and tutelary gods?

Truly the course of events has made the answer to this question easier than at first. We are driven by events to believe that a great moral blindness has befallen Germany; that its God, ceasing to be Christian, has become but Semitic; that it has lost the sense of the great imponderables; that the idolatry of the State has barrack-bound the conscience of the Church and stilled that witness of the kingdom of God which beards kings and even beheads them. We are forced to think that the cause of righteousness has passed from its hands with the passing from them of humanity, with the submersion of the idea of God's kingdom in nationality or the cult of race, with the worship of force, mammon, fright, and ruthlessness, with the growth of national cynicism in moral things, and with the culture of a withering, self-searing hate which is the nemesis of mortal sin, and which even God cannot use as He can use anger, but must surely judge. This people has sinned against its own soul, and abjured the kingdom of God. That settles our prayer for victory. We must pray for the side more valuable for the kingdom of God— much as we have to confess.

It would more than repay much calamity if we were moved and enlarged to a surer sense, a greater use, and a franker confession of the power of prayer for life, character, and history. There is plenty of discussion of the present situation, historic, ethical, or political, and much of it is competent, and even deep. There is much speculation about the situation after the War, at home and abroad. But its greatest result may be the discredit of elegant, paltering, and feeble types of religion, the end of the irreligious wits and fribbles, and the rise of a new moral seriousness and a new spiritual realism. Many will be moved, in what seems the failure of civilization, to a new reliance on the Church, and especially on the more historic, ethical, and positive Churches, which have survived the paganism of culture and which ride the waves of storm. Yet even these impressions can evaporate unless they are fixed by action. And the action that fixes them in their own kind is prayer—prayer which is really action. A religion of prosperity grows dainty, petty, sentimental, and but pseudo-heroic. We unlearn our fathers' creed that religion is, above all things, an act, that worship is the greatest act of which man is capable, and that true worship culminates in the supreme labour, and even sorrow, of real prayer. This is man at his utmost; and it has for its near neighbours all the great things that men or nations do. But when a nation must go to righteous war it embarks on one of the very greatest acts of its life, especially if its very existence as a servant of God's kingdom hang on it. A state of war is really the vast and prolonged act of a corporate soul, with a number of minor acts organized into it. It is capable of being offered to a God whose kingdom is a public campaign moving through history, and coming by the faith, toil, peril, sacrifice, grief, and glory of nations, as well as of hearts and souls. It is not possible to separate moral acts so great and solemn as the act of prayer (especially common and corporate prayer) and the act of war; nor to think them severed in the movement, judgment, and purpose of the Eternal. And we are forced into paradox again. The deeper we go down into the valley of decision the higher we must rise (if we are to possess and command our souls) into the mount of prayer, and we must hold up the hands of those whose chief concern is to prevail with God. If we win we shall have a new sense of power amid all our loss and weakness; but what we shall need most of all is the power to use that power, and to protect us from our victory and its perilous sequels, whether of pride or poverty. And if we do not win we shall need it more. There will be much to sober us either way, more perhaps than ever before in our history.

But that is not all, and it is not enough. As Christian people we need something to sanctify that very sobering, and to do for the new moral thoughtfulness itself what that does for the peacebred levity of the natural man. For such a purpose there is no agent like prayer—serious, thinking, private prayer, or prayer in groups, in small, grave, congenial, understanding groups—prayer with the historic sense, church-nurtured and Bible-fed. Public prayer by all means, but, apart from liturgical form, the more open the occasions and the larger the company the more hard it may be to secure for such prayer the right circumstances or the right lead. Public facility is apt to outstrip the real intimacy and depth with God. While, on the other hand, the prayer that freely rises and aptly flows in our audience of God may be paralysed in an audience of men. So that public prayer does not always reflect the practice of private petition as the powerful factor it is in Christian life and history. It does not always suggest a door opened in heaven, the insight or fellowship of eternal yet historic powers in awful orbits. It does not always do justice to our best private prayer, to private prayer made a business and suffused with as much sacred mind as goes to the more secular side even of the Christian life. Should ministers enlist? it is asked. But to live in true and concrete prayer is to be a combatant in the War, as well as a statesman after it, if statesmen ought to see the whole range of forces at work. The saintly soldier still needs the soldier saint. Yet so much prayer has ceased to be a matter of thought, will, or conflict, and religion therefore has become so otiose, that it is not easy even for the Christian public to take such a saying as more than a phrase. This is but one expression of a general scepticism, both in the Church and out, about prayer, corporate or private, as power with God, and therefore as momentous in the affairs of life and history. But momentous and effectual it must be. Other things being equal, a voluntary and convinced army is worth more than a conscript one. So to know that we are morally right means worlds for our shaping of the things that face us and must be met; and we are never so morally right as in proficient prayer with the Holy One and the Just. It has, therefore, a vast effect on the course of things if we believe at all in their moral destiny. More is wrought by it than the too-wise world wots; and all the more as it is the prayer of a great soul or a great Church. It is a power behind thrones, and it neutralizes, at the far end, the visible might of armies and their victories. It settles at last whether morality or machinery is to rule the world. If it lose battles, it wins in the long historic campaign. Whereas, if we have no such action with God, we lose delicacy of perception in the finer forces of affairs; we are out of touch and understanding with the final control in things, the power that is working to the top always; we become dense in regard to the subtle but supreme influences that take the generals and chancellors by surprise; and we are at the mercy of the sleepless action of the kingdom of evil on the world. It is a fatal thing to underestimate the enemy; and it is in Christian prayer, seriously and amply pursued, that the soul really learns to gauge evil's awful and superhuman power in affairs. I am speaking not only of the single soul, perhaps at the moment not chiefly, but of the soul and prayer of a society like the true Church or a sobered people. The real power of prayer in history is not a fusillade of praying units of whom Christ is the chief, but it is the corporate action of a Saviour-Intercessor and His community, a volume and energy of prayer organized in a Holy Spirit and in the Church the Spirit creates. The saints shall thus judge the world and control life. Neither for the individual nor for the Church is true prayer an enclave in life's larger and more actual course. It is not a sacred enclosure, a lodge in some vast wilderness. That is the weak side of pietism. But, however intimate, it is in the most organic and vital context of affairs, private and public, if all things work together, deeply and afar, for the deep and final kingdom of God. Its constant defeat of our egoism means the victory of our social unity and its weal. For the egoist neither prays nor loves. On the other hand, such prayer recalls us from a distraught altruism, teeming with oddities, and frayed down to atomism by the variety of calls upon it; because the prayer is the supreme energy of a loving will and believing soul engaged with the Love that binds the earth, the sun, and all the stars. So far is it from being the case that love to God has no sphere outside love to man that our love to man perishes unless it is fed by the love that spends itself on God in prayer, and is lifted thereby to a place and a sway not historic only, but cosmic.

Our communion with God in Christ rose, and it abides, in a crisis which shook not the earth only, but also heaven, in a tragedy and victory more vast, awful, and pregnant than the greatest war in history could be. Therefore the prayer which gives us an ever-deeper interest and surer insight into that eternal moral crisis of the Cross gives us also (though it might take generations) a footing that commands all the losses or victories of earth, and a power that rules both spirit and conscience in the clash and crash of worlds. As there is devoted thought which ploughs its way into the command of Nature, there is thought, still more devoted, that prays itself into that moral interior of the Cross, where the kingdom of God is founded once for all on the last principle and power of the universe, and set up, not indeed amid the wreck of civilization, but by its new birth and a baptism so as by fire. Prayer of the right kind, with heart and soul and strength and mind, unites any society in which it prevails with those last powers of moral and social regeneration that settle history and that reside in the creative grace of the Cross, which is God's true omnipotence in the world. "O God, who showest Thine almighty power most chiefly in having mercy and forgiving." Such speech as this may to some appear tall and rhetorical; but it would have so seemed to no father of the Church, ancient or modern, taking apostolic measure of the place and moment of Christ in society, history, or the universe.

If war is in any sense God's judgment on sin, and if sin was destroyed by the judgment in Christ and on Him, let us pray with a new depth and significance today, "O Lamb of God, that takest away the sin of the world, grant us *Thy* peace. Send us the peace that honours in act and deed that righteous and final judgment in Thy Cross of all historic things, and that makes therein for Thy Kingdom on earth as in heaven. Give peace in our time, O Lord, but, peace or war, 'Take the crown of this poor world.'"

Chapter Five

THE CEASELESSNESS OF PRAYER

Prayer as Christian freedom, and prayer as Christian life — these are two points I would now expand.

I. First, as to the moral freedom involved and achieved in prayer.

Prayer has been described as religion in action. But that as it stands is not a sufficient definition of the prayer which lives on the Cross. The same thing might be said about the choicest forms of Christian service to humanity. It is true enough, and it may carry us far; but only if we become somewhat clear about the nature of the religion at work. Prayer is certainly not the action of a religion mainly subjective. It is the effective work of a religion which hangs upon the living God, of a soul surer of God than of itself, and living not its own life, but the life of the Son of God. To say prayer is faith in action would be better; for the word "faith" carries a more objective reference than the word "religion." Faith is faith in another. In prayer we do not so much work as interwork. We are fellow workers with God in a reciprocity. And as God is the freest Being in existence, such co-operant prayer is the freest thing that man can do. If we were free in sinning, how much more free in the praying which undoes sin! If we were free to break God's will, how much more free to turn it or to accept it! Petitionary prayer is man's co-operation in kind with God amidst a world He freely made for freedom. The world was made by a freedom which not only left room for the kindred freedom of prayer, but which so ordered all things in its own interest that in their deepest depths they conspire to produce prayer. To pray in faith is to answer God's freedom in its own great note. It means we are taken up into the fundamental movement of the world. It is to realize that for which the whole world, the world as a whole, was made. It is an earnest of the world's consummation. We are doing what the whole world was created to do. We overleap in the spirit all between now and then, as in the return to Jesus we overleap the two thousand years that intervene. The object the Father's loving purpose had in appointing the whole providential order was intercourse with man's soul. That order of the world, is, therefore, no rigid fixture, nor is it even a fated evolution. It is elastic, adjustable, flexible, with margins for freedom, for free modification, in God and man;

always keeping in view that final goal of communion, and growing into it by a spiritual interplay in which the whole of Nature is involved. The goal of the whole cosmic order is the "manifestation of the sons of God," the realization of complete sonship, its powers and its confidences.

Thus we rise to say that our prayer is the momentary function of the Eternal Son's communion and intercession with the Eternal Father. We are integrated in advance into the final Christ, for whom, and to whom, all creation moves. Our prayer is more than the acceptance by us of God's will; it is its assertion in us. The will of God is that men should pray everywhere. He wills to be entreated. Prayer is that will of God's making itself good. When we entreat we give effect to His dearest will. And in His will is our eternal liberty. In this will of His ours finds itself, and is at home. It ranges the liberties of the Father's house. But here prayer must draw from the Cross, which is the frontal act of our emancipation as well as the central revelation of God's own freedom in grace. The action of the Atonement and of its release of us is in the nature of prayer. It is the free return of the Holy upon the Holy in the Great Reconciliation.

II. Then, secondly, as to prayer being the expression of the perennial new life of faith in the Cross. The Christian life is prayer without ceasing.

When we are told to pray without ceasing it seems to many tastes today to be somewhat extravagant language. And no doubt that is true. Why should we be concerned to deny it? Measured language and the elegant mean is not the note of the New Testament at least. $M\eta\delta\grave{\epsilon}\nu$ $\ddot{\alpha}\gamma\alpha\nu$, said the Greek—too much of nothing. But can we love or trust God too much? Christian faith is one that overcomes and commands the world in a passion rather than balances it. It triumphs in a conclusive bliss, it does not play off one part against another. The grace of Christ is not but graciousness of nature, and He does not rule His Church by social tact. The peace of God is not the calm of culture, it is not the charm of breeding. Every great forward movement in Christianity is associated with much that seems academically extravagant. Erasmus is always shocked with Luther. It is only an outlet of that essential extravagance which makes the paradox of the Cross, and keeps it as the irritant, no less than the life of the world—perhaps because it *is* the life of the world. There is nothing so abnormal, so unworldly, so supernatural, in human life as prayer; nothing that is more of an instinct, it is true, but also nothing that is less rational among all the things that keep above the level of the silly. The whole Christian life insofar as it is lived from the Cross and by the Cross is rationally an extravagance. For the Cross is the paradox of all things; and the action of the Spirit is the greatest miracle in the world; and yet it is the principle of the world. Paradox is but the expression of that dualism which is the moral foundation of a Christian world. I live who die daily. I live another's life.

To pray without ceasing is not, of course, to engage in prayer without break. That is an impossible literalism. True, "They rest not day and night, saying, Holy, holy, holy, Lord God Almighty, who wert, and art, and art to come." But it is mere poverty of soul to think of this as the iteration of a doxology. It is deep calling unto deep, eternity greeting eternity. The only answer to God's eternity is an eternal attitude of prayer.

Nor does the phrase mean that the Church shall use careful means that the stream and sound of prayer shall never cease to flow at some spots of the earth, as the altar lamp goes not out. It does not mean the continuous murmur of the mass following the sun round the world, incessant relays of adoring priests, and functions going on day and night.

But means the constant bent and drift of the soul—as the Word which was from the beginning (John 1:1) was πρὸς τὸν θεόν. All the current of its being set towards Him. It means being "in Christ," being in such a moving, returning Christ— reposing in this godward, and not merely godlike, life. The note of prayer becomes the habit of the heart, the tone and tension of its new nature; in such a way that when we are released from the grasp of our occupations the soul rebounds to its true bent, quest, and even pressure upon God. It is the soul's habitual appetite and habitual food. A growing child of God is always hungry. Prayer is not identical with the occasional act of praying. Like the act of faith, it is a whole life thought of as action. It is the life of faith in its purity, in its vital action. Eating and speaking are necessary to life, but they are not living. And how hidden prayer may be—beneath even gaiety! If you look down on Portland Race you see but a shining sea; only the pilot knows the tremendous current that pervades the smiling calm.

So far is this "pray without ceasing" from being absurd because extravagant that every man's life is in some sense a continual state of prayer. For what is his life's prayer but its ruling passion? All energies, ambitions, and passions are but expressions of a standing *nisus* in life, of a hunger, a draft, a practical demand upon the future, upon the unattained and the unseen. Every life is a draft upon the unseen. If you are not praying towards God you are towards something else. You pray as your face is set—towards Jerusalem or Babylon. The very egotism of craving life is prayer. The great difference is the object of it. To whom, for what, do we pray? The man whose passion is habitually set upon pleasure, knowledge, wealth, honour, or power is in a state of prayer to these things or for them. He prays without ceasing. These are his real gods, on whom he waits day and night. He may from time to time go on his knees in church, and use words of Christian address and petition. He may even feel a momentary unction in so doing. But it is a flicker; the other devotion is his steady flame. His real God is the ruling passion and steady pursuit of his life taken as a whole. He certainly does not pray in the name of Christ. And what he worships in spirit and in truth is another God than he addresses at religious times. He prays to an unknown God for a selfish boon. Still, in a sense, he prays. The set and drift of his nature prays. It is the prayer of instinct, not of faith. It is prayer that needs total conversion. But he cannot stop praying either to God or to God's rival—to self, society, world, flesh, or even devil. Every life that is not totally inert is praying either to God or God's adversary.

What do we really mean, whom do we mean, when we say, "My God"? In what sense mine? May our God not be but an idol we exploit, and in due course our doom?

There is a fearful and wonderful passage in Kierkegaard's *Enten-Eller* which, if we transfer it to this connection, stirs thoughts deeper than its own tragedy. The seduced, heartbroken, writes to the seducer.

"John! I do not say *my* John. That I now see you never were. I am heavily punished for ever letting such an idea be my joy. Yet—yet, mine you are—*my* seducer, *my* deceiver, *my* enemy, *my* murderer, the spring of my calamity, the grave of my joy, the abyss of my misery. I call you mine, and I am thine—thy curse for ever. Oh, do not think I will slay you and put a dagger into you. But flee where you will, I am yours, to the earth's end yours. Love a hundred others, but I am yours. I am yours in your last hour. I am yours, yours, yours—your curse."

Beware lest the whole trend of the soul fix on a deity that turns a doom. There is a prayer which makes God our judgment as well as one which makes Him our joy.

Prayer is the nature of our hell as well as our heaven.

Our hell is ceaseless, passionate, fruitless, hopeless, gnawing prayer. It is the heart churning, churning, grinding itself out in misery. It is life's passion and struggle surging back on itself like a barren, salt, corroding sea. It is the heart's blood rising like a fountain only to fall back on us in red rain. It is prayer which we cannot stop, addressed to nothing, and obtaining nothing. It calls into space and night. Or it is addressed to self, and it aggravates the wearing action of self on self. Our double being revolves on itself, like two millstones with nothing to grind.

And prayer is our heaven. It goes home to God, and attains there, and rests there. We are "in Christ," whose whole existence is prayer, who is wholly πρὸς τὸν θεόν for us. He is there to extinguish our hell and make our heaven—far more to quench our wrath and our seething than God's.

To cultivate the ceaseless spirit of prayer, use more frequent acts of prayer. To learn to pray with freedom, force yourself to pray. The great liberty begins in necessity.

Do not say, "I cannot pray. I am not in the spirit." Pray till you are in the spirit. Think of analogies from lower levels. Sometimes when you need rest most you are too restless to lie down and take it. Then compel yourself to lie down, and to lie still. Often in ten minutes the compulsion fades into consent, and you sleep, and rise a new man.

Again, it is often hard enough to take up the task which in half an hour you enjoy. It is often against the grain to turn out of an evening to meet the friends you promised. But once you are in their midst you are in your element.

Sometimes, again, you say, "I will not go to church. I do not feel that way." That is where the habit of an ordered religious life comes in aid. Religion is the last region for chance desires. Do it as a duty, and it may open out as a blessing Omit it, and you may miss the one thing that would have made an eternal difference. You stroll instead, and return with nothing but an appetite—when you might have come back with an inspiration. Compel yourself to meet your God as you would meet your promises, your obligations, your fellow men.

So if you are averse to pray, pray the more. Do not call it lip-service. That is not the lip-service God disowns. It is His Spirit acting in your self-coercive will, only not yet in your heart. What is unwelcome to God is lip-service which is untroubled at not being more. As appetite comes with eating, so prayer with praying. Our hearts learn the language of the lips.

Compel yourself often to shape on your lips the detailed needs of your soul. It is not needful to inform God, but to deepen you, to inform yourself before God, to enrich that intimacy with yourself which is so necessary to answer the intimacy of God. To common sense the fact that God knows all we need, and wills us all good, the fact of His infinite Fatherhood, is a reason for not praying. Why tell Him what He knows? Why ask what He is more than willing to give? But to Christian faith and to spiritual reason it is just the other way. Asking is polar co-operation.

Jesus turned the fact to a use exactly the contrary of its deistic sense. He made the allknowing Fatherhood the ground of true prayer. We do not ask as beggars but as children. Petition is not mere receptivity, nor is it mere pressure; it is filial reciprocity. Love loves to be told what it knows already. Every lover knows that. It wants to be asked for what it longs to give. And that is the principle of prayer to the all-knowing Love. As God knows all, you may reckon that your brief and humble prayer will be understood (Matt. 6:8). It will be taken up into the intercession of the Spirit stripped of its dross, its inadequacy made good, and presented as prayer should be. That is praying in the Holy Ghost. Where should you carry your burden but to the Father, where Christ took the burden of all the world? We tell God, the heart searcher, our heavy thoughts to escape from brooding over them. "When my spirit was overwhelmed within me, Thou knewest my path" (Ps. 142:3). So Paul says the Spirit intercedes for us and gives our broken prayer divine effect (Rom. 8:26). To be sure of God's sympathy is to be inspired to prayer, where His mere knowledge would crush it. There is no father who would be satisfied that his son should take everything and ask for nothing. It would be thankless. To cease asking is to cease to be grateful. And what kills petition kills praise.

Go into your chamber, shut the door, and cultivate the habit of praying audibly. Write prayers and burn them. Formulate your soul. Pay no attention to literary form, only to spiritual reality. Read a passage of Scripture and then sit down and turn it into a prayer, written or spoken. Learn to be particular, specific, and detailed in your prayer so long as you are not trivial. General prayers, literary prayers, and stately phrases are, for private prayer, traps and sops to the soul. To formulate your soul is one valuable means to escape formalizing it. This is the best, the wholesome, kind of self-examination. Speaking with God discovers us safely to ourselves. We "find" ourselves, come to ourselves, in the Spirit. Face your special weaknesses and sins before God. Force yourself to say to God exactly where you are wrong. When anything goes wrong, do not ask to have it set right, without asking in prayer what it was in you that made it go wrong. It is somewhat fruitless to ask for a general grace to help specific flaws, sins, trials, and griefs. Let prayer be concrete, actual, a direct product of life's real experiences. Pray as your actual self, not as some fancied saint. Let it be closely relevant to your real situation. Pray without ceasing in this sense. Pray without a break between your prayer and your life. Pray so that there is a real continuity between your prayer and your whole actual life. But I will bear round upon this point again immediately.

Meantime, let me say this. Do not allow your practice in prayer to be
arrested by scientific or philosophic considerations as to *how* answer is
possible. That is a valuable subject for discussion, but it is not entitled to
control our practice. Faith is at least as essential to the soul as science, and
it has a foundation more independent. And prayer is not only a necessity
of faith, it is faith itself in action.

Criticism of prayer dissolves in the experience of it. When the soul is
at close quarters with God it becomes enlarged enough to hold together in
harmony things that oppose, and to have room for harmonious contraries.
For instance: God, of course, is   always working for His Will and
Kingdom. But man is bound to pray for its coming, while it is coming all
the time. Christ laid stress on prayer as a necessary means of bringing the
Kingdom to pass. And it cannot come without our praying. Why? Because
its coming is the prayerful frame of soul. So again with God's freedom. It
is absolute. But it reckons on ours. Our prayer does not force His hand; it
answers His freedom in kind. We are never so active and free as in prayer
to an absolutely free God. We share His freedom when we are "in Christ."

If I must choose between Christ, who bids me pray for everything,
and the savant, who tells me certain answers are physically and rationally
impossible, must I not choose Christ? Because, while the savant knows
much about nature and its action (and much more than Christ did), Christ
knew everything about the God of nature and His reality. He knew more
of what is possible to God than anybody has ever known about what is
possible in nature. On such a subject as prayer, anyone is a greater
authority who wholly knows the will of God than he who only knows
God's methods, and knows them but in part. Prayer is not an act of
knowledge but of faith. It is not a matter of calculation but of
confidence—"that our faith should not stand in the wisdom of men, but in
the power of God." Which means that in this region we are not to be
regulated by science, but by God's self-revelation. Do not be so timid
about praying wrongly if you pray humbly. If God is really the Father that
Christ revealed, then the principle is—take everything to Him that
exercises you. Apart from frivolity, such as praying to find the stud you
lost, or the knife, or the umbrella, there is really no limitation in the New
Testament on the contents of petition. Any regulation is as to the spirit of
the prayer, the faith it springs from. In all distress which mars your peace,
petition must be the form your faith takes—petition for rescue. Keep close
to the New Testament Christ, and then ask for anything you desire in that

contact. Ask for everything you can ask in Christ's name, *i.e.* everything desirable by a man who is in Christ's kingdom of God, by a man who lives for it at heart, everything in tune with the purpose and work of the kingdom in Christ. If you are in that kingdom, then pray freely for whatever you need or wish to keep you active and effective for it, from daily bread upwards and outwards. In all things make your requests known. It will not unhinge such faith if you do not obtain them. At least you have laid them on God's heart; and faith means confidences between you and not only favours. And there is not confidence if you keep back what is hot or heavy on your heart. If prayer is not a play of the religious fantasy, or a routine task, it must be the application of faith to a concrete actual and urgent situation. Only remember that prayer does not work by magic, and that stormy desire is not fervent, effectual prayer. You may be but exploiting a mighty power; whereas you must be in real contact with the real God. It is the man that most really has God that most really seeks God.

I said a little while ago that to pray without ceasing also meant to pray without a breach with your actual life and the whole situation in which you are. This is the point at which to dwell on that. If you may not come to God with the occasions of your private life and affairs, then there is some unreality in the relation between you and Him. If some private crisis absorbs you, some business or family anxiety of little moment to others but of much to you, and if you may not bring that to God in prayer, then one of two things. Either it is not you, in your actual reality, that came to God, but it is you in a pose— you in some role which you are trying with poor success to play before Him. You are trying to pray as another person than you are—a better person, perhaps, as some great apostle, who should have on his worshipping mind nothing but the grand affairs of the Church and Kingdom, and not be worried by common cares. You are praying in court-dress. You are trying to pray as you imagine one should pray to God, *i.e.* as another person than you are, and in other circumstances. You are creating a self and a situation to place before God. Either that or you are not praying to a God who loves, helps, and delivers you in every pinch of life, but only to one who uses you as a pawn for the victory of His great kingdom. You are not praying to Christ's God. You are praying to a God who cares only for the great actors in His kingdom, for the heroic people who cherish nothing but the grand style, or for the calm people who do not deeply feel life's trials. The reality of prayer is bound up with the reality and intimacy of life.

And its great object is to get home as we are to God as He is, and to win response even when we get no compliance. The prayer of faith does not mean a prayer absolutely sure that it will receive what it asks. That is not faith. Faith is that attitude of soul and self to God which is the root and reservoir of prayer apart from all answer. It is what turns need into request. It is what moves your need to need God. It is what makes you sure your prayer is heard and stored, whether granted or not. "He putteth all my tears into his bottle." God has old prayers of yours long maturing by Him. What wine you will drink with Him in His kingdom! Faith is sure that God refuses with a smile; that He says No in the spirit of Yes, and He gives or refuses always in Christ, our great Amen. And better prayers are stirred by the presence of the Deliverer than even by the need of deliverance.

It is not sufficiently remembered that before prayer can expect an answer it must be itself an answer. That is what is meant by prayer in the name of Christ. It is prayer which answers God's gift in Christ, with whom are already given us all things. And that is why we must pray without ceasing, because in Christ God speaks without ceasing. Natural or instinctive prayer is one thing; supernatural prayer is another; it is the prayer not of instinct but of faith. It is our word answering God's. It is more the prayer of fullness even than of need, of strength than of weakness—though it be "a strength girt round with weakness." Prayer which arises from mere need is flung out to a power which is only remembered, or surmised, or unknown. It is flung into darkness and uncertainty. But in Christian prayer we ask for what we need because we are full of faith in God's power and word, because need becomes petition at the touch of His word. (I always feel that in the order of our public worship prayer should immediately follow the lesson, without the intrusion of an anthem. And for the reason I name—that Christian prayer is our word answering God's.) We pray, therefore, in Christ's name, or for His sake, because we pray as answering the gift in Christ. Our prayer is the note the tremulous soul utters when its chords are smitten by Him. We then answer above all things God's prayer to us in His Cross that we would be reconciled. God so beseeches us in Christ. So that, if we put it strongly, we may say that our prayer to God in Christ is our answer to God's prayer to us there. "The best thing in prayer is faith," says Luther.

And the spirit of prayer in Christ's name is the true childspirit. A certain type of religion is fond of dwelling on faith as the spirit of divine childhood; and its affinities are all with the tender and touching element in childhood. But one does not always get from the prophets of such piety the impression of a life breathed in prayer. And the notion is not the New Testament sense of being children of God. That is a manlier, a maturer thing. It is being sons of God by faith, and by faith's energy of prayer. It is not the sense of being as helpless as a child that clings, not the sense of weakness, ignorance, gentleness, and all that side of things. But it is the spirit of a prayer which is a great act of faith, and therefore a power. Faith is not simply surrender, but adoring surrender, not a mere sense of dependence, but an act of intelligent committal, and the confession of a holiness which is able to save, keep, and bless for ever.

How is it that the experience of life is so often barren of spiritual culture for religious people? They become stoic and stalwart, but not humble; they have keen sight, but no insight. Yet it is not the stalwarts but the saints that judge the world, *i.e.* that take the true divine measure of the world, and get to its subtle, silent, and final powers. Whole sections of our Protestantism have lost the virtue of humility or the understanding of it. It means for them no more than modesty or diffidence. It is the humility of weakness, not of power. To many useful, and even strong, people no experience seems to bring this subtle, spiritual intelligence, this finer discipline of the moral man. No rebukes, no rebuffs, no humiliations, no sorrows, seem to bring it to them. They have no spiritual history. Their spiritual biography not even an angel could write. There is no romance in their soul's story. At sixty they are, spiritually, much where they were at twenty-six. To calamity, to discipline of any kind, they are simply resilient. Their religion is simply elasticity. It is but lusty life. They rise up after the smart is over, or the darkness fades away, as self-confident as if they were but seasoned politicians beaten at one election, but sure of doing better at the next. They are to the end just irrepressible, or persevering, or dogged. And they are as juvenile in moral insight, as boyish in spiritual perception, as ever.

Is it not because they have never really had personal religion? That is, they have never really prayed with all their heart; only, at most, with all their fervour, certainly not with strength and mind. They have never "spread out" their whole soul and situation to a God who knows. They have never opened the petals of their soul in the warm sympathy of His knowledge. They have not become particular enough in their prayer, faithful with themselves, or relevant to their complete situation. They do not face themselves, only what happens to them. They pray with their heart and not with their conscience. They pity themselves, perhaps they spare themselves, they shrink from hurting themselves more than misfortune hurts them. They say, "If you knew all you could not help pitying me." They do not say, "God knows all, and how can He spare me?" For themselves, or for their fellows, it is the prayer of pity, not of repentance. We need the prayer of self-judgment more than the prayer of fine insight.

We are not humble in God's sight, partly because in our prayer there is a point at which we cease to pray, where we do not turn everything out into God's light. It is because there is a chamber or two in our souls where we do not enter in and take God with us. We hurry Him by that door as we take Him along the corridors of our life to see our tidy places or our public rooms. We ask from our prayers too exclusively comfort, strength, enjoyment, or tenderness and graciousness, and not often enough humiliation and its fine strength.

We want beautiful prayers, touching prayers, simple prayers, thoughtful prayers; prayers with a quaver or a tear in them, or prayers with delicacy and dignity in them. But searching prayer, humbling prayer, which is the prayer of the conscience, and not merely of the heart or taste; prayer which is bent on reality, and to win the new joy goes through new misery if need be—are such prayers as welcome and common as they should be? Too much of our prayer is apt to leave us with the self-complacency of the sympathetically incorrigible, of the benevolent and irremediable, of the breezy octogenarian, all of whose yesterdays look backward with a cheery and exasperating smile.

It is an art—this great and creative prayer—this intimate conversation with God. *"Magna ars est conversari cum Deo,"* says Thomas a Kempis. It has to be learned. In social life we learn that conversation is not mere talk. There is an art in it, if we are not to have a table of gabblers. How much more is it so in the conversation of heaven! We must learn that art by practice, and by keeping the best society in that kind. Associate much with the great masters in this kind; especially with the Bible; and chiefly with Christ. Cultivate His Holy Spirit. He is the grand master of God's art and mystery in communing with man. And there is no other teacher, at last, of man's art of communion with God.

Chapter Six

THE VICARIOUSNESS OF PRAYER

I

The work of the ministry labours under one heavy disadvantage when we regard it as a profession and compare it with other professions. In these, experience brings facility, a sense of mastery in the subject, self-satisfaction, self-confidence; but in our subject the more we pursue it, the more we enter into it, so much the more are we cast down with the overwhelming sense, not only of our insufficiency, but of our unworthiness. Of course, in the technique of our work we acquire a certain ease. We learn to speak more or less freely and aptly. We learn the knack of handling a text, of conducting church work, or dealing with men, and the like. If it were only texts or men we had to handle! But we have to handle the gospel. We have to lift up Christ—a Christ who is the death of natural self-confidence—a humiliating, even a crushing, Christ; and we are not always alive to our uplifting and resurrection in Him. We have to handle a gospel that is a new rebuke to us every step we gain in intimacy with it. There is no real intimacy with the gospel which does not mean a new sense of God's holiness, and it may be long before we realize that the same holiness that condemns is that which saves. There is no new insight into the Cross which does not bring, whatever else come with it, a deeper sense of the solemn holiness of the love that meets us there. And there is no new sense of the holy God that does not arrest His name upon our unclean lips. If our very repentance is to be repented of, and we should be forgiven much in our very prayers, how shall we be proud, or even pleased, with what we may think a success in our preaching? So that we are not surprised that some preachers, after what the public calls a most brilliant and impressive discourse, retire (as the emperor retired to close his life in the cloister) to humble themselves before God, to ask forgiveness for the poor message, and to call themselves most unprofitable servants—yea, even when they knew themselves that they had "done well." The more we grasp our gospel the more it abashes us.

Moreover, as we learn more of the seriousness of the gospel for the human soul, we feel the more that every time we present it we are adding to the judgment of some as well as to the salvation of others. We are not like speakers who present a matter that men can freely take or leave, where they can agree or differ with us without moral result. No true preacher can be content that his flock should believe in him. That were egoism. They must believe with him. The deeper and surer our gospel is the more is our work a judgment on those to whom it is not a grace. This was what bore upon the Saviour's own soul, and darkened His very agony into eclipse. That He, who knew Himself to be the salvation of His own beloved people, should, by His very love, become their doom! And here we watch and suffer with Him, however sleepily. There is put into our charge our dear people's life or death. For to those to whom we are not life we are death, in proportion as we truly preach, not ourselves, but the real salvation of Christ.

How solemn our place is! It is a sacramental place. We have not simply to state our case, we have to *convey* our Christ, and to convey Him effectually as the soul's final fate. We are sacramental elements, broken often, in the Lord's hands, as He dispenses his grace through us. We do not, of course, believe that orders are an ecclesiastical sacrament, as Rome does. But we are forced to realize the idea underlying that dogma— the sacramental nature of our person, work, and vocation for the gospel. We are not saviours. There is only one Saviour. But we are His sacraments. We do not believe in an ecclesiastical priesthood; but we are made to feel how we stand between God and the people as none of our flock do. We bring Christ to them, and them to Christ, in sacrificial action, in a way far more moral, inward, and taxing than official priesthood can be. As ministers we lead the sacerdotal function of the whole Church in the world—its holy confession and sacrifice for the world in Christ.

We ought, indeed, to feel the dignity of the ministry; we must present some protest against the mere fraternal conception which so easily sinks into an unspiritual familiarity. But still more than the dignity of the ministry do its elect feel its solemnity. How can it be otherwise? We have to dwell much with the everlasting burnings of God's love. We have to tend that consuming fire. We have to feed our life where all the tragedy of life is gathered to an infinite and victorious crisis in Christ. We are not the fire, but we live where it burns. The matter we handle in our theological thought we can only handle with some due protection for our face. It is one of the dangerous industries. It is continually acting on us, continually searching our inner selves that no part of us may be unforgiven, unfed, or unsanctified. We cannot hold it and examine it at arm's length. It enters into us. It evokes the perpetual comment of our souls, and puts us continually on self judgment. Our critic, our judge, is at the door. Self-condemnation arrests denunciation. And the true apostle can never condemn but in the spirit of self-condemnation.

But, after all, our doom is our blessing. Our Judge is on our side. For if humiliation be wrung from us, still more is faith, hope, and prayer. Everything that rebukes our self-satisfaction does still more to draw out our faith. When we are too tired or doubtful to ask we can praise and adore. When we are weary of confessing our sin we can forget ourselves in a godly sort and confess our Saviour. We can say the creed when we cannot raise the song. He also hath given us the reconciliation. The more judgment we see in the holy cross the more we see it is judgment unto salvation. The more we are humbled the more we "roll our souls upon Christ." And we recover our self-possession only by giving our soul again and again to Christ to keep. We win a confidence in self-despair. Prayer is given us as wings wherewith to mount, but also to shield our faces when they have carried us before the great white throne. It is in prayer that the holiness comes home as love, and the love is established as holiness. At every step our thought is transformed to prayer, and our prayer opens new ranges of thought. His great revelation is His holiness, always outgoing in atoning love. The Christian revelation is not "God is love" so much as "love is God." That is, it is not God's love, but the infinite power of God's love, its finality, omnipotence, and absoluteness. It is not passionate and helpless love, but it has power to subdue *everything* that rises against it. And that is the holiness of love—the eternal thing in it. We receive the last reconciliation. Then the very wrath of God becomes a glory. The red in the sky is the new dawn. Our self-accusation becomes a new mode of praise. Our loaded hearts spring light again. Our heavy conscience turns to grave moral power. A new love is born for our kind. A new and tender patience steals upon us. We see new ways of helping, serving, and saving. We issue into a new world. We are one with the Christ not only on His cross, but in His resurrection. Think of the resurrection power and calm, of that solemn final peace, that infinite satisfaction in the eternal thing eternally achieved, which filled His soul when He had emerged from death, when man's worst had been done, and God's best had been won, for ever and for all. We have our times of entrance into that Christ. As we were one with Him in the likeness of His death, so we are in the likeness of His resurrection. And the same Eternal Spirit which puts the preacher's soul much upon the cross also raises it continually from the dead. We overcome our mistakes, negligences, sins; nay, we rise above the sin of the whole world, which will not let our souls be as good as they are. We overcome the world, and take courage, and are of new cheer. We are in the Spirit. And then we can preach, pray, teach, heal. And even the unclean lips then put a new thrill into our sympathy and a new tremor into our praise.

If it be not so, how shall our dangerous work not demoralize us, and we perish from our too much contact with holy things!

The minister's holiest prayer is hardly lawful to utter. Few of his public would comprehend it. Some would dismiss it with their most opprobrious word. They would call it theological. When he calls to God in his incomprehensible extremity they would translate it into an appeal to Elijah (Matt. 27:47). For to them theology is largely mythology.

We are called at the present day to a reconstruction of the old theology, a restatement of the old gospel. We have to reappropriate and remint the truth of our experienced Christianity. But what a hardship it is that this call should search us at a time when the experimental power of our Christianity has abated, and the evangelical experience is so low and so confused as it often is! It must be the minister's work to recover and deepen this experience for the churches, in the interest of faith, and of the truth in which faith renders account of itself. Theological inadequacy, and especially antagonism to theology, means at root religious defect. For the reformation of belief we must have a restoration of faith. And a chief engine for such recovery of faith is for us what it was for Luther and his like—prayer. And it is not mindless prayer, but that prayer which is the wrestling of the conscience and not merely the cry of the heart, the prayer for reconciliation and redemption and not merely for guidance and comfort, the prayer of faith and not merely of love.

I saw in a friend's house a photograph from (I think) Durer just two tense hands, palms together, and lifted in prayer. It was most eloquent, most subduing. I wish I could stamp the picture on the page here and fit it to Milton's line:

The great two-handed engine at our door.

II

Public prayer is, on the whole, the most difficult part of the work of the minister. To help the difficulty I have always claimed that pulpit notes of prayer may be used. "The Lord's Prayer" itself is of this nature. It is not a prayer, but a scheme of prayer, heads of prayer, or buoys in the channel. But even with the use of all helps there are perils enough. There are prayers that, in the effort to become real, are much too familiar in their fashion of speech. A young man began his prayer, in my own hearing, with the words, "O God, we have come to have a chat with Thee." It was gruesome. Think of it as a sample of modern piety for the young! No prayers, certainly no public prayers, should be "chats with God." Again, other prayers are sentimental prayers. George Dawson's volume has this fault. The prayers of the Church should not be exposures of the affectional man. The public prayer of the Church, as the company of grace, is the saved soul returning to God that gave it; it is the sinner coming to the Saviour, or the ransomed of the Lord returning to Zion; it is the sanctified with the Sanctifier; it is not primarily the child talking to the Father— though that note may prevail in more private prayers. We are more than stray sheep reclaimed. We are those whose defiant iniquity has lain upon Christ for us all.

But the root of the difficulty of public prayer lies farther back than in the matter of style. It lies in the difficulty of private prayer, in its spiritual poverty, its inertia, its anemia. What culture can deal with the rooted difficulty that resides there, out of sight, in the inner man of the heart, for lack of the courage of faith, for sheer spiritual fecklessness? Yet the preparation for prayer is to pray. The prayer of the Church is learned in the chamber. The culture needed in the practice of prayer. It is only prayer that teaches to pray. The minister ought never to speak before men in God's name without himself first speaking to God in man's name, and making intercession as for himself so for his people.

Intercession! We are properly vigilant that the minister do not sever himself from his people in any sacerdotal way. But for all that, is the minister's personal and private prayer on exactly the same footing as a layman's? It is a question that leads to the distinction between intercessory and vicarious prayer. The personal religion of the minister is vicarious even when it is not intercessory. Great indeed is the spiritual value of private intercession. The *intercessory* private prayer of the minister is the best corrective of the *critical* spirit or the grumbling spirit which so easily besets and withers us today. That reconciliation, that pacification of heart, which comes by prayer opens in us a fountain of private intercession, especially for our antagonists. Only, of course, it must be private. But the minister is also praying to his people's good even when he is not interceding on their behalf, or leading them in prayer. What he is for his Church he is with his whole personality. And so his private and personal prayers are vicarious for his people even when he does not know it. No Christian man lives for himself, nor believes for himself. And if the private Christian in his private prayers does not pray, any more than he lives, unto himself alone, much more is this true for the minister. His private prayers make a great difference to his people. They may not know what makes his spell and blessing; even he may not. But it is his most private prayers; which, thus, are vicarious even where not intercessory.

What he is for his Church, I have said, he is with his whole personality. And nothing gives us personality like true prayer. Nothing makes a man so original. We cannot be true Christians without being original. Living faith destroys the commonplaceness, the monotony of life. Are not all men original in death? *"Je mourrai seul."* Much more are they original and their true selves in Christ's death, and in their part and lot in that. For true originality we must be one, and closely one, with God. To be creative we must learn with the Creator. The most effective man in history was he who said, "I live; yet not I, but Christ liveth in me." What a reflection on our faith that so much piety should be humdrum and deadly dull! Private prayer, when it is real action, is the greatest forge of personality. It places a man in direct and effective contact with God the Creator, the source of originality, and especially with God the Redeemer as the source of the new creation. For the minister personality is everything—not geniality, as it is the day's fashion to say, but personality; and prayer is the spring of personality. This impressive personality, due to prayer, you may often have in "the peasant saint." And in some cases its absence is as palpable. Hence comes vulgarity in prayer, essential vulgarity underlying much possible fineness of phrase or manner. Vulgarity in prayer lies not so much in its offences to good taste in style as in its indications of the absence of spiritual *habit* and reality. If the theology of rhetoric destroys the theology of reality in the sermon, how much more in prayer!

Prayer is for the religious life what original research is for science— by it we get direct contact with reality. The soul is brought into union with its own vaster nature—God. Therefore, also, we must use the Bible as an original; for, indeed, the Bible is the most copious spring of prayer, and of power, and of range. If we learn to pray from the Bible, and avoid a mere *cento* of its phrases, we shall cultivate in our prayer the large humane note of a universal gospel. Let us nurse our prayer on our *study* of our Bible; and let us, therefore, not be too afraid of *theological* prayer. True Christian prayer must have theology in it; no less than true theology must have prayer in it and must be capable of being prayed. "Your theology is too difficult," said Charles V to the Reformers; "it cannot be understood without much prayer." Yes, that is our arduous puritan way. Prayer and theology must interpenetrate to keep each other great, and wide, and mighty. The failure of the habit of prayer is at the root of much of our light distaste for theology. There is a conspiracy of influences round us whose effect is to belittle our great work. Earnest ministers suffer more from the smallness of their people than from their sins, and far more than from their unkindness. Our public may kill by its triviality a soul which could easily resist the assaults of opposition or wickedness. And our newspaper will greatly aid their work. Now, to resist this it is not enough to have recourse to prayer and to cultivate devotion. Unfortunately, there are signs in the religious world to show that prayer and piety alone do not save men from pettiness of interest, thinness of soul, spiritual volatility, the note of insincerity, or foolishness of judgment, or even vindictiveness. The remedy is not prayer alone, but prayer on the scale of the whole gospel and at the depth of searching faith. It is considered prayer—prayer which rises above the childish petitions that disfigure much of our public pietism, prayer which issues from the central affairs of the kingdom of God. It is prayer with the profound Bible as its book of devotion, and a true theology of faith for half of its power. It is the prayer of a mind that moves in Bible passion, and ranges with Bible scope, even when it eschews Bible speech and "the language of Canaan."

And yet, with all its range, it is prayer with *concentration.* It has not only thought but will in it. The great reason why so many will not decide for Christ is that Christ requires from the world concentration; not seclusion and not renunciation merely, but concentration. And we ministers have our special form of that need. I am speaking not of our share in the common troubles of life, but of those specially that arise from the ministerial office and care. No minister can live up to his work on the casual or interjectional kind of prayer that might be sufficient for many of his flock. He must think, of course, in his prayers—in his private prayers—and he must pray his faith's thought. But, still more, in his praying he must act. Prayer is not a frame of mind, but a great energy. He must rise to conceive his work as an active function of the work of Christ;

and he must link his faith, therefore, with the intercession which covers the whole energy of Christ in His kingdom. In this, as in many ways, he must remember, to his great relief and comfort, that it is not he who is the real pastor of his church, but Christ, and that he is but Christ's curate. The final responsibility is not his, but Christ's, who bears the responsibility of all the sins and frets, both of the world and, especially, of the Church.

The concentration, moreover, should correspond to the positivity of the gospel and the Bible. Prayer should rise more out of God's Word and concern for His kingdom than even out of our personal needs, trials, or desires. That is implied in prayer in Christ's name or for Christ's sake, prayer from His place in the midst of the Kingdom. *Our* Prayer-book, the Bible, does not prescribe prayer, but it does more—it inspires it. And prayer in Christ's name is prayer inspired by His first interest— the gospel. Do not use Christ simply to countersign your egoist petition by a closing formula, but to create, inspire, and glorify it. Prayer in Christ's name is prayer for Christ's object—for His kingdom, and His promise of the Holy Ghost.

If we really pray for that and yet do not feel we receive it, probably enough we have it; and we are looking for some special form of it not ours, or not ours yet. We may be mistaking the fruits of the Spirit for His presence. Fruits come late. They are different from signs. Buds are signs, and so are other things hard to see. It is the Spirit that keeps us praying for the Spirit, as it is grace that keeps us in grace. Remember the patience of the missionaries who waited in the Spirit fifteen years for their first convert. If God gave His Son *unasked,* how much more will He give His Holy Spirit to them that *ask* it! But let us not prescribe the form in which He comes.

The true close of prayer is when the utterance expires in its own spiritual fullness. That is the true Amen. Such times there are. We feel we are at last laid open to God. We feel as though we "did see heaven opened, and the holy angels, and the great God Himself." The prayer ends itself; *we* do not end it. It mounts to its heaven and renders its spirit up to God, saying, "It is finished." It has its perfect consummation and bliss, its spiritually natural close and fruition, whether it has answer or not.

Chapter Seven

THE INSISTENCY OF PRAYER

In all I have said I have implied that prayer should be strenuously *importunate*. Observe, not petitionary merely, nor concentrated, nor active alone, but importunate. For prayer is not only meditation or communion. Nor ought it to be merely submissive in tone, as the "quietist" ideal is. We need not begin with "Thy will be done" if we but end with it. Remember the stress that Christ laid on importunity. Strenuous prayer will help us to recover the masculine type of religion—and then our opponents will at least respect us.

I would speak a little more fully on this matter of importunity. It is very closely bound up with the reality of prayer and of religion. Prayer is not really a power till it is importunate. And it cannot be importunate unless it is felt to have a real effect on the Will of God. I may slip in here my conviction that far less of the disbelief in prayer is due to a scientific view of nature's uniformity than to the slipshod kind of prayer that men hear from us in public worship; it is often but journalese sent heavenwards, or phrase-making to carry on. And I would further say that by importunity something else is meant than passionate dictation and stormy pertinacity— imposing our egoist will on God, and treating Him as a mysterious but manageable power that we may coerce and exploit.

The deepening of the spiritual life is a subject that frequently occupies the attention of religious conferences and of the soul bent on self-improvement. But it is not certain that the great saints would always recognize the ideal of some who are addicted to the use of the phrase. The "deepening of the spiritual life" they would find associated with three unhappy things.

1. They would recoil from a use of Scripture prevalent in those circles, which is atomistic, individualist, subjective and fantastic.

2. And what they would feel most foreign to their own objective and penetrating minds might be the air of introspection and self-measurement too often associated with the spiritual thus "deepened"—a spiritual egoism.

3. And they would miss the note of Judgment and Redemption.

We should distinguish at the outset *the deepening of spiritual life* from the *quickening of spiritual sensibility.* Christ on the cross was surely deepened in spiritual experience, but was not the essence of that dereliction, and the concomitant of that deepening, the dulling of spiritual sensibility?

There are many plain obstacles to the deepening of spiritual life, amid which I desire to name here only one; it is prayer conceived merely, or chiefly, as *submission, resignation, quietism*. We say too soon, "Thy will be done"; and too ready acceptance of a situation as His will often means feebleness or sloth. It may be His will that we surmount His will. It may be His higher will that we resist His lower. Prayer is an act of will much more than of sentiment, and its triumph is more than acquiescence. Let us submit when we *must*, but let us keep the submission in reserve rather than in action, as a ground tone rather than the sole effort. Prayer with us has largely ceased to be *wrestling* But is that not the dominant scriptural idea? It is not the sole idea, but is it not the dominant? And is not our subdued note often but superinduced and unreal?

I venture to enlarge on this last head, by way of meeting some who hesitate to speak of the power of prayer to alter God's will. I offer two points:

I. Prayer may really change the will of God, or, if not His will, His intention.

II. It may, like other human energies of godly sort, take the form of resisting the will of God. Resisting His will may be doing His will.

I. As to the first point. If this is not believed the earnestness goes out of prayer. It becomes either a ritual, or a soliloquy only overheard by God; just as thought with the will out of it degenerates into dreaming or brooding, where we are more passive than active. Prayer is not merely the meeting of two moods or two affections, the laying of the head on a divine bosom in trust and surrender. That may have its place in religion, but it is not the nerve and soul of prayer. Nor is it religious reverie. Prayer is an encounter of *wills*— till one will or the other give way. It is not a spiritual exercise merely, but in its maturity it is a cause acting on the course of God's world.[1] It is, indeed, by God's grace that prayer is a real cause, but such it is. And of course there must be in us a faith corresponding to the grace. Of course also there is always, behind all, the readiness to accept God's will without a murmur when it is perfectly evident and final. "My grace is sufficient for thee." Yes, but there is also the repeated effort to

---

1. This position is excluded by Schleiermacher's view of religion as absolute dependence, because that leaves room for no action of man on God. And it is one of the grave defects of so great a saint as Robertson.

alter its form according to our sanctified needs and desires. You will notice that in Paul's case the power to accept the sufficiency of God's grace only came in the course of an importunate prayer aiming to turn God's hand. Paul ended, rather than began, with "Thy will be done." The peace of God is an end and not a beginning.

"Thy will be done" was no utterance of mere resignation; though it has mostly come to mean this in a Christianity which tends to canonize the weak instead of strengthening them. As prayer it was a piece of active co-operation with God's will. It was a positive part of it. It is one thing to submit to a stronger will, it is another to be one with it. We submit because we cannot resist it; but when we are one with it we cannot succumb. It is not a power, but *our* power. But the natural will is not one with God's; and so we come to use these words in a mere negative way, meaning that we cease to resist. Our will does not accept God's, it just stops work. We give in and lie down. But is that the sense of the words in the Lord's Prayer? Do they mean that we have no objection to God's will being done? or that we do not withstand any more? or even that we accept it gladly? Do they not mean something far more positive—that we actively will God's will and aid it, that it is the whole content of our own, that we put into it all the will that there can be in prayer, which is at last the great will-power of the race? It is our heart's passion that God's will be done and His kingdom come. And can His kingdom come otherwise than as it is a passion with us? Can His will be done? God's will was not Christ's consent merely, nor His pleasure, but His meat and drink, the source of His energy and the substance of His work.

Observe, nothing can alter God's grace, His *will* in that sense, His large will and final purpose—our racial blessing, our salvation, our redemption in Jesus Christ. But for that will He is an infinite opportunist. His ways are very flexible. His *intentions* are amenable to us if His *will is* changeless. The steps of His process are variable according to our freedom and His.

We are living, let us say, in a careless way; and God proposes a certain treatment of us according to our carelessness. But in the exercise of our spiritual freedom we are by some means brought to pray. We cease to be careless. We pray God to visit us as those who hear. Then He does another thing. He acts differently, with a change caused by our freedom and our change. The treatment for deafness is altered. God adopts another treatment—perhaps for weakness. We have by prayer changed His action, and, so far, His will (at any rate His intention) concerning us. As we pray, the discipline for the prayerless is altered to that for the prayerful. We attain the thing God did not mean to give us unless He had been affected by our prayer. We change the conduct, if not the will, of God to us, the *Verhalten* if not the *Verhaltniss*.

Again, we pray and pray, and no answer comes. The boon does not arrive. Why? Perhaps we are not spiritually ready for it. It would not be a real blessing. But the persistence, the importunity of faith, is having a great effect on our spiritual nature. It ripens. A time comes when we are ready for answer. We then present ourselves to God in a spiritual condition which reasonably causes Him to yield. The new spiritual state is not the answer to our prayer, but it is its effect; and it is the condition which makes the answer possible. It makes the prayer effectual. The gift can be a blessing now. So God resists us no more. Importunity prevails, not as mere importunity (for God is not bored into answer), but as the importunity of God's own elect, *i.e.* as obedience, as a force of the Kingdom, as increased spiritual power, as real moral action, bringing corresponding strength and fitness to receive. I have often found that what I sought most I did not get at the right time, not till it was too late, not till I had learned to do without it, till I had renounced it in principle (though not in desire). Perhaps it had lost some of its zest by the time it came, but it meant more as a gift and a trust. That was God's right time—when I could have it as though I had it not. If it came, it came not to gratify me, but to glorify Him and be a means of serving Him.

One recalls here that most pregnant saying of Schopenhauer: "All is illusion—the hope or the thing hoped." If it is not true for all it is true for very many. Either the hope is never fulfilled or else its fulfillment disappoints. God gives the hoped-for thing, but sends leanness into the soul. The mother prays to have a son—and he breaks her heart, and were better dead. Hope may lie to us, or the thing hoped may dash us. But though He slay me I will trust. God does not fail. Amid the wreck of my little world He is firm, and I in Him. I justify God in the ruins; in His good time I shall arrive. More even than my hopes may go wrong. I may go wrong. But my Redeemer liveth; and, great though God is as my Fulfiller, He is greater as my Redeemer. He is great as my hope, but He is greater as my power. What is the failure of my hope from Him compared with the failure of His hope in me? If He continue to believe in me I may well believe in Him.

God's object with us is not to give just so many things and withhold so many; it is to place us in the tissue of His kingdom. His best answer to us is to raise us to the power of answering Him. The reason why He does not answer our prayer is because we do not answer Him and His prayer. And His prayer was, as though Christ did beseech us, "Be ye reconciled." He would lift us to confident business with Him, to commerce of loving wills. The painter wrestles with the sitter till he gives him back himself, and there is a speaking likeness. So man with God, till God surrender His secret. He gives or refuses things, therefore, with a view to that communion alone, and on the whole. It is that spiritual personal end, and not an iron necessity, that rules His course. Is there not a constant spiritual interaction between God and man as free spiritual beings? *How* that can be is one of the great philosophic problems. But the fact that it is is of the essence of faith. It is the unity of our universe. Many systems try to explain *how* human freedom and human action are consistent with God's omnipotence and omniscience. None succeed. *How* secondary causes like man are compatible with God as the Universal and Ultimate Cause is not rationally plain. But there is no practical doubt that they are compatible. And so it is with the action of man on God in prayer. We may perhaps, for the present, put it thus, that we cannot change the will of God, which is grace, and which even Christ never changed but only revealed or effected; but we can change the intention of God, which is a manner of treatment, in the interest of grace, according to the situation of the hour.

If we are guided by the Bible we have much ground for this view of prayer. *Does not Christ set more value upon the importunity than on submission?* "Knock, and it shall be opened." I would refer also not only to the parable of the unjust judge, but to the incident of the Syrophenician woman, where her wit, faith, and importunity together did actually change our Lord's intention and break His custom. Then there is Paul beseeching the Lord thrice for a boon; and urging us to be instant, insistent, continual in prayer. We have Jacob wrestling. We have Abraham pleading, yea, haggling, with God for Sodom. We have Moses interceding for Israel and asking God to blot his name out of the book of life, if that were needful to save Israel. We have Job facing God, withstanding Him, almost bearding Him, and extracting revelation. And we have Christ's own struggle with the Father in Gethsemane.

It is a wrestle on the greatest scale—all manhood taxed as in some great war, or some great negotiation of State. And the effect is exhaustion often. No, the result of true prayer is not always peace.

II. As to the second point. This wrestle is in a certain sense a resisting of God. You cannot have wrestling otherwise; but you may have Christian fatalism. It is not mere wrestling with ourselves, our ignorance, our selfwill. That is not prayer, but self-torment. Prayer is wrestling with God. And it is better to fall thus into the hands of God than of man—even than your own. It is a resistance that God loves. It is quite foreign to a godless, self-willed, defiant resistance. In love there is a kind of resistance that enhances it. The resistance of love is a quite different thing from the resistance of hostility. The yielding to one you love is very different from capitulating to an enemy:

> *Two constant lovers, being joined in one,*
> *Yielding unto each other yield to none—*

i.e. to no foreign force, no force foreign to the love which makes them one.

So when God yields to prayer in the name of Christ, to the prayer of faith and love, He yields to Himself who inspired it, as he sware by Himself since none was greater. Christian prayer is the Spirit praying in us. It is prayer in the solidarity of the Kingdom. It is a continuation of Christ's prayer, which in Gethsemane was a wrestle, ἀγωνία with the Father. But if so, it is God pleading with God, God dealing with God—as the true atonement must be. And when God yields it is not to an outside influence He yields, but to Himself.

Let me make it still more plain. When we resist the will of God we may be resisting what God wills to be temporary and to be resisted, what He wills to be intermediary and transcended. We resist because God wills we should. We are not limiting God's will, any more than our moral freedom limits it. That freedom is the image of His, and, in a sense, part of His. We should defraud Him and His freedom if we did not exercise ours. So the prayer which resists His dealing may be part of His will and its fulfillment.

Does God not will the existence of things for us to resist, to grapple with? Do we ourselves not appoint problems and make difficulties for those we teach, for the very purpose of their overcoming them? We set questions to children of which we know the answer quite well. The real answer to our will and purpose is not the solution but the grappling, the wrestling. And we may properly give a reward not for the correct answer, but for the hard and honest effort. That work is the prayer; and it has its reward apart from the solution.

That is a principle of education with us. So it may be with God. But I mean a good deal more by this than what is called the reflex action of prayer. If that were all it would introduce an unreality into prayer. We should be praying for exercise, not for action. It would be prayer with a theological form, which yet expects no more than a psychological effect. It would be a prayer which is not sure that God is really more interested in us than we are in Him. But I mean that God's education has a lower stage for us and a higher. He has a lower will and a higher, a prior and a posterior. And the purpose of the lower will is that it be resisted and struggled through to the higher. By God's will (let us say) you are born in a home where your father's earnings are a few shillings a week, like many an English labourer. Is it God's will that you acquiesce in that and never strive out of it? It is God's will that you are there. Is it God's will that you should not resist being there? Nay, it may be His will that you should wisely resist it, and surmount His lower, His initial, will, which is there for the purpose. That is to say, it is His will that you resist, antagonize, His will. And so it is with the state of childhood altogether.

Again: Is disease God's will? We all believe it often is— even if man is to blame for it. It may be, by God's will, the penalty on human ignorance, negligence, or sin. But let us suppose there were only a few cases where disease is God's will. It was so in the lower creatures, before man lived, blundered, or sinned. Take only one such case. Is it God's will that we should lie down and let the disease have its way? Why, a whole profession exists to say no. Medicine exists as an antagonism to disease, even when you can say that disease is God's will and His punishment of sin. A doctor will tell you that resignation is one of his foes. He begins to grow hopeless if the patient is so resigned from the outset as to make no effort, if there be no will to live. Resistance to this ordinance of God's is the doctor's business and the doctor's ally. And why? Because God ordained disease for the purpose of being resisted; he ordained the resistance, that from the conflict man might come out the stronger, and more full of resource and dominion over nature.

Again, take death. It is God's will. It is in the very structure of man, in the divine economy. It is not the result of sin; it was there before sin. Is it to be accepted without demur? Are doctors impious who resist it? Are we sinning when we shrink from it? Does not the life of most people consist in the effort to escape it, in the struggle for a living? So also when we pray and wrestle for another's life, for our

dear one's life. "Sir, come down ere my child die." The man was impatient. How familiar we are with his kind! "Do, please, leave your religious talk, which I don't understand; get doing something;

cure my child." But was that an impious prayer? It was ignorant, practical, British, but not quite faithless. And it was answered, as many a similar prayer has been. But, then, if death be God's will, to resist it is to resist God's will. Well, it is His will that we should. Christ, who always did God's will, resisted His own death, slipped away from it often, till the hour came; and even then He prayed with all His might against it when it seemed inevitable. "If it be possible, release Me." He was ready to accept it, but only in the last resort, only if there was no other way, only after every other means had been exhausted. To the end He cherished the fading hope that there might be some other way. He went to death voluntarily, freely, but—shall we say reluctantly? ἑκών, ἀέκοντί γε θυμῷ—resisting the most blessed act of God's will that was ever performed in heaven or on earth; resisting, yet sure to acquiesce when that was God's clear will.

The whole of nature, indeed, is the will of God, and the whole of grace is striving with nature. It is our nature to have certain passions. That is God's will. But it is our calling of God to resist them as much as to gratify them. They are there as God's will to be resisted as much as indulged. The redemption from the natural man includes the resistance to it, and the release of the soul from what God Himself appointed as its lower stages— never as its dwelling-place, and never its tomb. So far prayer is on the lines of evolution.

Obedience is the chief end. But obedience is not mere submission, mere resignation. It is not always acquiescence, even in prayer. We obey God as much when we urge our suit, and make a *real* petition of it, as when we accept His decision; as much as when we try to change His will as when we bow to it. The kingdom of heaven suffereth violence. There is a very fine passage in Dante, Parad. 20:94 (Longfellow):

> *From fervent love, and from that living hope*
> *That overcometh the divine volition.*
> *Not in the way that man o'ercometh man;*
> *We conquer it because it will be conquered,*
> *And, conquered, conquers by benignity.*

It is His will—His will of grace—that prayer should prevail with Him and extract blessings. And how we love the grace that so concedes them! The answer to prayer is not the complaisance of a playful power lightly yielding to the playful egoism of His favourites. "Our antagonist is our helper." To struggle with Him is one way of doing His will. To resist is one way of saying, "Thy will be done." It was God's will that Christ should deprecate the death God required. It pleased God as much as His submission to death. But could it have been pleasing to Him that Christ should pray so, if no prayer could ever possibly change God's will? Could Christ have prayed so in that belief? Would faith ever inspire us to pray if the God of our faith must be unmoved by prayer? The prayer that goes to an inflexible God, however good He is, is prayer that rises more from human need than from God's own revelation, or from Christian faith (where Christian prayer should rise). It is His will, then, that we should pray against what seems His will, and what, for the lower stage of our growth, *is* His will. And all this without any unreality whatever.

Let us beware of a pietist fatalism which thins the spiritual life, saps the vigour of character, makes humility mere acquiescence, and piety only feminine, by banishing the will from prayer as much as thought has been banished from it. "The curse of so much religion" (I have quoted Meridith) "is that men cling to God with their weakness rather than with their strength."

The popularity of much acquiescence is not because it is holier, but because it is easier. And an easy gospel is the consumption that attacks Christianity. It is the phthisis to faith.

Once come to think that we best say "Thy will be done" when we acquiesce, when we resign, and not also when we struggle and wrestle, and in time all effort will seem less pious than submission. And so we fall into the ecclesiastical type of religion, drawn from an age whose first virtue was submission to outward superiors. We shall come to canonize decorum and subduedness in life and worship (as the Episcopal Church with its monarchical ideas of religion has done). We shall think more of order than of effort, more of law than of life, more of fashion than of faith, of good form than of great power. But was subduedness *the* mark of the New Testament men? Our religion may gain some beauty in this way, but it loses vigour. It may gain style, but it loses power. It is good form, but mere æsthetic piety. It may consecrate manners, but it impoverishes the mind. It may regulate prayer by the precepts of intelligence instead of the needs and faith of the soul. It may feed certain pensive emotions, but it may emasculate will, secularize energy, and empty character. And so we decline to a state of things in which we have no shocking sins—yes, and no splendid souls; when all souls are dully correct, as like as shillings, but as thin, and as cheap.

All our forms and views of religion have their test in prayer. Lose the importunity of prayer, reduce it to soliloquy, or even to colloquy, with God, lose the real conflict of will and will, lose the habit of wrestling and the hope of prevailing with God, make it mere walking with God in friendly talk; and, precious as that is, yet you tend to lose the reality of prayer at last. In principle you make it mere conversation instead of the soul's great action. You lose the food of character, the renewal of will. You may have beautiful prayers—but as ineffectual as beauty so often is, and as fleeting. And so in the end you lose the reality of religion. Redemption turns down into mere revelation, faith to assent, and devotion to a phase of culture. For you lose the *power* of the cross and so of the soul.

Resist God, in the sense of rejecting God, and you will not be able to resist any evil. But resist God in the sense of closing with God, cling to Him with your strength, not your weakness only, with your active and not only your passive faith, and He will give you strength. Cast yourself into His arms not to be caressed but to wrestle with Him. He loves that holy war. He may be too many for you, and lift you from your feet. But it will be to lift you from earth, and set you in the heavenly places which are theirs who fight the good fight and lay hold of God as their eternal life. ❦

THIS LIFE AND THE NEXT:
The Effect on This Life of Faith in Another
1918

Chapter One

IS LIFE'S BREVITY ITS VALUE?

George Eliot's "Jubal." The effect of life's brevity on its value. Death good for
life only as it promises life beyond. The moral action of immortality on life due
to the enhanced value of personality.

I am not proposing to speak about the grounds in this life of a belief in
another, but about the reaction of that belief upon this life. It is not a
question about the basis of a belief in immortality, but about its moral
rebound. We often hear from pulpits of the effect of this life on the next;
but this is not a pulpit, and what we are now to dwell on is rather the
reaction of the next life on this. Sometimes we are bidden to turn from
considering what we do for posterity to realise what posterity does for
us— which is much. Mr. Benjamin Kidd lectured in 1906 at the Royal
Institution on this subject. "The significance of the Future in the theory of
organic evolution." Well, it is great. But the future has a greater
significance still for our *spiritual* evolution. Posterity does much for our
souls. We are to think, then, of the reflex action on us of the idea of
immortality, or, in a more Christian way, the power over us of an endless
life in Christ, where the gain in dying is but more of our career in Christ.
If to live is Christ, to die is more Christ.

May I be personal and reminiscent? The formative part of my life was
spent in a world ruled by the giants of the Victorian days, of whom one of
the most potent was George Eliot. And I can well remember when her
poem, "The Legend of Jubal," came out in *Macmillan's Magazine*. I was a
student in an ancient university in a far northern city. A few of us seized
the magazine as soon as it could be bought, and took it out for
consumption one morning by the banks of the Highland river that there
ends in the North Sea its passionate yet pensive life. George Eliot was not
at her best as a poet, and I do not think that "Jubal" is as much read now
as her lyric with the same motive, which probably will live in the
anthologies.O may I join the Choir Invisible,

> *Of those immortal dead who live again*
> *In souls made better by their presence, etc.*

But "Jubal" was more dramatic, more picturesque, and at the same time more philosophic, which appealed to us as we then were. It had a story, and it had reflection. And one passage that impressed myself deeply that morning was the lines describing the tender value given to life by the new sense of its mortality. According to this legend, death had never entered the world till an accident brought it. As the finality of the sleep came home to the race, its effect was revolutionary. And the nature of the effect was more feverish energy, and an affection tender because brief.

> And a new spirit from that time came o'er
> The race of Cain; soft idlesse was no more,
> But even the sunshine had a heart of care,
> Smiling with hidden dread—a mother fair
> Who, folding to her heart a dying child,
> Beams with feigned joy that but makes sadness mild.
> Death now was lord of life, and at his word
> Time, vague as air before, new terrors stirred,
> With measured wing now audibly arose
> Thrilling through all things to some unknown close.
> Now glad content by clutching haste was torn,
> And work grew eager, and device was born.
> It seemed the light was never loved before,
> Now each man said, "I will go and come no more."
> No budding branch, no pebble from the brook,
> No form, no shadow, but new dearness took
> From the one thought that life must have an end.
> And the last parting now began to send
> Diffusive dread through love and wedded bliss,
> Thrilling them into finer tenderness.
> Thus to Cain's race death was tear-watered seed
> Of various life, and action-shaping need.

Now, who does not feel the touching truth in this? Who has not clung with new tenderness to the dear one whose days are numbered? How many have recognised their angels only as they were leaving them? Even in health who has not stayed the impatient word, at the remembrance that the time together is at most so short, and might be shortened to an hour? Who has not felt a new fascination in the world's beauty as our lease of it runs out, even if we have had many fits of disillusion about it?

But what if this became our general attitude to the world If the ruling feeling of society were that of brief life, sure sorrow, and eternal loss! If this feeling became a social principle! If we all lived in the conviction that death ended all, and was no new departure! What would the effect of that be? Would it not be like that of alcohol—first bustle, then blight, excitement and then stupidity? If we only looked forward to Jubal's goal, to immersion in the All—

> *Quitting mortality, a quenched sun wave,*
> *The all creating presence was his grave.*

would there be much creative vigour left in life under that doom?

A far greater poem on immortality came from the Victorians than George Eliot's. There was "In Memoriam." And we can call it great, whatever critical reserves we may have about certain aspects of that spiritual achievement to-day. It is a poem that ought to be read and studied to-day more than ever before. Our preachers of comfort and hope should make much of it, and, even if they quote little, draw much from it, while they add something. It is better and holier than ghosts for the comfort and making of the soul. Well, there is a line in it which is very true to the psychology of sorrow. Unless we can be sure of love's immortality, Tennyson says, a blight would come on love, it would be

> *Half dead to know that it could die.*

So it would be. It would take the energy out of us, and the zest, if we came, habitually and collectively, to believe that death ended all, and that we only survived in our life's resultant among men, and not in its personality with God.

We might grant that death teaches us much as to the value of life, and that life without death would become a very hard and coarse thing. With the abolition of death would vanish the uncertainty which educates faith, the mystery, the tragedy, which makes life so great, the sense of another world which gives such dignity and meaning to this, the range of sympathy that flows from believing that our affections are not for this world alone. Erase death, and Tithonus tells us life sinks at last into drab weariness. Its noblest, dearest interest ebbs and fades. Its tragedy and its chivalry both go. We should end by having no concern but feeding, drowsing, prancing and feeding again. Love, valour, pity, sacrifice; charm, music and all the nameless spell of nature and of personality; courtesy and reverence, all the sweet fine things of life that are tributes to soul, and that death seems to cut short most painfully—those are the things which would really die out if we succeeded in indefinitely averting death.

But, of course, it is not death that preserves these after all. It is the conviction that death is a crisis which opens a new phase of life. It is the conviction, latent or patent, of immortality and spiritual growth in it. How much more true is St. Paul: "Wherefore, my beloved brethren, be ye steadfast, immovable, ever abounding in the work of the Lord, for as much as ye know that your labour is not in vain in the Lord." The work is the Lord's. It is there not simply to meet man's need, but God's purpose. That purpose is a greater action-shaping power than our need is. It is not true to suggest, as this poem does, that death, understood as final, could have set afoot the new future of energy or desire, the eagerness of work, the strength of society, or the tenderness of affection. For men were already living in a city, "The City of Cain," before the accident took place or the stimulus of death came in. The enterprise of civilisation had started well on its way. Did it need an accidental death to stir in the children of the first murderer the terrors that made life tragic, intense, and pathetic? It is not the poverty and brevity of life that draws out its resources; it is its sense of fulness and power. It is strength that is the root of action, not need. "Action-shaping need," yes, but not action-creating. Action *shaping*! Yes, but what *inspires* action—moral action as distinct from mere energy, mere movement? What makes the good will which attends at all to the needs of others and does not just feed our own? A stream is not effective which just spreads out and flows into each hole it finds. It dies of diversion. That phrase was a piece of eggshell which clung to George Eliot from the hatching of her mind by George Henry Lewes, as anyone may see who reads his now forgotten books. Need may shape action, but it does not create action; which is the child of wealth not poverty, of the soul's fulness and not of its death. We were created by God not out of his poverty and his need of company, but out of his overflowing wealth of love and his passion to multiply joy.

The passage is fine poetry; it is true to certain phases of experience, but it is a pathetic fallacy all the same. It partakes of that very sentimentalism in religion which the author's school unduly despised,—and succumbed to. Sentiment has its dear place, but it is demoralising to construe life by the sentiment of its phases instead of the revelation in its conscience. Love is not fondness. Sentiment is not life. Sentimentalism is not cherishing sentiment but living by it, at the cost of moral realities. Like art, it is life's friend, but not its guide. And it is the peculiar peril of a religion of love which is not understood as holy love.

Of course it would be unfair to say that with the decay of a belief in immortality morality would straightway cease. At least that would be putting it too bluntly. All morality would not cease. The nobler souls would still for a time find goodness good. And the rest would find incumbent on them a utilitarian ethic in the interest of the society of which they -were a part. For a long time at least this would be so. But all the time there would be question whether a utilitarian ethic is really moral, whether you find your moral soul in it or not.

This finding of the soul raises an issue more direct and just. Would moral vigour, courage, enterprise, civilisation continue to rise and progress under the condition supposed? Would the disbelief in immortality lead in the end to the finding of the soul or the losing of it? Would it lead to the gain of public morale or its loss? For I mean the phrase less in the theological sense than the sociological. Even if the disbelief in our soul's future did not arrest morality, would it not lead to a lowered sense of that which is behind morality and is the condition of it—the value of personality? And would that not in the end produce the same effect as the relaxation of moral sanctions—especially on society? Public morality would sink to class egoism or national patriotism, and finally it would be abjured. The moral value of the individual would sink—as it has done in Germany, for instance, where there is no general belief in immortality, and where the individual withers and the State is more and more. And this means the corruption of the State itself, which ceases to be a moral entity, and becomes the prey of the militarist gamblers in power. The people would be brutalised. The citizen would really cease to be a citizen. The free elector would disappear and become *Kanonen-futter* fed up to the guns. Under such a creed the vital natural man would cease to concern himself with posterity; therefore he would slacken in public concern. His interests would be but egoist, and his activity but for the order of the day. He would say of everything, "it will last my time." His policy would be from hand to mouth, with a growing tendency to the mouth and its egoism. The shortening of the soul's career would lead to the impoverishment of its interests. It would be emptied and not merely curtailed.

Pantheism or Positivism, of course, does not think so. It says that each moment left would receive an increase of value, like the Sibylline books. If you reduce the supply you increase the price of life. Well, that looks plausible if you treat moral realities and moral issues commercially, if you regulate the soul by economics, or politics by mere prudence. But that course has been a failure. We are now on the other tack. We try to regulate economics by the soul, wages by the standard of living, profits with a prime regard to wage. The soul does not work by the law of supply and demand. You do not increase the value of mankind by decimation. To reduce population is not the way to a vigorous and lasting community.

Nor is it so if we reduce the content of each life by stopping it at a point. On the contrary each person would then drop to pursue the line of least resistance. If I am to die in six months I won't get new clothes. If I must get them, shoddy will do. A jerry-built house will serve me; and the children can move to a new one when this begins to crack. Burdens would be thrown on the aftercomers. Those upon whom the end of the world should come would be crushed under the silt of the obligations left to them before it arrived. Neglect would not be felt to be criminal. Whereas the sense that each moment is of value for an eternal life is like the soul's sense that it is not its own but is the subject and property of Christ—it raises the soul's sense of its dignity, and therefore raises also its inner wealth and energy. The things it does are worth while. And it *will* matter to us a hundred years hence what we do to-day or omit. If there were no other consideration, there would be this. If I am to be extinguished at seventy I need not be too much concerned about my soul's perfection, to say nothing of becoming perfect as God is. And that is the end of moral effort in due course. The pursuit of perfection is a greater moral influence than the passion for power.

The finality of death in the *vital* sense leads to all the low temperatures in life which I have been describing. Its finality in the *moral* sense leads to all the enormities which we associate with the doctrine of a double predestination.

Clearly in this life some are better off than others, and some are morally better. That means, if there be a ruling power in human affairs, a doctrine of election in one sense or another. Now, to a doctrine of election we do not need to object. Aimer *c'est choisir.* Love is preferential. But two things we must insist on. First, it is not an election to prerogative, privilege, and exemption, but to God's own responsibility, service, and sacrifice. The Captain of the elect came to serve. For it is an election of love. On th·t the Gospel is clear. And second, it is the action of a moral process that goes on after death. The fate of the soul is not finally determined then. Those lives and those generations which were elect here were chosen for the service and good of those whose turn was not to come in this life Education, or experience, which begins in this life does not fructify in certain cases till another. An election to a certain place in this life does rot mean that we are condemned to that place for ever. Death does not fix the moral position of the soul irretrievably. Other methods of moral discipline lie beyond. We cannot be occupied there with the sordid trivialities which engage so much of our time here. That is to say, we are not predestined for ever to the place or state in which we die. Does that not take the sting out of a doctrine of predestination? We are all predestined in love to life sooner or later, *if we will.* An election is to certain stages and methods of endless growth. It is selection for cycles and crises of moral evolution. It is not that some are chosen for eternal life and some are doomed to eternal death. That was a nightmare which grew from the association of the truth of election with the falsehood of death's finality. And its tendency is to reduce the value of the soul, like the notion that death is final in the sense of extinction. It is a doctrine which for the popular mind has blighted the great name of Calvin, and prevented us from realising him as one of the very greatest makers of history, and the creator through Puritanism of modem democracy. Calvin only applied consistently that idea of death's finality which all Protestants held. Take his doctrine of election, relieve it of the notion of death's absolute arrest, and you have a great panorama of development which makes this life organic, with all the possibilities of an endless growth beyond. It is the abuse of Calvinism, as it is the abuse of purgatory, that has done the mischief. So we discard the extreme of orthodoxy as we do the extreme of negation about the finality of death. And we realise the immense effect exerted on this life and its uses by the faith of another life, which is the continued action of the Kingdom of God and the discipline of the moral soul. But why did predestination, as a matter of fact, not lower personality? Why was it the religion of the strongest men of the day and for long after—the makers of history? Why did it not act like Fatalism in Islam? Because it was the action not of a Fate but of a living God and a free God of Grace, however distorted the conception of His mode of action. The greatness of God's free and holy sovereignty overbore the weakness of the rest of the creed. He was a living God and a free, and not a force, a process, or a fate. And the history of Calvinism shows that a supreme concern for God's freedom is the best motive and guarantee for man's.

Chapter Two

THE EGOISM OF IMMORTALITY

The egoism of Christ. The fear of punishment and the hope of heaven. Demoralisation possible. But my neighbour's immortality. The worth of our mortality to God. The egoism of the anti-egoists. Immoral immortality.

The belief in immortality has been charged with egoism. But there is egoism and egoism. And in Christ Himself there is a unique combination of self-sacrifice and self-assertion.

In what sense can we say there was an egoism in Jesus? "Eternal life is to believe in Me," "Because I live ye shall live also," "I shall judge the world," "Inasmuch as ye did it to these ye did it to me." These, with many similar claims, indicate what, in a mere man, would be egoism carried even to imperial megalomania Yet it does not offend us. It offends us no more than the egoism of God—who is a sole and jealous God—or love's egoism with its monogamy (the social counterpart of monotheism) and its exclusive right. As a matter of fact, the egoism of Christ is in the same category as the absoluteness of God; and such egoism in God is the blessing of the world. It is its moral stability. It is its holiness. To worship it is not to be infected with egoism, but to lose it. To glorify God is to find our soul, which is lost in its own pursuit. It is not egoism to court an immortality which is the communion and obedience of His absolute life.

It might, of course, be said that we should not speak of an egoism in God, and that we had better betake ourselves to a less familiar but more fitting word, and speak of His Egoity. But that hardly meets the case if by the new term we think to avoid the idea that God seeks His own. He does seek His own, since He can seek no higher. Like us, He must seek the highest. Could He devote Himself only to an inferior? His grace to us is a debt to Himself. And our faith is a faith that nothing is well with us until we are at His service in that quest, that seeking of His own. For He is a holy God, with a life self-determined and turned in on Himself with an infinite self-sufficiency, just as surely as He is a God of love with a life outgoing. He is at once self-contained and communicative. Without a centripetal force the heavens cannot stand. It were a slack piety, and one drawn from our sentiment more than from His revelation, to treat Him as one whose whole concern is to give, with nothing in His energy of that self-regard which makes a character worth much to receive. An effusive God cannot be a holy God, and such love is not divine. It is not self-seeking, therefore, to cherish an immortality of divine service. Man's true self is the worship of God's. But to this point I shall return.

I do not mean to say much on the common theme (however valuable) of the effect on this life of a doctrine of retribution, of rewards and punishments, in another. For this is not the only action of a belief in immortality. And some might say it was not the chief. They might say its chief effect was on the soul's belief in itself and its dignity. They would question the worth of goodness done for a reward. Many would ask how reward consists with grace, a wage with a free gift—deep points these that I do not stop to discuss here. As to punishment, they might also go on to say that the fear of it has been more debasing than the hope of reward; because people as they grow worse tend to think more about punishment, while as they grow better they think less of reward. The reward is not a motive with the people who deserve best, but the punishment is a motive with the people who deserve least. And in a religion of moral redemption a doctrine cannot be of chief value if it weigh more with the bad than with the good.

Also, I will do little more than mention the effect of the waning belief in eternal torment, both upon life and upon some public matters like capital punishment, or war. If the hangman fixes a soul in a certain state for ever, I do not see how any crime could justify any State in the capital sentence; nor do I see how it could morally go to war. But there does follow on the decay of this belief a certain levity about death, judgment, and the soul. The soul is taken more lightly if its sin is no more than this life or a brief purgatory can deal with. The whole meaning of life is lowered. And with life's reduced value there comes a reduced sense of life's sanctity and public order. This levity of doctrine has gone beyond a protest against the eternity of punishment, and has led to dropping the idea of any hell or judgment at all, as if we could cheat judgment by dying. And so it leads to the loss of such life-wisdom as begins in fear, and rises to reverence and awe. It is all part of the loss of moral tone in religion through the general abeyance of the sense of the holy and of sin.

In the matter of reward, it is charged by some that an immortal life, as it involves the infinite expansion of the self, magnifies our egoism, makes us take ourselves too seriously, and thereby tends to develop an anti-social frame of mind which cannot bear to be out of anything and always wants the front. The criticism itself reflects the old anti-social individualism. But there is no doubt that some forms of the belief do have the effect named. It is so in Islam, which is mostly a religion of conquest rather than of civilisation. It was so even with the Moors in Spain. But it is so also nearer home. Germany means civilisation, but by racial dominion. If the doctrine of immortality is held only on subjective grounds, it is quite likely to end in religious egoism. It is a fundamental principle of all I say on the subject that a sure belief in immortality does not rest where philosophy puts it, but where religion puts it. It is not founded on the nature of the psychic organism, but on its relation to Another. I mean that if it is based on the indestructible nature of the soul substance, or upon an untamed passion for adventure, or upon endless curiosity, or upon our instinct and thirst for personal perfection, or upon our native moral greatness, or upon any such stoic forms of self-esteem, or even self-respect, it is quite likely (if you go on far enough to give scope for its gravitation) to end downward in a supreme care for *my* immortality, whatever becomes of yours. And that ends in people elbowing each other out of the way to get at the elixir of life, or to dip in this Bethesda pool for eternity. But these are philosophic considerations, or æsthetic or egoistic concerns, which are not really religions. They detach man from God, the Lord and Giver of Life. At least they do not found on man's union with God. They set him, with his claims and presumptions, over against God, as the deadly way of Pharisaism was. Man may come thus to behave like a spoilt beauty, unschooled in duty, and craving for attentions without end. The Creator may even be reminded that He has made the soul immortal, that He cannot recall the initial gift of life, and that the soul bears stamped on it a signed concession of eternal rights. All that is egoist enough, or can become so. And I do not remember where we have Christian warrant for believing that man was created immortal.

But the case is quite altered if I am not thinking chiefly about my living for ever. I may be thinking of some dearer to me than life, for whose salvation beyond the grave I would risk my own. Or I may be thinking of the immortality of the race; which is a more potent influence on the present than a multitude of individual immortalities, because the efficiency of an organic group is greater than the sum total of the efficiencies of its units. A nation is great, a crowd is not. But still more is the case altered if I am thinking about our glorifying God for ever whether as a soul or as a race. All is different if I am thinking of what my soul means for others. Most of all when I am thinking of what it means for

God and not of what it means for me, if I am not making Him to serve my egoism, if I am not thinking of the paradise of Heaven but of the purpose of God and His righteousness. If my immortality is due to God's gift, it is due to His *incessant* gift and creation, and not to an infinite lease of life which He signed at the beginning. That is to say, it can go on only by communion with Him. But that is not the communion of love between equals, but of grace between unequals. And whatever we owe to God's grace glorifies Him far more than it glorifies us. What man tends to say, whether he do it naïve or philosophically, is, "Because I live I shall live." But what Christ says, and what faith hears is, "Because I live ye shall live also." He alone has life in Himself, and we have it by His gift and by union with Him either here or hereafter. It makes a vast difference between the philosophic and the religious treatment of immortality when we remember this—that in the Bible the supreme interest and the final ground of immortality was not the continuity of an organism, physical or psychical, but of a relation. The ground of the belief was not that such an organism must go on, but that a life in God, and especially in the risen Christ, could not die. The philosophic way is egoist, however large and fine; it does justice to that excellent creature man. It is anthropocentric. The other way (of faith) is concerned with God, His stake in us, His purpose with us, and our service of His Kingdom and honour. It is theocentric.

If this were a mere matter of debate and we wanted to make a point, we might, of course, remind an objector that if there is egoism in some of the hopes of immortality, there is egoism in many of the results of its denial. If death be dissolution, self knows that it has but a short time, and must make the most of it. And there is no power to forbid or limit. So it piles gain on gain, power on power, pleasure on pleasure, with an energy that nothing abates or deflects, and with a deep sense of the resources of money to neutralise consequences, still pain, and avert death. So duty easily comes to be a negligible quantity. And the man is ruled by the will to live with all his might the little span on which he may count. But the events round us would show, if nothing else did, that such brief egoism in due course reduces the value and power of each ego even to enjoy. It reduces the value of moral personality, and society sinks to worse than death.

But it is not here a mere matter of debate and of making points. Let it be owned that in cases it has happened, and does happen, that the passion for poring on a future life has starved the passion due to this life, and bleached it of reality. (Though, to tell the truth, I wish more people pored on these things now.) It has taken the monk out of his helping place in the world into a hiding place; and it has put him into a cellular self, regardless of either the goods or the duties of this life. By his celibacy it robbed the world of the propagation of the best lives to an extent only equal to that in which by this war we have lost them. But the hope that produces such a result does not get its substance from positive faith, which is occupied with Christ and not with our future, and with a Christ who had much sense of life's joy and zest. The dream of a life to come can be used only to pamper the self; and that means to empty of reality the life that now is. It is a non-moral faith; for if social duty be unreal, all is unreal. Our real and great hope is not that one day we shall die to the world, but that this day we live to others and to God.

To such misled people as I have named the future was a hope that starved the present. But there are those to whom it is a fear, which also crushes it. The dread of hell is an obsession that has distorted many lives. But that again has been because their future was more to them than Christ was, and they were more tied in self than freed in a Saviour. With a keen conscience and a vivid imagination, a future that is merely life prolonged and not reborn may well become filled with fears and loaded with care. But in Christ the future is given us filled with a regenerate power and glory, where fear is sanctified into penitence and vigilance, sorrow glorifies God and becomes service, and love is realised in ready obedience. Our total ignorance of a future which faith does not fill with Christ can be a more debasing source of fear than a hell which we know serves the purposes of God. Without Christ and the love of Him, the past and the future may equally loom upon us, and beetle over our present.

And not upon us only. We are unsure and anxious not only about ourselves, but about the loved and lost. If our personal outlook be a blank we can perhaps be Stoics, but what of them? Is it any comfort to our love, does it not add a sting to death and put a slur on love, that they may have ceased to be? It is one thing to commit them to Christ, who fills (and is) our future and theirs; but it is another thing to trust to Christ neither ourselves nor them. And yet to-day there are thousands who have far more passion to see their dead than to know Christ; one word from a *revenant* were worth all that Christ has said or could say; a frame of mind which not only disappoints moral hope, but leaves them too easy victims to the occult and all its train. It is neither religion nor ethic, but magic. It does not produce religious belief. "If they believe not Moses and the prophets, neither would they believe to Christian purpose if one rose from the dead." One does not like to seem untender to the bereaved, but surely it is a poor ending to high-minded people when they find in West End mediums a certainty about their dear ones which they had renounced in Christ, and more comfort in the ghosts' banalities than in the power or silence of Him. It is always an unstable frame of mind and a low form of faith to be, even in the name of love, more anxious about immortality than about being in Christ or in God's Kingdom. And it is dangerous, because it exposes affection to the advances of magic, the variation of temperament, and the spell of the occult—as if the chief secret of life were in the preternatural or the subliminal and not in a moral revelation. But, on the other hand, we can so view the other life in Christ, and so care for the righteousness of His endless Kingdom that we give up the dearest souls to its historic service with tears of such noble sorrow as the mother weeps in sad joy when she sends of her daughter as a bride.

Chapter Three

THE EGOISM OF GOD

The immortals not an elite. The egoism of God is the blessing of the world. The moral paradox and miracle of holy love.

To keep saying that our immortality is not so much a matter of our psychical structure, but of our relation to God. And not to God only, but also to our fellows. Let us think of the future not only religiously, as God's gift to us, but ethically, as the destiny of others rather than of ourselves, or as the destiny of our whole kind. Its issues go to the horizon of the whole race. If the future do not belong to them all as it does to us we become an elite. The immortals become a caste. They exist, not in grades of glory (which we may well think), but in a monopoly of prerogative. Without are dogs. If we are more concerned about our own future than about that of our kind we destroy the Kingdom of God. We turn moral considerations out of the large action of history, and we cut the tap root of the unity of mankind, which at the last lies in the conscience and its salvation. The Christian believes in the unity of man only because he believes in the righteousness of the universal Kingdom and the new Humanity in Christ. Also, if we are more concerned about a future compensation for the ills and losses of life to ourselves than to others, we soon come to treat them as our tools. If there be no compensation, such as only another world can give, to these millions of sufferers, all silent but for a Pleader in heaven, and unknown except to the mercy that forgets nothing—if there be no compensation to these dim and common populations of age after age, that fact reduces their whole value, and therewith the value of the soul everywhere. And with that goes the concern at last for human life or suffering. Men come to seem not worth compensating. God has not cast His mantle over their mangled corpses. But we cannot so leave them. If they do not ask, we must ask for them. We must press God to take order for them. Otherwise we lose respect, to say nothing of love, for them. We belong then to a caste and not to mankind. And if the caste so formed be a coarsely egoist, if it be a militarist, caste, with a dynastic caste within it; and if, moreover, the belief in the soul and its destiny die out in that land, then the lives of the millions are but food for the guns, and even the caste itself becomes the vassal of the dynasty. And the whole of Humanity becomes but the manure in which this monopoly grows.

But a bold spirit may go further and say that the God of the everlasting Kingdom is but an Egoist. He is a dynast. The very unity of the race may be but the footstool of His throne. If his object in our eternal life is His own eternal glory, that transfers the egoism to Him. It makes Him the Arch-Egoist, the Cæsar of heaven. And how can an Egoist worship the Arch-Egoist, however much he might envy Him? There is a kind of thinking, more or less popular, which takes to that somewhat crude criticism as the liberal way. That is its form of protest against the domineering sovereignty of God in the old orthodoxy, for which it has nothing but protest—no interpretation. The Church in preaching a holy God, a jealous God, a sole God, is charged with preaching an egoist God; and the Christian course, it is said, must be to discard Him for a God whose holiness is only purity, and whose being as pure love is wholly spent in bestowing Himself on His creation without a thought of His own self or dignity. He keeps us immortal for our good, and He is not thinking of His own sanctity or glory at all.

But this is as one-sided as orthodoxy could ever be, and for moral man much more fatal. It makes God but the servant of man, the father of a spoilt child. Man picks up all the egoism such a God discards. The Christian revelation is a God of *holy* love and not of hearty love only; but this tendency drops the holy and keeps only to the love. It offers us a God of dear motherhood and not holy fatherhood. It has taken this swing in the rebound from an orthodoxy that made everything of God's justice and nothing of His love. But if we cannot hold both sides of a paradox we are not fit for the kingdom of heaven. The God of holy love is a paradox. He is not only a mystery; we might even welcome that in an a æsthetic way. But He is an aggressive mystery; and that irritates us. He combines two things which, as thoughts, we can adjust in no theology; but we can grasp them by a faith of their reconcilement in a person with whom we have to do—a moral reconcilement, and not one worked out by the process of an idea.

Consider. A God of holy love, a God whose love we do not only enjoy but worship, must be a God that orbs into a perfect sun as well as sheds His goodly rays. He must be a God concentrated as much as a God communicative; else what can He communicate? He does owe something to that closed self which blesses all to their fill. Except as a real self He cannot bless. He would have nothing to give. His self-revelation would only be effusion. But His transcendence in the Old Testament does not cease in His condescendence in the New. It even rises to the place the *Holy* Spirit takes there as a constituent of Godhead. His love is homeward bound as well as outward bound. If it go forth always, it also returns incessantly on Himself. Systole is as endless as diastole. And the synthesis of these two movements can only be realised in the energy of His living person; it cannot be set out in any rational harmony. It involves the miracle of personality and will. That the holy should ever touch the sinful is the great miracle of moral reality. A holy God is more than altruist. His holiness is not egoism. His absolute founds every relative, and does not destroy it.

In the Bible, things, or places, or people are holy which are set apart for God; God is holy as He is set apart for Himself. Things are holy as they are for God; He is holy as He is for Himself. We are holy as belonging to Him; He is holy as belonging to Himself, as absolute possessor of Himself, by gift of none. He is possessor of Himself, and of all in Him that houses and blesses us. In the Father's heart are many mansions. For the creature to be holy is *to be for God;* for God Himself to be holy is *to be God.* His holiness is the complete accord of His will and His nature. It is not an attribute of God; it is His name, and being, and infinite value. But if the holiness do not go out to cover, imbue, conquer, and sanctify all things, if it do not give itself in love, it is the less holy. It is but partial and not absolute. As holy He must subdue all and bless all. God's holiness is the fundamental principle not of our worship only, but of His whole saving revelation and economy of love. It is the moral principle of both love and grace. It is love's content, it is what love brings or grace gives. And it is the warrant of love's eternity. For only the holy can love for ever and for ever subdue the loveless; only the holy can thoroughly forgive so as to make His holiness dear. In God's holiness are perfectly balanced the two things which correspond to Egoism and Altruism with us. They are warp and woof of Him. That heaven moves in the harmony of its centrifugal and its centripetal powers. If we fasten on either at the cost of the other we fly from our orbit and come to grief. Luther (but half decatholicised) seized on the love, and we have modern Germany, with its deadly docility, its soft piety, and its hard practice. Calvin (with the moral thoroughness of Redemption) seized by preeminence on the holy, with a seeming hardness which has brought the freedom and security of the world. The two had coexisted in Catholicism in a naïve and dormant way; and they had to dispart in these two reformers on the way to a synthesis which we have not yet reached in practice, but which the great Catholicism of the future must see.

The egoism of the absolute God is not egoism. It makes the relativity of all. It is not selfishness but selfhood. It is the security of blessing for all. The egoism of God is the blessing of the world. It is His possession of His own holy soul. If He did not possess His soul how should He give His spirit to us? It is not the egoism of an individual that we have to do with, but the universal self-containedness, self-constancy, self-identity. It is the eternal totality (if we speak Latin) or the holiness (if we speak Saxon) of all things in righteous love. It is love's power, in every contact with creation, to remain itself, assert itself, establish itself, and always come home to itself, bringing its sheaves in our souls. It is the absoluteness and eternity of the moral and spiritual world, the security and certainty of the conquest, government, and uplifting of the Universe. The worship of the absolute selfhood of the holy Lover by those who live in Him is the source in us of permanent power to quell our egoism in the sacrifices of love. Naturally we love love because it is lovely. Yet it might be helpless. We do not love spiritually till we are perfectly sure of its infinite power. And that lies in its holiness. Because it is holy it is almighty, and we trust it for eternal victory. The idea of a Fate behind Him that might destroy Him and that keeps Him on a long chain would also destroy religion; we could not worship a God who was but our stoutest comrade under a Fate which bound us both. He would not be a holy God. And we can worship no less.

God's holy love is the egoism not of the fragmentary individual but of the absolute fulness and perfect personality which gives every person or soul its place, wealth, and joy. It is the egoism of the sacrificial God of the Cross, lifted up to draw all men unto Him. And an immortality which shares such egoism as that is our last destiny as the image of God.

Chapter Four

DE MORTUIS

The egoism of the will to live is qualified by the suicides and the martyrs. Demoralising sacrifice. False consolations and true. Prayer for the dead.

We have seen that when we speak of another life we mostly mean a second cycle of this life better oiled. The immortality of the soul means for us mostly a continuance, under better and smoother conditions, of that self-asseveration, conscious or unconscious, which makes life here. It expresses that revolt from extinction which gives zest and verve to our natural world, and which may be, after all, but a part of our egoism. But we have also seen that a belief so great as Immortality has come to be in Christianity cannot rest at last upon the instinct of a mere egoism distended. Such a basis would reduce its moral value, *i.e.* its ultimate value for life. We should lose life in our anxiety to prolong it. The Christian ground for immortality is that the Lord hath need of him.

But when our life-hunger has been discussed it is not all. Is there no such thing as the passion for death? If we long for Immortality, we also have, in cases, both the wish and the power of suicide. If we could only be sure of extinction by it! Sleep! Ay, but what dreams may come! In like manner the racial instinct is an adumbration of the instinct for immortality, and emerges in us when religion does; but there is also celibacy, whether as a preference, or a power, or a duty. These are two sets of extremes, life with its refusal in death, or love with its refusal in celibacy. And each extreme seems to cross the other's drift—life at war with death, love with celibacy. But there is one point in which the two agree. They agree in asserting the soul's power over nature. The one, life, asserts that the soul has power to transcend nature and live down circumstances; the other, suicide that it has power to slip out of circumstances, to foil nature, and to stop when nature says go on. The one, love, can rejoice over untoward fate; the other, celibacy, can wear down instincts the most primal and powerful. And if the soul is so in control of nature, then it need not end with nature. It is not wholly dependent on it. Thought does not depend on brain. Still, let us not overpress certain points in the argument. I only note that, when we urge the passion for life as an argument for its duration, the disgust or indifference for life must also be taken into account. The attenuation of life, by loss of interest in it, is closely associated with its brevity.

There is a farther qualification that we have already marked on the passion to live. The desire for immortality may not be a desire for my immortality, but for that of another life more dear to me than my own. That would greatly affect the note of my daily life. Indeed such a love might point towards my own suicide were I certain that it would ensure the continuance of the other's life beyond. I am ready to die; he is not. If my death could be thought to give him chances in a future life which he has thrown away in this I would welcome it. I might even cause my own death for his sake, and trust the motive to win me mercy. If my ceasing to live entirely could ensure him a life of goodness and happiness, I should gladly go out that he might have a fuller life. "Blot me out of the Book of Life." "I could wish myself accursed of God for my brethren's sake." I would part with my immortality for his if I had the power. Indeed, in some cases, so far as people have the power, it is done. Some lives are thus given for others, not by an act of pistol or poison, but by long days of sacrifice; and sometimes, alas! these very days crush the soul itself and grind it down. You will meet with a long life sacrifice in which the soul seems to sink in the moral scale with every year, and the service itself becomes sordid. This is one of the most pathetic of moral mysteries. The cross that was taken up was more than the moral power could carry. It shows that sacrifice is not in *itself* a moral or an elevating thing. The habit is not sustained by any sense of a compensating future or an unfailing God. There is often, indeed, no regard for a future life at all. That is a common type of parenthood among unspiritual people. All warmth or beauty in the relation dies in the habit or duty of it. But take it at its best. Would it alter, would it vanish, if immortality came to be generally disbelieved?

Again, at a time like the present, the interest of countless bereaved hearts is not in immortality for themselves, but for those who have been caught away either unfulfilled, or unprepared, or worse than unprepared, by the wickedness of war. What do our ideas of the unseen warrant us to say to the bleeding hearts and fearful minds of those left upon earth?

At the outset, I venture to think that it is a surrender of Christianity to find from ghosts a comfort and hope about the unseen which we do not draw from Christ. It is amoral. It is another religion and a debased. It is the renunciation of the moral element in religion for quite an inferior mysticism (magic). It is a non-moral mysticism which gets from some Bond Street medium a faith which the soul fails to receive from Christ or His apostles and saints. But that by the way.

May we say in consolation to the bereaved that every martyr patriot goes straight from the held of death to the side of the Saviour? May we say that in the way of comfort; as if a death for a great cause, to whose side the man sprang at a patriotic call, wiped out the vices of a lifetime, or the betrayal of innocent hearts? We could say no such thing. We may not forget our moral gospel so far as to speak like that. If these souls go straight to the presence of the Saviour, it is to the Judgment seat of Christ, where we must all stand. Yes, but it is where nothing is neglected or forgotten, nothing glozed, and nothing set down in malice, but good and bad are in scales perfectly and kindly just. It is quite as false, on the other hand, to quote the bad old phrase about the tree lying as it has fallen. It does not. It crumbles. Or it is moved away. It is turned to some good account. We may be quite sure that, if a cup of cold water to a disciple do not lose its reward, so an act of sacrifice for a righteous cause cannot go without its moral value for God, and a corresponding effect on the soul. And the finest thing that that soul ever did, though it will not atone for a lifetime of things foul, yet must have its full value for the personality in a sphere where such things tell more than they do here. There shall never be one lost good. The closing sacrifice does all that is in it to do. It is not wasted. But it does not do what it is beyond heroism itself to do for the soul. It does not save. Yet it may be the moment of his conversion. It may open his moral eyes. It may begin his godly sorrow. It may be the first step in a new life, the beginning of repentance in a new life which advances faster there than here. We threw away too much when we threw Purgatory clean out of doors. We threw out the baby with the dirty water of its bath. There are more conversions on the other side than on this, if the crisis of death opens the eyes as I have said. And, while it may be true that some mephistophelian spirits are born dead into that world as some are into this, is it not true also that for others we can only say that the manner of their leaving life became them better than anything they did in it, and it is the first step to a *new* life, and not only *another* life? If a man do not at once receive the prodigal's robe, at least he has the entree of the father's domain.

How natural in this connexion to turn to prayer for the dead. Prayer for the dead is healthier than tampering with them. Prayer is our supreme link with the unseen—with which otherwise we have no practical relations. We should resume prayer for the dead, were it only to realise the unity of the Church and our fellowship with its invisible part. In Christ we cannot be cut off from our dead nor they from us wherever they be. And the contact is in prayer.

No converse with the dead is so much of a Christian activity as prayer for them. There is no part of the practical Christian life which is so intimate and effectual as prayer. It colours and shapes us more than the obvious forms of action do. It is the work which chiefly influences the growth of faith and the quality of character. Life is affected from its foundation by whether we pray or not, and by how we pray. It is the main practical interest between this life and the life unseen. And we shall pray or not pray, we shall pray one way or another way, according as we believe in a future life, and hope for ourselves, or for those dearer than ourselves. Which is the better, to put them in God's hands and pray for them, or to bring strange devices to pass to conjure them up? If we believe in a continued life through spirits and not through Christ, if a medium mean more than a Mediator for our contact with the unseen, the manner of our prayer will be accordingly. If we discard Christ's moral revelation, and say we get more if one seem to rise magically from the dead, we pass into another religion, and prayer sinks accordingly. If Christ's voice do not come to us from beyond the grave, if all we hear is but the dull sound and hard effort of a miner's pick trying to meet ours in a tunnel between the two worlds, the note of our prayer and of our life is going to be deeply affected. It will lose the infinite moral value of union with the intercession of Christ, crowning His moral and final victory of a *holy* Cross. Or if we go on to say that death ends all, it ends all prayer. It not only stops the soul that prays, but the thought of it paralyses the soul and its prayer in life.

On the other hand, if death fix and settle all, if the tree lies for ever as it falls, prayer is much affected, and so life. One form of prayer is then excluded—prayer for the dead (though they need our prayer more if they are suffering yonder). Yet it would be easier to maintain a belief in immortality if we were encouraged so to pray. It would give us a practical relation with the other side, and to other immortality than our own. As it is, we have little direct and practical contact with immortality so far as the day's life goes. No act of that life brings us into direct and practical connection with the world of the dead. It is a dream; it is a world not realised. It does not belong to the strong and active side of our life. There is always about a life that works outward on another a certain note of distinction which is not made up for by any enthusiasm of Humanity. I knew an agnostic of a very fine kind who shortened his life by his devoted service to the very poor in a low part of London. There was to me a certain halo about him. And yet it is a different kind of spell that invests a life lived in the power of an endless life, a life that dwells with immortality daily.

I venture to say, then, that the instinct and custom of praying for our dearest dead, or our noblest (like many of the soldiers by whose pain and death we live), should be encouraged and sanctified as a new bond for practical life between the seen and the unseen, where we have bonds all too few. Nothing in our Christian belief is against it, and there is a good deal for it. It would never have been lost but for the abuses of purgatory, masses, and the commerce which the Church made of a magical influence on another world. But we threw away too much when we made a clean sweep. We are bidden to pray for everything that is not trivial, *"In everything* making your requests known," and to cast every real care on God. There is nothing serious that we may not bring to the Father. A widow praying who does not know where her next shilling is to come from means more to the Father than a full choral service, and more engages His heart. And it is serious enough that half our heart, and all its treasure, should be snatched into the unseen. With that unseen our only sure link is the God to whom we pray. But He is as much the God of our dead as of us; and He is a God from whom they cannot be severed as they are from us. May our prayer to our common Father not put into petition what is always in our thoughts, and put into words what is always in our heart? If we name them before God, what are we doing in our way but what He does in His, and calling things that are not as though they were?

There are those who can quietly say, as their faith follows their love into the unseen, "I know that land. Some of my people live there. Some have gone abroad there on secret foreign service, which does not admit of communications. But I meet from time to time the Commanding Officer. And when I mention them to Him He assures me all is well."

There is another world. It is not a mere unseen, unknown. It is not blank being, but full of feature, character, power, reality. We do not fall into it over the edge of a bottomless abyss. It is not clean cut off from this life. All kinds of processes run out into it, and they carry current both ways. For Christian people the supreme link, the Grand Commissure (if I might so speak) of both worlds is Christ. The absolute unity of Christ's soul in its victory over death and dread, in its exorcism of the occult powers, gives us the spiritual unity of seen and unseen. His great delivery for a pagan world was not from death, but from inferior and accusing spirits haunting, distracting, and debasing life. His living person is as real yonder as here, as real here as there. It is the last effective in both worlds. He *is* a living person. He is not inert substance, a mere continuity of essence, a mere prolongation of some great kind of being, or vitality, or principle, or tendency. He *is* the House of many mansions. He is more. He is King and Lord. His unity is one of action and reaction. In Him the other world acts on this, and this world on the other. But our chief action from this world on the other is prayer. And our other world is God. Prayer is action in the God in whom our dead live. Were they in hell, it is still God's hell. How can prayer help, either in nature or in grace, being prayer for our dead? Can we think of them there and not pray? Can we think of them there not praying, and for us, as even Dives prayed for his family at a very early stage of his new moral growth? They, too, in proportion as they feel the atmosphere of the other world,—are they not caught up, and carried on, in the stream of the great intercession? Believers at least are all in Christ, and surely not outside that intercession in His name and power. In the early Church, says Dr. Swete, it was a wellspread opinion, and apparently unrebuked, that the dead in Christ pray for the living. "No belief which was not actually an article of faith was more general, or more deeply cherished in Christendom." Paul has no protest against Baptism for the dead. There is nothing apostolic or evangelical that forbids prayer for them in a communion of Saints which death does not rend. It is an impulse of nature which is strengthened by all we know of the movement of grace. The arguments against it are apt to be more theologically pedantic than spiritually proficient. And they do not seem to have much heart.

Chapter Five

THE PRACTICE OF ETERNITY AND THE EXPERIENCE OF LIFE

The moral psychology of the saints. The change wrought by age on the soul's direction. But also in the soul's interests. The effect on life of the antepast of Eternity.

There is much to be yet written about the psychology of spiritual change, and especially of conversion and of the new birth which gives us our true eternity. For eternal life means more than immortality. We may hope for better light on the process when there are more cases, and more thorough, and more intelligent cases of the new birth among people with the modern mind and the psychological insight. The psychology of sainthood has not yet had the attention which has been given to the psychology of the natural man. The reason is partly because spiritual people are somewhat shy of revealing themselves, partly because they are shy of analysing the hour of their best spiritual experience. For to dissect may be to kill it; it shrivels at the critical touch; and we can examine but its memory. But we have some analogies—and large analogies, not small. The soul's immortality beyond death may be shown to have a relation to the new birth, similar to that which the new birth has to the origin of the natural egoist man.

It is not so hard to speak of conversion if we mean by it no more than a change of direction, a turning round and moving the other way. But more than that is meant when it is described as regeneration, as a new birth. It is a change in quality, and not in mere movement or behaviour. It means a greater crisis in the growth of the moral personality than the mere reversal of the machinery; a new type of motor is put into the mill.

It has been pointed out that we can mark in the long course of the moral life a slow change, which we may well call a slow conversion, because it is a change in the direction of our interest. In youth, says Paulsen, speaking of the course of the natural life, our interest is turned mainly upon the future; in maturity it is turned upon the present; and in age it reverts more and more to the past. Such a change is gradually wrought by experience upon the direction of the soul. And it is brought about by our approach to another life. For what are youth, maturity, and age? Are they not all relative terms and stages, which we measure by their distance from a fixed point—namely, death. They draw their meaning from some close to which they move. Their particular meaning comes from their various distance from death. But that means from eternity. For death is the point where all men enter a relation with eternity which gathers past, present, and future all into one infinite simultaneity.

Youth, maturity, and age, I say, gradually undergo in us the great conversion of interest that I have described when they are spread out and successive; but they must undergo a greater change still when we enter at death an eternity in which they all coexist in a timeless way, and act simultaneously and collectively on us. And the frequent contemplation here of such contact with eternity must greatly affect life. If the conduct of our life is much affected by the gradual passage to age as I have put it, without our being very conscious of the change; if the history of our soul must be still more affected when we pass death, and find all the stages of life in a timeless simultaneous action on us, must not life be vastly affected in those who also accustom themselves spiritually to confer with eternity during the whole of life's passage, who make frequent excursions into the unseen, and who deliberately expose their soul at intervals during their whole life to the spiritual influence which condenses all successive stages in a timeless spiritual experience. To dwell devoutly on such an eternity must much modify the natural development. It must hasten it by anticipation, and ripen us faster than any experience of life can which is merely ethical and reflective. It moralises in a transcendent way the time process, the successive stages of life. And especially so as we look back on life; it sublimates the retrospect.

Let me linger on this. Paulsen finely says (speaking of the spiritual and reflective life) that when we come to age and look back on our moral growth, we are much less interested in recalling the good times we had than we were when we anticipated them in youth; and we are more arrested by the memories of our faults than of our pleasures. As to these, we prefer to dwell on the pleasures we have given, or the help we have brought—on the amount of service we have put into life. And we are more concerned than we once were about the loss we have caused, the lives we have stunted, the wrongs we have done; or about the wrongs and losses which our success has cost, even when we meant no ill, just by the course of things. That is to say, our outlook on life is more moral and less selfish in its retrospect than in its prospect. We become alive to the preoccupation of our old egoism and the cruelty of our youth—or at least its crassness and insensibility. And does this not show what the larger effect of eternity must be? Is that not the inverted value we shall see in looking back on life when we are converted by entering Eternity? And is it not the value we should see if we entered Eternity in spirit here? If during life we let the influences of eternity, of life in its simultaneity, play on us deliberately and in advance; if we court, by the culture of our spiritual life in Christ, the revelation of eternity in God, with whom is no after nor before; if we let it all act on our soul from there; should we not be doing much to anticipate the verdict of age, and to avert many of the regrets of eternity? The last judgment would then be always at work on us. We should live in it and its power and glory. We should in a short time fulfil a long time. By the Eternal Spirit, we should so number our days that we turn our hearts to moral wisdom faster than we are changed by the mere lapse of the years. For the knowledge that we court with pains has a value that does not belong to what is forced on us, or what just sinks in subconsciously.

But this means for Christians placing ourselves in ever closer rapport with Christ's holy love, and especially with the holiness in it and the conquest that means. The real power of immortality is the eternity of the holy. It is philosophically put, the invincibility of the moral absolute. Holiness, with its eternal moral conquest, is the eternal thing in love itself, it is the only guarantee of love's final victory. As we take home eternity from Christ, it is the holy we take home in love. It is the holy as what might be called the ingrain, the tissue, the physiognomy of eternal love, the content and quality of it, the gift and power it brings, the warp to its woof. It is to this supreme moral power that we expose ourselves for our cleansing, our shaping, nay, our new creation—which is something beyond love's power except as holy. And it is as moral persons that we do so, for the holy is a moral idea, it is a moral power. Therefore it is not the mere duration of the soul that concerns us, not the continuance of a *process* more or less natural by which we are swept in, but the immortality of the moral personality which is reared by our *action,* our personal action of response. And the influence of holiness, of God, on that active personality is supreme, because the true eternity is His standing act, it is Himself in that pure holy action which is the native energy of His being. He is not a static being into whose kind love we sink, but He is the eternal Energy we join, which constitutes all being, and binds in holy action the coherent universe—the love which, as holy, moves the earth and all the stars. He is the most influential environment of the moral soul. For His holiness does not merely act on man as an object, as it does on the natural world; but it so acts on him that he returns the act as a subject; it is a case of reciprocal action in a rising scale. It is communion. And we know, not as science knows, but because we are first known by what we know, because His knowing us is the cause of our knowing Him. The object of our knowledge is the eternal Subject that knows. An eternity which begins by knowing us must have a very different effect on our life from an eternity which we but know, and to which we but look forward.

Chapter Six

IMMORTALITY AS PRESENT JUDGMENT

It is a vocation rather than a problem. Life is another thing if we confuse these. Immortality is a destiny rather than a riddle. Live immortally. Choose; do not argue. To live for Eternity is much, but to live Eternity is more.

Like every other Christian doctrine, that of the soul's immortality needs to be moralised and brought home to our daily life without losing its mystic spell. And in this interest we might regard the following considerations.

The trouble about the doctrine of immortality has been increased by the fact that so many have turned it from an imperative task to a leisurely theme. It has passed from a practical task to be but a theoretical problem, from a Gospel to our will to be a riddle to our wits. From a "concern" it has become an enigma. From a vocation it has turned a question. From a matter of conscience and duty it has become a matter of poetry and speculation. It has been made to rest not on the free grace of God but on the dim presumptions of man. The faith of it has turned from a gift of God to a result of ours.

And this greatly affects its influence on life. We should begin with the fact, if we are Christians at all (for it just means our part and lot in the Christ Who vanquished death), and we should act accordingly. I do not see how a true believer in Christ can doubt the immortality of those who are Christ's (and He claims all), or require occult assurance of it, which means finding Him unsatisfactory. But if you do not so begin and so act; if, instead of beginning with the belief, you expect only to end with it, how long do you think you will take to arrive at a conclusion? It may take a long time, for some all their lives, for others more. Meantime how are you to be living? If so great a thing is true about life, it must have, and must be meant to have, an effect equally great on life's practice. Our belief about such a fact of personality when it finds us must greatly colour life. Is it an immortal soul that is living life out? If so, and if you begin, and for long go on, speculating pro and con, then all that makes the power of immortality and its action on your soul is lost out of your first stage. Your soul must lose irreparably in the end if that *plastic* stage is not living the immortality out as a power or principle, but is only working towards it in a hope rather than a faith. It must make a great difference to life if it is not spent under the power of an eternal life but only under its possibility, not in living out the immortality but only in weighing it, considering whether there is any such thing to live out. If you do not believe in it you cannot live it. And if you are not living an immortal life you are living something different and inferior; and the effect of this for life's tone and value must correspond. It is not something that begins when we die, but something that begins with us and lives forth in our life. Death is not the solution of the riddle, but a crisis of the power. And it may be the coming home of judgment on you for treating as a riddle what is a power.

Immortality is really a destiny pressing on us by Christ in us; it is not a riddle that just interests us. It is not chess, it is war. It is a duty bearing on us, it is not a theme that attracts us. When duties turn to mere problems and destinies become but intellectual toys, it is an evil time. It is not well when we stop doing in order to discuss. We cannot safely turn the will's duty over to thought. Duty is a thing we must do. For effect on life we must own it practically, not debate its existence. The gifts of God are not there to be looked in the mouth but to be lived in the heart. There is no Christian question about our duty to obey the immortal call; the only possible question is as to the form of obedience; or it is the question whether we are obeying it or not. Our immortality lies on us with that kindling weight, that weight of glory, that weight of wings. Weight but not pressure. The wings that add to our weight yet lift us from the ground. "My soul cleaveth to the dust; quicken Thou me according to Thy winged word." Such a word, gift, and destiny is our immortality. Our Christian business is to crystallise it. It is an obligation; it is not a mere stirring in us. It is a duty on our person and action; it is not a mere process of our natural organism, to whose stream we have just to yield ourselves. Life is not just a stream which we have reason to think flows on beyond a certain point, or continues when it disappears round a certain bend. It is not an inevitable movement towards the future. It is rather a doom from the past, a work in the present, or a destiny from above. We cannot tarry to argue if there is an immortality awaiting us; we must obey the immortality urging and lifting us. We do not move to a possible mirage of a city of God; the citizenship is within us. Ask, am I living as immortal—not as one who will be immortal? Do not waste time asking if there is a coming eternity; ask, what must I do to give effect to my present eternity; how shall I be loyal to the eternal responsibility in me and on me? Is my faith a life? It must make a great difference to life whether we treat our eternity as a present or a future, as a power or as a possibility, as a duty or as an ideal—whether our Christ is a Bystander or an Occupant of us. Our immortality is really our judgment and its joy of righteousness; it is not a mere condition of judgment, nor the region of it. It does not become a mere venue, a mere stage for judgment, a set scene. Nor does it provide a mere asbestos either for future flames, or for the happier incandescence. It has no existence apart from a content of weal or woe. And that content depends on us (under grace). Our immortality is not just the glory (or gloom) of going on and still to be. It is not mere duration. There is no such thing, no such abstraction. Our eternity is something that remains when all its events have passed. It is the state of a soul, the content and quality of its life, when events in a sequence cease, when they have come and gone with the soul's verdict on them, and the reaction of such a verdict on the soul. It is good or evil according to choice. It is a disparting to one of two great seas. It does not call chiefly for contemplation but decision. What Paul did in speaking to Felix was not to persuade him of immortality; it was to turn immortality from a curious interest to a crushing crisis, from a curious interest hovering about life, and discussible at the tables of roués, to a searching judgment on life's interior. It was preaching that Felix did not like with wine and walnuts. The salons shun it, and the reviews ignore it. Nor was it in the nature of popular preaching. It did not carry the accent either of culture, or of sentiment, or of mere urbane consideration. It did not humour the instincts of the heart, nor hallow the graces of the home. It did not agitate the questions that occupy the periodicals on the one hand, nor those that captivate the young on the other. But it was the kind of preaching which brings the other life into this, which shapes our behaviour in time by the nature of an immanent eternity (whether we speak of public conduct or private), which transmutes time into eternity and does not simply prolong it. It translates a present, it does not discuss a future. It does more than educate, it converts. It does more than enlarge our moral horizon, or manipulate the themes of moral culture. It makes the new heaven and the new earth wherein dwelleth righteousness.

That is a sample of the way we must rescue the spiritual for the ethical, moralise our theology, and make creed practice. However much religion may be life, theology is deeper life. It rises deeper in God's life, it goes deeper into ours. It moralises all by its origin in the holy. A theme like Immortality, at least—we do it wrong, being so majestical, to explore it but as a cavern with our torches, instead of honouring it as our light and sun and showing it forth accordingly. It is much to live for Eternity, to live Eternity is more.

Chapter Seven

ETERNITY WITHIN TIME, TIME WITHIN ETERNITY

The other life then is the other life now. The timeless in Time. Time's Sacrament. We are Eternal each moment. Eternity and progress.

"This is eternal life," says Jesus, "to know God, to know Me." It is a thing indwelling with us, it is not a thing outside that awaits us. It is ourselves in a phase, in a new relation. Myself am hell; myself am my own heaven. It is not a realm we enter, nor an influx that enters us. Moral though it be, it is a mystic thing now rather than a future then, an inner presence not an outer goal, a power rather than an expectation. It is to know God as holy love. But it is not to know Him as an object, not to know Him as science knows, not to know Him in a cognition, which sees a thing at the other end of our observation or of our thought. It is to know Him by an inner appropriation. It is by an interpenetration. We know what begins by knowing us. We know because we are known. It is the kind of knowledge which does not give power but is power, where our self is not just enhanced but lost, and only in that way found in its fulness. The Christ, who knew God best, had power over all; but it was power to give as to Him it was given, and to give to His own eternal life. Eternal life is much more than contact; it is living communion with spiritual and eternal reality. And on that reality's initiative. Real love is not that we loved God but He us.

Eternal life is not so inward that it ignores the world as phantasmal. Especially it does not ignore history. Unhistoric spirituality is often a danger to faith. Some say it is one of the greatest to-day. The true spirituality is rooted in history. It springs from an incarnation of action. It is not a matter of illumination. It does not arise from a mere emanation of light. It is knowing God in Christ the Redeemer. The resurrection to immortality crowns the redemption from guilt. It is not the lone soul with the Alone, ignoring two millenniums of revelation and its saints. It is not intuition, mystic and gnostic. It is in a historic Mediator. Is that a piece of theology? Is a Mediator between the eternal spirit and the finite an unreality, an intrusion? The mystic soul may impatiently think so, but the moral soul finds such mediation the way to reality; and the mystic experience is not quite trustworthy about reality. The pagan gods had not mediators, because they were not real or good gods; but the living God has a living Revealer. To know the living God is to know Christ, to know Christ is to know the living God. We do not know God *by* Christ but *in* Him. We find God when we find Christ; and in Christ alone we know and share His final purpose. Our last knowledge is not the contact of our person with a thing or a thought; it is intercourse of person and person. We meet God in His coming in Christ, meet Him there on His own tryst, and find there that we know only because we were first known. We do not infer from Christ to God. And in Christ we *have* Eternal *life,* we do not simply qualify for it, we do not just take the needful steps.

The true spiritual intuition looks through the historic Christ. Otherwise it is apt to be individual and not social. It may haunt a cell and retire from a church. It is more devout than sacramental. It is not historic and it is not moral in its nature. It is more prone to visions than revelations; it is more mystic than positive. It develops subjective frames rather than objective powers. It often craves fusion with God rather than communion. From the abeyance of the moral note it tends to think of process more than action, of imagination more than conscience, of elation more than sympathy, of an evolution instead of a redemption. It is more interested in sanctity than in righteousness. It lives on an inner light rather than a redeeming power, a charity rather than a righteousness, a group of saints rather than a Kingdom of God. Its immortality is a beatific vision rather than the reciprocal energy of eternal life. Christian intuition turns on our insight into Christ, which to an extent varies with temperament; but Christian faith turns on Christ's action on us and for us, which is removed from our variations, and can be met and answered well by some whose spiritual penetration is not yet subtle, vivid, or vocal.

Another life—what is the other life *then* but that which is the other life *now?* What is it but the eternal life which is our true life here, only viewed as going on, viewed in amount rather than in kind, in extent rather than quality, as prolonged rather than intense, as expressed in terms of time, duration or quantity, instead of worth? We ask, how long, instead of how rich, how full, we live. Some will remember the Spinozist description of the two disparate aspects of the great reality. Spinoza spoke of these aspects as thought and extension. And there was only an empirical connexion between them. Well, the two aspects of eternal life correspond. We may view it quantitatively, extensively, as everlasting, or qualitatively *sub specie eternitatis,* as moral. Now are these, like extension and thought, irrelevant to each other and disparate? Are we quite ignorant of what *has* these features, of that whose physiognomy they are? The life that goes on—is it not the life of moral personality? That is soul, that is reality. When we speak of another life we think of our life as enduring; but it is the continuance of the same eternal life which is our good as souls here—intense at each immeasurable moment, infinite in each particle, as it were, and royal in its quality, whatever its extent may be. It does not matter for the moment whether we think of its imperative as that of conscience or that of love. It is the great shaping and guiding power, whose influence is real out of all proportion to our sense of its range.

Even when by the other life we mean the eternal life in its aspect of duration, we still prize it only for its quality. We want it, not because there is a lot of it, but because it is good. Without that quality it would be a Tithonus burden, and we might well shrink from it. The same thing makes it precious both there and here. It is its intrinsic excellence and influence. It is its excellence and influence over what we call nature. It is its quality, not simply as enhancing us (which is after all but an extension or aggrandisement of our Ego), but as regenerating us, as giving us another centre, which is the source of another value, and so makes a new creation. It is as holy that the soul is permanent, it is in virtue of its quality. It is as holy that God Himself is eternal, in incessant moral victory. Thus, as we shall see later, we connect immortality very closely with the new birth, which is the foundation of Christian ethic.

As to natural ethic it might plausibly be said that it could go on in our posterity for its own sake even were immortality denied. Truth (it is even held) would be a good thing were there none to believe it, and kindness were all hearts dust.

> *It comforteth my soul to know*
> *That though I perish truth is so.*

That is in some ways absurd. (Yet read Isa.51:6.) It is a very individualist view. As was long ago said, pagans have an ethic but paganism has not. Even if a case could be made out from the good pagans—that virtue was good in its own right, their failure was to get people in general to believe and act on it, whose brief life would be a merry one at all costs. But for Christian ethic the view that goodness was indifferent to immortality could not be made even plausible. To abolish a future life would be to abolish the eternal life of the present (*i.e.* the Eternal Spirit, or the Eternal Christ), which takes the place of the natural man, and makes the Christian soul and its conduct. If you destroy the permanency, you do not leave the quality unaffected. The new power is of God's Spirit. It is absolute, timeless. If at a point it could cease, it would be struck at the heart; its absoluteness, its divinity would cease—"Half dead to know that it could die."

When we speak of eternal life we are apt to think of it as a second order of things, which might be developed out of time or inserted into it, but which is less obvious, less real, more ghostly and metaphorical. But, if we come to consider closely, all the deepest life is timeless; and the more life there is the more timeless it feels. The more intensely we live the less we take note of passing time. Life is full of the present the more vital it is. But what does that mean? The present? Suppose we look into that. Should I be metaphysical (and therefore an enemy of the human race) or should I be but psychological (and a favourite of the hour) if I took this line? What is the present? Has it any real existence? Is any fixed point of time conceivable? Can you arrest any moment? Have we not to do with something that is not so much a point in time as timelessly interior to time, and to all its movement through what we call points? Each moment of time is outwardly but a spark at the contact of past and future, a point that is gone before you can say it is. What is the present, outwardly seen, but the briefest flash in the perpetual becoming of things. And we master it only by pressing into its inwardness, by union with that perfect *being* which has a *becoming* only in us and our history. The moment is a "shoot of everlastingness." There is no present, because there is no time. An abounding life which is all present, even if not all conscious, is timeless. But not as a dreamy entity or velleity might be. It is eternal as a moral act or personality is. It expresses itself chiefly in action, and an act, in its nature, as the act of a spiritual personality, is a timeless thing. As an act of the spirit it partakes of the energy eternal. The great acts of the great personalities at a point of history are superior to time, interior to it, and beyond it. So also their bodies mock space, and five feet of corporeality may mould the soul of man for ever. The greater we grow the less are we the victims of time or space, and the more we are immortal. And the more we live in our true and active immortality the more greatly we live— most of all as we live in Christ, whose whole person went into one eternal and redeeming act.

Eternity is thus beyond time only in the sense of being deep within it. "He hath set eternity in their hearts." It is within our interior, and beyond it above it in that way. It is more interior. It inhabits our inner castle.

"Religion is not the perception of the infinite; it is having the infinite within us." That makes the moral value of Immortality for life. We are living now the life beyond. Time and space are rather distilling our eternity than preparing for it. Think of the automatic reaction on our soul of our resolves and deeds, so that what we have been makes us what we are. Think then, more deeply still, of the power, the eternity, moulding these wills and deeds. Our eternal life is not at the end of our days but at the heart of them, the source of them, the control of them. Time is there to reveal or to deposit Eternity, not to qualify for it. Eternity does not lie at the other end of time, it pervades it. We can invert our way of putting it. Time is, as it were, the precipitate of eternity—should I say the secretion of it? Time is the living garment of the God in us. And it can be not only transparent but permeable. It has the sacramental, the miraculous power to pass us into eternity at each moments and not only when we die. Time is divine in the sacramental, and not in the essential, sense. That is, the divine thing is achieved in the souls time makes, whether time be a form of the eternal consciousness or not. Time is divine in function if not in being. "For religion," says Schleiermacher, "immortality means being one with the Infinite in the midst of finitude. It means to be eternal at every moment." We have begun eternity. We began it at birth. The sacramental value of time I will discuss further in the next chapter.

But does that not farther mean this, that life and history are there to let God get out rather than to let man get on? We go forward really only as we can take God with us and realise His Kingdom. The grand interest of man is not progress but eternity, not length but wealth of days, and wealth moral and spiritual. Above progress is the Kingdom of God—a conception that is replaced in the fourth gospel by the idea of Eternal Life. It is eternity, it is the Kingdom of God, that is the standard to decide what is progress and what is not.

This is the point where religious liberalism comes to grief, especially in its popular forms. It becomes secularised as the march of mind. But a life which realises that its great interest is not progress but eternity must be concerned about much else than the advance of culture. It must be a life very different from one to which progress is everything. It can rest. It is not always on the move. It can be guided and steered. It has a worship. It has at least a pole star and a compass. It must be much higher than a life of mere progress, and so much the more real. As we draw nearer death by age, and immortal things become more real to us, it is a commonplace to say that we tend to grow more conservative. But why is it the case? It is not that we grow lazy and reactionary, but rather because eternity is set deeper in our heart. We become more alert in a certain direction. We become more sensitive to what is deep than to what is lively, to a searchlight than to the flares, to what is the sure, permanent, and timeless thing in all movement. We realise more the goal eternal, which rules within every point of progress as its true ground, which has a quality and a command of its own to stamp upon all movement, a norm (and not only a law) to set on all change, and which, therefore, is the only test we have whether a movement is progress or not. The great interest is not progress; it is the eternity which all along the line looks forth from what we call progress (or looks in on it), and passes a judgment on it. The eternal element in us measures the events which teach, impress, and even shape the soul. The soul remains when these are gone. It passes judgment on them when they are dead. The eternal soul reacts on its impressions. It selects some as making for its true progress, and rejects others which make the other way. Its ever-abiding eternity is the measure of its neverabiding times and phases. Eternity saturates and shapes time, time but clothes and serves eternity. And the soul, as eternal, by an epigenetic[1] power on its environment, selects some directions of change for its own, and discards others. It is thus the real creative power in things. It exercises over them all a creative criticism, appreciative, selective, and expansive. This idea of a creative criticism from above is more positive and Christian than that of creative evolution. It does more justice to personality, and pays it more respect. To be judged or chosen is a nobler thing than to be hurried on by a stream. Though evolution itself is a great step to the assertion of that moral eternity within time which the mere thinker is apt to ignore. For it gives room for that election, that choice, which must always be associated with the notion of a personal God in relation to His world. The conviction of that eternity which is the true immortality, of that timeless simultaneity and compatibility of things, is what really sets up the idea of progress; since, as I say, only an eternal and final standard which is at once ground and goal, and which unites in itself both causation and finality, enables us to describe any movement in time as progress or the reverse. And it is therefore of first moment for the form and colour of life, personal or social.

---

1.   The theory of development known as epigenesis is different from that called preformation in having a selective action on its environment. All is not in the germ in miniature, which is a simple body without structural sign of its discriminating power.

Chapter Eight

LIFE A SACRAMENT

Time sacramental of Eternity. How part and lot in the Eternal raises the common tasks and tragedies of life beyond the sordid.

It is quite true that time is a gift to us as immortality is. But time is given us that we may become free of it, and may reach the undying spirit and quintessence of time. Our business in time is to resist it even while we appropriate it. We take the honey from the flower we have to struggle to enter and are soon to leave with a struggle. The soul, shaped as it is by the events of time, has yet in the end more power to determine them. A soul like Christ's, immersed in a year's events, can yet be creative for history. Our growth in time (if we may change the image) is to resist its petrifaction, to resent our burial in time, and the sealing of the grave. And this we can only do immortally—by rising always into the timeless heaven, and in Christ continually ascending by the experience of a constant new creation. The second death is to miss the second creation. We grow in soul if we feel spiritually younger to-day than yesterday, and to-morrow than to-day. We are less loaded with years because we are more lifted in the eternal. We taste the rejuvenescence of immortality, where ends meet and things come full circle. We live where the Father for ever meets the Son, the first the last, the beginning the end, age youth, and all things return for their completion to the perfection in which they began. Time is sacramental of Eternity.

As we follow up this line of reflection, I say, there is borne in on us something more than the religious significance of life. There comes home to us not only its solemn but its sacramental value. Life means more than even the poets tell. It has more than an imaginative worth. It has more than a supernatural. It has more than an everlasting. It has a holy and eternal worth. I mean that not only is it involved in the process or tragedy of the Universe, but it is partner in the solution of that tragedy in God. History is not only reconciled, it is charged with the message and power of reconciliation. Even art can embalm life in amber. It can cast on it the æsthetic spell, and for a time transport us to another world. It can make our noisy lives seem moments in the energy of the eternal silence. But a greater than art is here. There is a greater secret than even art commands in the relation of the soul and the Holy. The action in time of the Holy and Eternal Spirit of our Redemption is greater than that of genius. We are told indeed by many a seer that "the momentary life of to-day is a factor in the procession of all time and being." Philosophy can teach us that, whether it get it home or not, whether there be much help in it or not. But we have to do with more than a procession of being, or a dance of ideas; and we have to do with getting that something more home to people. We have to do with an eternal providence, with a heart of love eternal, and with a will absolute over the hearts and in the wills of men; and we have to do with a public faith in it. I mean something more than dogmatics—certainly more than dogmatics as a sort of Palladium we carry about in an ark. I have in mind the riddle of the painful earth, for which theology must be some kind of solution. We have to connect up earth's tragedy with God's.

The tragedy of the plodding peasant, dragging a rheumatic existence from the soil, and dying alone and brokenhearted with his daughter's shame or his son's crime—we have to integrate that with an eternal tragedy, an immortal solution of it, and a final joy. We have to link it with God's disappointment in His son man, His grief and His joy and His victory in His Son Christ. Is there any experience possible to the soul, is there any power at work on it, any revelation, any redemption, whereby the very horrors of world-war and wickedness can be made sacramental of the fulness of joy? Can they be underagents for the last righteousness and angels of the last judgment which secure the last peace? Is it a delusion, or is it Time's sacramental secret, that a person, like Christ, of two thousand years ago, is as near us all now as He was to men then? Have we with us a power of life by which these two millenniums do not divide us from Christ, like a world of mists and seas, but unite us—as commerce and invention make the ocean a bond and not a gulf? Is it a dream that the issue in His Cross is greater, and more creative, than all the issues of history? Why do the heathen rage but for the Kingdom of God's Son? And have we a power by which ephemeral lives are not only absorbed in a stream universal but become revelations and energies from a person of absolute love? Can they become channels of the Holy Ghost, in the power of One Who was more than a channel, and more than a revelation—Who was the incarnation of God the Redeemer? That is what the Cross of Christ as the source of His Spirit proposes to do with them. The victory of an immortal Redeemer becomes the effective point and principle of life's most sacramental significance. It is the source of any worth life can have not only to God but among us *for* God, as the vehicle of the Eternal Spirit, as a human priest to human kind. The power which makes life most deeply sacramental is its new creation by Christ. The eternal life that Christ's Cross won for us in the Eternal Spirit acts on us so timelessly that it can give the meanest life the eloquence of the spiritual world. It makes it that it can be not only an object but a channel of supernatural blessing, and not only a channel but a medium. That miraculous power which turns the historic Christ from a memory to be the most real presence, and even constituent, of our life today, that power which makes Him Who is so far off the most near, and changes the temporal to the eternal—that is what makes the true sacramental power in life, and transfigures it with the glow of something that lifts it and lights it for ever. Nothing makes the poor man's toil so full of worth and price as the work of Christ the Spirit. Nothing so lifts into eternal significance the loves, sorrows, drudgeries, tragedies of the poor men of the dull fields. It has done it in cases innumerable. Nothing so makes them know themselves, and seem to others, to be worlds more than mere atoms bubbling in a seething cauldron, or drifting in a desert dust, whirled in a universe of meaningless sound and fury. Such certainty as Christ can give, and does give, of a life beyond life by our partnership of it in Him fills the humblest soul with such power and price that the men of genius can neither fathom it (though they feel it) nor can they give, far less guarantee, that which they may divine of its wealth. The commonest life means worlds both Godward and manward. That is the sacramentality of life. The most Christian poets are those who, like Wordsworth, Burns, or Barnes, breathe that note from huts where poor men lie. And the warrant for it is its Creator, its new Creator—the power of the Eternal spirit by which that poor man Christ Himself won the endless victory over time, death, and the world. The simple have known that as they could know nothing else. And it made life for them, and for all who could read them aright, because they shared the same faith, full of staying power, mystic eloquence, and conclusive bliss. "Grave in the sight of God is the death of His loyal and loving ones."

Chapter Nine

IMMORTALITY AND THE KINGDOM OF GOD

Absence from able publicists of either idea. But the only perfection is in a common realm and a common King.

We have admitted that the belief in another life has been cherished on lines so individual that its effect on this life has really been to increase the natural egoism instead of concealing it. That has happened because it has been dismoralised—first, because the notion of eternal life has dropped to that of endless life, and second, because it has been narrowed down from the idea of the Kingdom of God. It is on this latter that I would now dwell.

The Kingdom is more than a social idea, but as a social idea it dominates the synoptics. In the Epistles it retains its social note as the ideal Church. In the fourth Gospel it appears more mystically, and therefore more individually, as eternal life. To put it technically, the eschatology becomes a transcendency, and the last things are not simply the end things but the ground things, the dominants. As the Church went on to grow more external and egoist this idea shared in the fall. Both the Kingdom and its eternal life became debased by contact with the paganism they overcame. But now we are returning to the larger and holier note. The Kingdom of God is the emergence into the life of history, both by growth and crisis, of that saving sovereignty which is the moral power and order of the spiritual world. The coming of the Kingdom is the growth or the inroad of God's Will on earth to be what it always is in peace and glory in Heaven. I am thinking of what we have in the very opening of the Lord's Prayer, where the phrase "as in heaven so on earth" belongs to each of the three first petitions, and not only to its next neighbour. "Hallowed be Thy Name" as in Heaven so on Earth; "Thy Kingdom come" as in Heaven so on Earth. As if it should say, "There is a realm at the heart of things where all is already won and well, all is Yea and Amen. And access to it is not barred to faith on earth. And it is the real workshop of history." Our commerce with that country alters much, the whole complexion of our social discussion changes, when we seek to measure and adjust all things by their obedience to this power and their movement to this goal. All changes its note and method when we seek first that Kingdom. That is the new creation in which dwells immortality.

Now it is quite true that to-day there is better thinking and writing in social or national subjects than there ever was in the world before. It is writing also much ruled by the ethical note. But even the best of it is for the most part, less than historic in its range, and it moves only in the middle register of thought. Its eye is not on the history of the whole soul. And it represents spiritually neither revolt nor faith, but indifference (probably more apparent than real). It is not for God's enemies, but neither is it for God as it is for man. To read it you would not guess that we were in a Christian country with a long Christian tradition shaping its society. You would receive the impression that its religion had no more to do with affairs than a harem, that it is kept behind the purdah. In all the able and interesting speculation of the publicists about either the causes or the consequences of the present convulsion, it is one of the most significant things that hardly any reference is made to the eternal Kingdom of God, ranging from earth to heaven; and no express guidance is taken from distinctive principles of the Kingdom's ethic. Insistence on a world-righteousness, and on judgment accordingly, is treated as an outburst, more or less amusing, of obsolete Puritanism. If such be the mark of civilisation, and if the Kingdom of God yet be the fundamental nisus in and under all the civilisations, it must be that offence comes and war. Our social science is written as our novels are—as if there were no such thing among the powers of life as the Kingdom of God and its religion, as if religion were not the ruling passion of the race (to say nothing of its contents being the key of history), as if a supreme regard to an eternal life made no vital difference to the conduct of life. All is written as if the power which has done the most to make history was an illusion now outgrown, as if the Kingdom of God were a superstition of pietists in holes and corners, or a figment of theologians who mistook for effective realities certain fantasies of the first century. Any thinker would be more or less discredited with the leading writers on social or political questions, however profound a historian, if he announced that he was to measure everything in the light of the principle of Christ's established Kingdom of God emerging into human affairs. Even with the far flung monitions and deep old judgments of the war booming in our ears that is so. Reconstruction in its wake is approached with a mind which seems to have no sense of any but economic or philanthropic quantities. The treatment of the war as a function of judgment by that Kingdom on a whole civilisation which ignores it would be regarded as a piece of pulpit fustian which the preacher has sunk to be expected to say. And that means that religion, the deepest religion, and especially the religion of the long future, is regarded (if at all) but as a private affair, that there is no idea of eternity as the greatest of public interests and public powers, but that we can best prepare citizens for life by teaching civics. There is no sense of a Church as the trustee of man's last social weal, nor of the reign of a holy God as active and decisive in our common life. When you begin discussing the Church with such people they discuss Churchmen; just as when I criticise democracy I am often tripped up with the fatuous remark what capital fellows the trades' union leaders are. But no judgment can be really recognised as such, it cannot be recognised as a movement of the Kingdom of God, and a solemn effect of its righteousness, except by a conscience taught by God. Calamity on a worldly soul but hardens it. And the fool brayed in a mortar is a shrewd fool still.

Now, since that is so, the chief public work of the Church as the trustee of eternal life, and the way to its recovery of public influence in this life, must be so to acquire the deep historic conscience of the holy as to evangelise with its righteousness the corporate nation and not only the souls in it; to create public repentance and new purpose; to Christianise political conduct; to press the reality of the Kingdom of God in history and affairs; to make it the dominant it was for the Person who has most moulded history; and to do this in such a way that it shall not only become credible but luminous for public life—at least with those for whom the moral interest of society is supreme. Much of the current talk about the Church's duty after the war where it is not pietism is journalism, mostly empiric, the work of people who have no special preparation, no serious discipline in ethic, history, philosophy, or theology for such matters, but as taken from some other job for this. People who have no real part or lot in the Church are very eager to exploit it as an asset for some vague ideal. They know much in a way, but not in a way to teach them that the Church has made modern history. And they vindicate their claim to be realists "without any nonsense" by calling on the Church to change front with every new formation of social phases and public events, just as they would urge the House of Commons. The Church may only change front in so far as it can do so without changing its ground. And when it comes to selecting the time and type of change, the Church has really no more fools in it than literature or business. But more and more the Church must feel that its ground is the Kingdom of God set up by the moral and creative crisis for history of the Cross of Christ. The real ground of a Christian belief in the soul's future and the future of humanity is the reality of God's Kingdom there put in action as, in a new creation, planting heaven, founding earth, and leading history (Isa. 52:16), there put into subtle control of human affairs, and made the goal of human history as the new destiny of each soul. It is true all the same that if the Church realised as it should its own ground, its first concern might be the less bustling but more biting task of its own reconstruction. One is amazed at the naïve facility with which it devises machinery for the new situation without a misgiving that that situation is largely due to a defect, not to say a falsity, in its own grasp of the Gospel, which calls for something like a conversion in itself as the preacher.

Our preoccupation with the interests of another life (I have said) may be of a degree or kind to damage the soul it would save, and the Kingdom it should serve. It may encourage the same egoism which is the ruling power in civilisation, which is bound to quarrel with the movement of the Kingdom, and which it is the work of a real revelation to convert or destroy. I mean by egoism profiteering in religious things to the loss of public soul; and by a real revelation I mean a revelation which redeems even more than it reveals, plants us on a new centre, and changes our conscience much more than our conceptions. In an ethical religion which is also social the immortality of a personal being is valuable as an increase of life for others, and especially for God and His Kingdom. If we are more they are more. The very Fathers are not perfect till we Sons of the later day come in (a fact which should end the tyranny of patristics). By a perverted religion we can overdo the care of our soul, which we have to master and not to fuss, and which is in better hands than ours; but we cannot be too much occupied with the Kingdom of God and our lot there. This is a more vital doctrine for Christianity than the immortality of the soul, because it includes it. The historic righteousness, the holiness of God, which makes His Kingdom, is an infinitely greater matter than the realisation of the superior self. Indeed, is there any hope of our coming to our own, our ownest own, in life except as God does Who is our life, and Whose own we are? We cannot truly or finally realise ourselves except in the service and spread of the Kingdom of God. (Only let us not be too self-conscious in this matter of service. The man who is always fussing about his duty needs our vigilance.) It is this Kingdom which is the standard of all progress, and the test by which we tell it from degeneration. It is only to this service that all else is added, and especially moral growth. That is to say only in the active love and service, not simply of God, but of the Kingdom of God and His Christ, are the full powers of the soul released and its resources plumbed. The Kingdom of God is only another phrase for the energetic fulness of man's eternal life— here or hereafter. It involves a millennium, the moral organisation of society in considerate sympathy, but it is much more. It is the greatest object in the world; and life's chief end is not even the highest stage or phase of itself, but to glorify and to enjoy for ever in His realm a God of holy love. Without such a goal and its service there is nothing to keep alive in us always a living sensibility of feeling or imagination—as there is nothing without it to bind the nations together by their conscience. That is the Kingship of God, which is more than His Kingdom.

It has been said, in a slashing way which impresses some, that amid our present circumstances the only choice open to Society is between Utopia and Hell. But what is Utopia, and how reach it? How pass from the mere anomalies of Society to the paradox of moral power and peace? Hell is easy; and our Utopias are not hard; they kindle us easily. But this is hard. For these cannot bring themselves to pass. We slide down, but we have to struggle up. And where are we to find the power to climb, or the guidance? We must be carried, for we cannot go. We faint and fail till we wait on the Lord. The soul in due course subsides on itself, and its prospects starve and shrivel; but, forgetting itself in God's Kingdom after a godly sort, the soul rises to the righteousness of it and all its rich entail. Here in our present life we are not what it is in us to be because of the limitations which beset us within and without. Each stunted soul is a drag upon every other. We cannot love each other as we should, nor even as we long to do, because of something that lies on us like frost, and ties us with invisible threads. We cannot move as we would. Or if we do, at the first step to our neighbour's heart our foot is frozen by reserve, or it stumbles on his invisible fence. And this may be so even with those who are nearest us. But in a life of eternal reconciliation, which is not sympathetic only but constructive, which is not a kinder family only but a godlier Kingdom, it will be otherwise. We shall not lose our individuality, but the barriers will fall down in a spiritual telepathy and tact: We shall talk across our fences. For the features of our idiosyncrasy, the physiognomy of our soul, limits though they be, are not limitations. They are frontiers and not barriers. They make contour and character, not insulation. The individual, as he becomes a living person, has powers infinitely expansible and reciprocal. As the soul grows thus perfect it grows at once more capacious and more communicative. For it is such persons only, and not mere individuals, that can interpenetrate. Each has wealth to give, and room to receive the rest. We grow by such mutual interpenetration. Hearts swell into each other. We assimilate each other. We know as we are known. We live ourselves into each other. We rise to each other, or we stoop to raise. None without the rest can be made perfect. And the common perfection is guaranteed by the Kingship of an indwelling God. Our powers increase there by much more than addition. And that more is what makes a meeting a Church—it is the Holy Ghost. The new creation is a new combination of the old powers, with an eternal life as the secret of the blend.

But the longer we dwell on this new life, and dispose ourselves to it, so much the more we inhabit another world. And the change, the reaction on our life, is great as we live such another world into this. We acquire both the devout life and the brotherly. The immortality of the soul can only be realised as our part and lot in an immortal fellowship deeply active every day. This is what saves it from being an egoist burden or a bore. But it is first a fellowship of Christ.

To preach the Kingdom without preaching the knowledge of Christ may be still to serve Him; but to preach it with an ostentatious silence about Him is of Antichrist. The one is the twilight of the morning, the other of the evening.

Chapter Ten

IMMORTALITY AND REDEMPTION

The theology of it and the psychology. The ethic of it. The holy the guarantee of the eternal. The difference of faith and experience.

All this goes to hint that it is not quite satisfactory to speak so much of the soul's immortality when we speak of its future. For, as I say, if that mean an immortality native and intrinsic to it, it may be but an expanded egoism. Or else we are leaving out those souls in whom the passion to bless others becomes ready to be shut out from the presence of God and a share in His eternity. Is it not better, then, to have less to say about the soul's immortality and more about God's new creation—less about a life in heaven or hell and more about life in Christ or without Him? We can be more sure about the new creation than about the natural immortality of the soul. I do not wish to prejudge the question about conditional immortality. But I venture to suggest that for religious purposes it is better to approach the matter theologically than psychologically, in terms of the first creation and the second, of nature and grace. These theological terms are better, surer, more objective than the terms which do not go beyond aspirations, premonitions, tendencies, probabilities, which have no real leverage on life, or at least do not give it footing, and are apt to become but pursuits, or even hobbies, of leisure. Our immortality is the new work of God on us rather than the continuation of a psychical process, the uncoiling of an infinite spring, or the fruition of a spiritual tendency. Immortality is a gift, a creation. We do not simply arrive; we were invited and we are fetched. As the second creation it is more of a creation than the first. For it is creation not out of a chaos but a wreck. It is the recreation of a decreation. Our perfection (though it is anything but an annexe) is more created from us, than developed out of us. We are born again into an uncreated world, as the first birth placed us in a world created. And the moral thereof for life is that we grow more perfect when we dwell upon what we may receive rather than on what we may become, and when we conquer our recalcitrance and not merely our inertia.

When I speak of our immortality as a work of God I do not necessarily mean a sharply and obviously miraculous act. And I certainly do not speak of a wing added on to us, a *donum superadditum.* That is not how a personality is regenerated. It is not even how it grows. But I would go deeper than any thaumaturgy, and think of the way the new creation is related to the old. We do not pass from the one to the other by a jolt, radical and revolutionary as the change is. The old life and the new are not parted by a bottomless pit. It is a constitutional revolution. I mean God did not create the first world of nature without reference to the second of grace. His grace is not but a new strategy to save an unforeseen reverse. He did not give us a natural freedom without knowing that He had in reserve freer resources still, which were more than able to recover any abuse of it. He had the new creation in view when He issued the first. The second was provided for in the first, and we are to live the first in the interest of the second. Though nature cannot of itself culminate in grace, at least it was not put there without regard to grace. Grace is Nature's destiny. We are born to be saved. The soul that in its freedom threw away with its freedom its immortality and its God yet was not thrown out of the compass of redemption and regeneration. Any immortality worth having is always of God's grace; it is not a matter of going on and still to be. It is not a mere realisation of a created self but a rescue of it. The soul's true destiny is not achieved under God's benevolence; it is bestowed by His grace. If it go on and on it is not because of the ever new creative action of Him Who is the source of fresh value more than of continued being, and Who makes life not only long but precious. If we think only of the soul's immortality we shall be bandied to and fro by diverse presumptions. But if we think of an incessant new creation as the source of the new life by a new birth, then our whole soul's habit will settle from the oscillations of self on the fidelity of God, or the constancy of the divine Energy, or the faithfulness of the new Creator. The one is the way of reflection and its presumptions, the other of faith and its certainty. And it makes all the difference to life which of these is our ruling note. Only one of them makes a thing really and finally religious out of the life we would prolong. The fidelity of God will mean more for our destiny than the simplicity of the soul, its indissoluble simplicity, and certainly more than its constancy. His Holiness, and the constancy which in Him is fidelity, is the warrant of our personality. Nothing can separate us from the holy love of God in Christ. And nothing but the faith of that love enables us to say that.

We do not believe the greatest things on the ground of experience, but only in the medium of experience, by way of an experience, by a miracle of the Spirit which takes place only in experience, and gives us our

Authority. It is in that plane, though not on that ground. The matter of our immortality is one of the cases where faith must outrun experience. We cannot experience our own Eternity as we can Christ's. Our faith is in One for whom there is no after nor before, to whom, therefore, the far future is already an experience, and our destiny already an achievement. I cannot experience the far future (Paul would have said) by any faith; but for me to live is Christ. My career is Christ, the risen and immortal. He has subdued everywhere everything fatal to my soul. Apart from Him there are perils to it I cannot conceive. I do not know, in my most religious moments, what may happen to my future an the long, long course of things. How can I be sure of an *Eternal* God, One from whose hands nothing can pluck me ever? All the religious are not. How can I tell that between now and then there may not be some fatal incursion upon heaven which even the vast love of God may be powerless to withstand—just as all the love my dearest spend on me can not avert my death and parting? I may be plucked from His hand, as lives here are snatched away from our love unspeakable. Is God's unspeakable love also invincible? That is the question. Is He able to keep what I trust to Him? I have no means of being sure about this, nor can I live as if I were, unless I know and experience Christ; unless I know Him not simply as the Lover of my soul but as the Victor for it for ever, nay, the very constituent of it; unless His love is the Holy One's love, love absolute. The Christian revelation is not just God is love, but God's love is omnipotent. If I know Him as the final Redeemer, who has beaten down Satan, or all that Satan means, for ever, I trust the saving power of His personality as I can never trust the indestructibility of my own. To faith it is more certain that He cannot be broken than that I cannot. He cannot be broken short as time might suddenly cease. The holy nature and quality of His work for me, and for man's whole destiny, is a mightier matter than mere duration. It is only His salvation, His redemption, that gives duration any moral value, any value for eternity. But if this is so, then the belief that it is so gives a distinct complexion to both religion and life. The habit of my soul will be different, first, if I believe in its future, and second, and still more, if I believe in it for these reasons—reasons moral rather than psychological, more ethical than philosophical, more theological than ethical, and therefore more religious in a religion of moral redemption—reasons of faith more even than of hope. The foundation of the moral is the supermoral.

Chapter Eleven

ETERNITY AND NEW BIRTH

Does the great change re-furbish or regenerate? Do we need more a fuller life or a changed? Immortality is the continuance less of the soul than of its change. Meaning of the new creation. Not an annexe, nor a surrogate, but a reconciliation of the soul. The idea of Resurrection as the nexus of that life and this.

The subject I have in hand is practically the relation of immortality and ethic, of Christian ethic and natural, of Christ and conscience. Is our immortality just a new discovery, or is it a new birth? Is the Christian conscience but the natural refined, or is it the natural reborn? Christ's relation to the conscience—is it to develop its culture or to reconstitute its power? Is it to subtilise its acumen, or is it to give it a new quality and a new principle corresponding to the new centre on which it is set and the new life which Christ now lives in us—a life new in proportion as He is of God more than of man? Is conscience the voice of God, or (more humbly) the ear which may hear it? The work of Christ—is it refurbishing or regeneration? Is our key changed, or only the clef? Is conversion but a fresh stimulus, or is it a real revolution in the quality of the moral life, the source of its power, and the direction of its movement? Is the new birth but a somewhat exaggerated metaphor for a new departure, for turning over a new leaf? Is the passage from the natural to the eternal life but an ascent of the spiritual nature, or is it a leap and a venture of faith? These are questions which are of first moment for the effect on life of that new birth into our true immortality.

We hear of many who are eating their heart out because circumstances do not allow them a fuller life. But it is not more life and fuller that we want. We need a different life, a life not simply with a new light on it but a new power in it and a new footing under it. We need a new centre, not a transformation but a transposition. We need the completion not of the soul but of its radical change. The growing spiritual life, and not the natural, goes on beyond the greatest of its crises, in death, and goes on reversing its past all the time. That goes on into which we are being changed as personality grows by a constant revolution in our egoism. (I refer to the allusion to Paulsen in Chapter V.) If life goes on for ever, it goes on coming round full circle, and reflecting an absolute change, an inversion of values which are presaged in the moral estimates of age compared with youth. If it is an absolute change, that means life going on for ever in an ascending spiral where looking back is looking down. For the eternal, in the qualitative sense of rich life and full, could not continue such if it did not include the quantitative also of long life, and time to work itself out. Grace would then simply be irrelevant to nature, and not related at all. Nothing can ensure to us indestructible being except a power which delivers us, by a higher way than mere persistence, from the mutations of time or space—which delivers us from their demoralisation. Only what is eternal in the moral sense could ensure eternity in the temporal sense, for "morality is the nature of things." Eternity is time not simply prolonged, nor only sublimated, but hallowed, morally regenerated for the holy. That which protects us from time to that which delivers us from evil. So the kingdom of an endless heaven is the Kingdom of a *holy* God. And it is the fruit not of *Christus Consummator* but of *Christus Redemptor.*

I dwell on this to point out that any discussion of Christian ethic which does not start with moral regeneration is by so much the less Christian. In the Christian faith "we die but once, but we are born twice." Immortality is precious as the continuance of that which has set life in quite another than the natural key, moved it into a new rhythm, and made its verdicts more than those of the natural judgment rarefied, or the rational just spiritualised. It is behaviour in a new dimension. Have I not said that that is no true, and it is certainly no Christian, belief in immortality which hankers for a life after death just to give the old egoism supernatural opportunities, and to furnish the old desires with superior facilities for getting their head and their bread? Did not even the Pharisees likewise? They believed in a resurrection, but not in immortality as Christ understood it. For him newness of life meant more than a return to life, for however long; it meant a new order of life and love. But for them it only meant a better chance for the old passion; it meant just making good the damage in earth's disappointments; it did not necessarily mean a higher stage of aspiration, or a change of quality in the desire. They need not be born again, as even their best, like Nicodemus or Hillel, must from Christ's point of view. Their divine future meant but the happier perpetuating of such national and social ambitions as filled the horizon of many a zealot in his public career. Christ thought of a new heaven and earth; they thought of a smooth running repristination, the restoring of dominion to Israel. He thought of immortality as a worship; they thought of it as a reward, the return to them, repaired, of what death had taken away. For Christ the true resurrection and the true immortality meant a new ethic born of the spirit; for them it was worldliness re-established and endowed, with security of tenure.

In these remarks I have had partly in view the admirable book of Dr. Rashdall, *Christ and the Conscience.* No book on Christian ethic so good has appeared among use But I cannot agree with its religious foundation. The prolegomena seems to me to be vitiated by the absence of the idea of regeneration in connexion with Christian ethic. I am not going to argue here whether we are to think of regeneration in the baptismal, and subliminal, not to say magical, way, or in the evangelical and ethical way. It is enough for my present purpose to recognise that in both cases it represents a change as real and miraculous as grace and the Spirit's life must always be. It is not to be identified with sanctification. Nor is it to be reduced to a development of sympathetic power, nor to a culture of the moral judgment. Christian ethic is not simply the top story of all natural ethic. It is supreme in another sense than merely superlative. There is a new "creative synthesis"(Wundt). There is an element of crisis, and a new life given. We are born into a new world. We are lifted to a new plane. We ascend there in a new atmosphere. When we die it is into an immortality which is only a new departure in the old rebirth and its new life. It is but a new grasp of the grace in which we had died to nature, and yet in losing it found it.

There is a crude way of criticising the idea of a new creation and reducing it to a mere metaphor by asking whether the old soul is destroyed and a new identity put down on its site. We all know that that could not be. It is not even a new wing built on. Of course the new man must find his points of attachment in the old, but he cannot have his foundation there. The truth is the newness of the new creature is less in himself than in his tenant. Christ lives in him. And the newness in the man corresponds to the new and original thing in Christ. If in Christ there was nothing essentially new, if He was but man at his spiritual best, we could not so speak. But all that makes Him the Son of God goes to differentiate the new creature He inhabits. It is a real novelty, it is not a fresh stimulus that we have. And if that be so, it means much for the tone and style of our life. It gives us a creative revelation; and a fresh experience is not a revelation. The new creation is not in me so much as in Him Whose unique soul and life inhabits me as souls do souls. My knowledge is reborn beyond all science because I am known by Him whom I know; my life is reborn beyond all nature because it is now not lived by me but lived into me. The new master makes the new man. The relation of son to God, which is intrinsic to Christ by His nature, becomes ours by His gift; we are sons in Him. He is Son in Himself. He is our immortality. We do not in the new creation get a new identity, but a new kind and quality of moral power, a new unity of soul by His Reconciliation. The new man is the destruction of the old man as forgiveness destroys—forgiveness, and not sheer oblivion, forgiveness, which is but the negative action of eternal life in a Reconciliation drawing on all the unity of God, rising, that is, from His holiness. The new thing in Christ's revelation of God was not a new attribute, but the unity in holy love of all His attributes, conflicting before. It was the revelation and action of God as holy in His love, with all that that entails. And so the new thing in us is not a new quality or faculty, but the unity of our warring selves and our divided heart in Christ's name and power. It is the Reconciliation with God and ourselves. It is the θεῖου τι in the life of an organism which marks even a mollusc from a mosaic, which no analysis can discern, no invention reproduce, and no mere continuation create. It is like the unity in a work of art, which the best copyist cannot give. It was thus that Shakespeare used Plutarch. Art makes a chord instead of a clang.

I knew not if, save in this, such gift be allowed to man
That out of three sounds he frame not a fourth sound but a star.

The new and qualitative element in immortality is what connects it with the new birth, and gives it the greatest of all influences upon our conduct of life, were it only that it fortifies the will to live, to say nothing of living to divine effect. Our present life is deepened by such an immortality; whereas a mere indestructibility would become a thin ghostliness, with an air of Sheol and a Tithonus burden. Love receives thus a solemnity which guards it from levity, and which fixes its colours in fixing its destiny. We live and love to glorify an immortal God in Christ. We labour to be accepted of Him. He harmonises the passion for life and the longing for death. The faith of a Christian immortality blesses our present life also by taking its concern off itself and its interests. We are not too preoccupied with our own personal prospects. We are lost in the desire of God's Kingdom and its fulness. And so our very personal growth is more free and full. For the self-preoccupied do not grow; they do not advance; they only rotate, and wear their axis out. But that is a complaint which every form of immortality will not cure. An immortality that we project from ourselves, as the grand presumption from our being what we are, does not rid us of that egoism. An immortality which does not proceed from God's gift in Christ is but an imaginative one, which seems now sure now dim. But, losing our souls in Him, we find in His eternity a life we never found while we called our souls our own. In union with Him we live in His grace, be it here or there. We shall have a very different interpretation of His world and His ways in it, a very different theology, according as we are thinking of the release of our powers or the glory of His grace.

This gives room for the idea of Resurrection, whatever we may think of its form or body. The other life reacts on this because it is still, through all crisis or miracle, organic with it. And what integrates the other life into this life's history is the idea of resurrection. The New Testament connects the idea of immortality with that of resurrection. Its nature is given in Christ's. It is not the resurrection of the flesh but of a body—not of matter but of form. Its idea of resurrection means something very much more than the repristination of the old life under happier circumstances. That, I have said, is but Jewish, and Pharisaist, and Moslem. It thought the old desires were to be refurbished, the old ambitions facilitated, the old life well warmed and oiled for an elect. But that was sheer egoist eudæmonism, the cult of selfish happiness and individual well being. It only gave the old hunger better cooking. The idea of immortality had to be moralised. And that was done first, by the notion of sanctification and perfection, but, second, by the close association of these with the new life of past duty and relation. The other life was that life going on to perfection and coming to itself in a crisis. It was in an organic moral connection with this. Christ came back to give effect to what He had done. He came back, His body (not His flesh), His person came back to be the Holy Spirit of all He had done. That is the real value of the doctrine of resurrection. It gives the next life a realism drawn from its moral reality common and continuous with this. Our life beyond is in a moral relation of causality with this. Moral causation is broken as a bondage but not as a power. We take with us the character we made. All discussion of what body we come in is beside the point; and we have no data. What happens to this physical body is indifferent to faith, and it is left to reverence. We are reverent to the corpse, and not prudent. It will not be wanted again. We do not mummify our dead; we even burn them. But still the idea of Resurrection is the integrating factor between the next life and this. Even the new nature does not come *per saltum.* We return to an old haunt. We put on an old fashion if not the old garment. We grow in the old soil. So the next life has much effect on this by making the new present of infinite worth and moment. Our character here starts our destiny there. This is one of the things that make it such an abuse to rely on another life to make good our neglect here. The deliberate postponement of repentance here in the hope of doing it there only deepens its unlikelihood. We fix the impenitent temper. We return yonder to the habit of putting off which we acquired here.

It may be added that, as we pass into no lone immortality, the social bearings of the next life on the present are great. We so worship here as worshipping with the greater part of the One Church there—the Unseen. The dead are the majority; and we are in communion with them in Christ. Even for society outside the Church the authority of history means much. For the dead, I say, are the majority; and if they are not extinct they are still in some organic connexion with history and with the present. The future is in some sense their resurrection. They revisit us if only in the resultants of their deeds. And we still meet in the undying Lord. In Christ the past with its souls means much for us and our future. We are debtors both to ancestry and posterity, both unseen. We live as those who are come to a general assembly and Church of the first born (for the youngest dead are senior born to us in the unseen). We are come to a city of the living God, and a heavenly Jerusalem, and an innumerable company of heavenly ones. And we cannot live our public life as if we were cut off from either life or society on the other side. We are all in the one historic purpose of God. We are in the lower parts of the same Kingdom of God, and in the advance battles of the soldiery of faith. The dead still have a vote where votes are not counted but weighed. Let us not ignore their weight, their tradition, in public things. They still belong to the constituency of the Christ Whom we have to put in command of affairs. Ignoble peace always renounces the sacrifices of the noble dead, and still crucifies them afresh.

Chapter Twelve

THE FRUCTIFICATION OF FAILURE

The future is the fruition of failure here. Eternity holds the key of history, the meaning of progress, the interest of tears. All opens out in that light. The pathos of the past.

There are those who are not geniuses, with a ruling passion to realise themselves and get themselves out, but they have more affinity with the meek saints, who have striven for souls without any effect apparent. To such it may come with some cheer to remember that, if death is not a blight but a blessing, the seed they sowed here will be reaped yonder. As the Old Testament lives and works in the New so our discipline, long latent here, bears fruit yonder. Death is like the leaf between the Old Testament and New Testament. Or as the old Bible lives on, and lives larger, in the growing Church, so the instruction at came to little here may yonder bud and seed. Christ died like a corn of wheat sinking into the ground to rot, but His harvest grows all over the world. So our fruitless efforts for souls will germinate yonder, as the mummy wheat is said to sprout in soil to-day. Historic Christianity is working its greatest results in the unseen world, and far more mightily, perhaps, there than here, as the spiritual climate is so much more congenial. When we are disappointed with the historic results of the Gospel, and ask with even despair

And is the thing we see Salvation?

the answer is that it is not, except in process. Indeed the thing we see most obviously to-day is the result of neglecting God's salvation and kingdom. But there is a realm far within all that goes on here where these things are not neglected, but are ruling, judging, and creative powers. The effects of Christianity are greater, its salvation is greater, where we do not see than where we do. Which helps us patiently to believe how great they will be in the future and unseen stretch of earth's history. There is a region where the triumph of the cross is assured and realised as it is not yet here. And our contributions to it here do not come to their fruition till they take effect in a land that is their own. It seems far off, but the same faith that works for it sees it. It we paint for eternity it is eternity painting through us. For after all eternity is doing far more for time than time is doing for eternity. "Time is the mercy of Eternity." Think of that phrase of Blake.

Time is there by the initiative of Eternity, by the Grace of God, to make
eternity accessible. He forestalls us with every good. We love Him
because He first loved us, and became incarnate in creation for us. Time is
not the mistake of Eternity. The Eternal did not darkly blunder on man's
suffering soul. The old Providence does not desert us when we go out of
life's door. The souls that go into eternity know themselves as they never
did before. The spirit is more to them than ever before. Their spiritual
acquirement while they were here opens out upon their sight. Think of the
grand leisure of Eternity, the leisured receptivity of soul, its feeding in a
wise passiveness. How things will break open on us, and be reconciled.
And not only its poverty but also its wealth will be enriched. Lessons,
facts, thoughts, sacrifices, verses, hymns, that were here overwhelmed
with the life mean and coarse, stand out, open out, fructify, take command
there. Memories become powers. Old faces become fresh blessings. The
once dear becomes the ever solemn. Even if the once despised become
terrible it is as the terrible things in righteousness answer us from the God
of our Salvation. And all through Death. All things are in a new light.

> *Thou takest not away, O Death,*
> *Thou strikest; absence perisheth,*
> *Indifference is no more.*
> *The future brightens on our sight,*
> *For on the past has fallen a light*
> *That tempts us to adore.*

Yes, the old companion body, so mangled once, and even so abused,
and made the servant of sin, is clothed with a new tenderness through a
new repentance, and the soul shall still feel a respect and affection for its
old home. In a theatre once I saw a packed audience brought to a dewy
silence like the half hour in heaven, while a young girl on the stage
caressed a child to sleep with words they had all known long, and
memories they had known longer still, sung to a grave sweet melody.

> *O, the auld hoose, the auld hoose,*
> *What though the rooms were sma',*
> *How many cherished memories*
> *Do they like flowers reca'l*
> *The auld hoose, the auld hoose,*
> *Deserted though ye be,*
> *There ne'er can be a new hoose*
> *Will seem sae fair to me.*

So, I thought, the spirit might look back from its immortal repentance upon the mangled body left on Flanders fields, wherein had grown up a young soul's pathetic tragedy. And the very repentance, not being hopeless, would not be fierce but tender, and the poor shieling of flesh would receive from across the misty seas of death a reverence we knew not while we lived therein.

And if you complain that this is sentiment and fancy I will say it is that and more. It is at least a parable of what I said was in the heart of the doctrine of resurrection, of the new meaning, effect, and dearness of all that took place in time, all that came closest to life, all that was the medium of experience. It is a parable of all the blessings we misprised, all the monitions we ignored, all the teaching we resented, all the discipline that chafed us, and all the sacrifices we coolly took as our due. The loving faces we too little loved will not rise up to accuse us, though their very blessings will reproach us. They will not reproach, though reproach will be ours. For it is love's native land this, its song is of mercy and justice, its very judgments are full of grace, and its severities make for praise. And their past, through which we who are left here are now toiling, and struggling, and crying, appears already to certain eyes, for whom we once worked and wept, to be

> *Ennobled by a vast regret,*
> *And by contrition sealed thrice sure.*

Chapter Thirteen

L'ENVOI

To live is Christ, to die is more Christ. We pass into a genial native land.

You cannot dwell too much on the death and resurrection of Christ as the revelation of God's immortal love, so long as you do not hide the fact that they are powers and not mere lessons, and that they make together one crucial, final act of divine majesty and mercy. They make up the act which is the central and unflagging energy of the world's last reality as moral reality. They are one act of decisive, and final power at the moral centre of the Universe; and that is real omnipotence. Unless we can say that, the centre of our religion does not coincide with the centre of the moral cosmos; our faith and our ethic lead a double life; and in a religion of universal and moral redemption that cannot be. Therefore Christ went out in the one grand moral activity of all being, and not in a mere submission, passivity, or martyrdom. He certainly did not simply subside into an allcreating presence, as one vortex swirls away to make room for another in a vast sea which boils with them. His death and resurrection made the greatest thing His great historic and cosmic person did. Nay, it was the greatest thing that God ever did. When God raised Christ from the dead it was the greatest of all His works. It was the new creation of the world. It certainly was the greatest thing ever done for the soul.

Christ's death meant power and victory over sin's spiritual guilt and moral bondage; His resurrection meant victory over sorrow, nature, and the bondage of the world. Together they make a glory greater and surer than nature's joy. More than the morning stars sang together at this new creation—the Father was well pleased. Nothing created could express the Holy Father's joy as He found Himself in the victory of His equally holy Son. A new value was given to the natural life from its spiritual Lord. It became more active, more precious, and dear. We learned to paint for Eternity. Clutching haste died, and crude feverishness. "I pass but do not cease. I go to those who have gone. I go to Him in whom is no after nor before, and in whom all work is Yea and Amen. To die is Christ. It is gain—gain in reality. I go nearer to the great reality, the eternal holy love. I do not just sink into the Unseen, I move deeper into God and the

Kingdom of God. I see His face. I am rapt into the energies of the Eternal. Here I am not where I should be, because others are not. But I go where all souls are filled with Christ; where the public opinion is the Holy Ghost; where all moves in righteousness, service and worship." What an accession to our best life here to believe that. What a gain to the value of these things here, when, even if we do lead a buried life, it is among the roots of the fruit eternal where the river of life flows by. The same Christ Who is the reality and power of that life beyond is the reality and value of this. To live here is to live the Christ that rules eternity. To die is more of that Kingdom.

Doubt and distraction about our destiny do not stimulate work nor ennoble feeling, though a morbid tenderness they may breed. They kill work. They reduce it to mere restlessness. Mere activity is not work. We do not then run a race set before us; we dawdle, or we scamper; we flutter before pursuing doom like a fowl before a train. And these uncertainties about our future, these blank misgivings, debase feeling rather than elevate it. But how the revelation of Christ's eternity as ours has ennobled love. It has given love a new value for the modern world, and yet made the parting full of hope. The more free we are made from life and the world the more we find in both. But Jubal was not freed, only swallowed up. He was reabsorbed; he was not redeemed. But Christian death is the only close which is more of a beginning than an end.

The foundation of our true immortality is in a redemption. Eternal Life is a new *gift* to us by a new act, a new creation. It is a second birth. It is not a case of evolution but of revolution. It is not the development of a power or an ideal immanent to the world or Humanity. It is a gift of God, through an act of God. And thus it is the only means of passing to our moral perfection. To evade that act of God is to turn religion to a piece of æsthetic. In an ethical religion we are redeemed. We do not glide into heaven; we are taken, not to say plucked, into it. There is no straight line or smooth ascent to our high places—that is shown by the calls to severe self-denial of earthly good.[1] And these calls join with the certainty of judgment to make life grave, or even tragic, as Eternal Life makes it great and glorious. For our race the Kingdom of God can only come by the

---

1. There is another life, hard, rough, and thorny, trodden with bleeding feet and aching brow, the life of which the cross is the symbol, a battle which no peace follows this side the grave; which the grave gapes to finish before the victory is won; and—strange that it should be so—this is the highest life of man. Look back along the great names of history- there is none whose life has been other than this.—3. A. Froude, England's *Forgotten Worthies.*

Cross, by crisis, by a breach with the natural life, though not a disruption of it. It is this new relation to a holy Creator and His eternity that gives the final value to life's chief assets and its best dreams. Eternal Life is the enhancement and warrant of human joy and weal. It is the fixing of its finest colours. It is the last Amen. Do not flee the world; overcome it by good. "There is no time so miserable but a man may be true" The force you have to use on yourself is really a function of the power of new life which carries you, an energy of the righteous kingdom. If you break with the world it is in the power of the life which serves and saves it. If Christ live in you all humane affection, all love of man or woman, will be in the service and worship of God. A new power of service comes from that faith. In the vast certainty that Christ has charged Himself with our immortality our minds and hands are set free to serve others. We escape from ourselves, our introspection, our culture of immortality. We escape our anxious self-concern. So little is Christian immortality a piece of egoism. We do not see the prospect as a field for imaginative enjoyment, nor as a food for our mere comfort. If Christ is our life our future is not our own. Our ruling passion is not greed of life. We do not do just what we must do to keep death at bay. We begin living the eternal life here, with its endless selfless energy, vaster than we feel, and surer than we know. That life is not a mere spirituality but a sanctity; for we are not mystic beings in our destiny, but moral and holy. So to live is the life of faith— which is not another piece of work, but the new life which is the source of all work, and which has for its ventures all the capital of Christ's life behind it.

The other life is not the negation and arrest of this. Nor is it mere restitution—as if we might then pursue all the old egoist dreams and appetites only with better machinery than here. That were pagan, Moslem. It were at best but happiness. And the Christian idea is not happiness and it is not power, but it is perfection—which is the growth of God's image and glory as our destiny. ❦